Saratoga Springs

NEW YORK

A BRIEF HISTORY

Timothy Holmes

THE History PRESS

Published by The History Press
Charleston, SC 29403
www.historypress.net

All images, unless otherwise noted, are from the 375,000 negatives in the George S. Bolster Collection of the Saratoga Springs History Museum, taken primarily by Harry B. Settle and Bolster as well as other, earlier photographers. They are reproduced with permission from the Saratoga Springs History Museum.

First published 2008
Second printing 2013
Third printing 2014

Manufactured in the United States

ISBN 978.1.59629.452.3

Library of Congress Cataloging-in-Publication Data

Holmes, Timothy.
Saratoga Springs : a brief history / Timothy Holmes.
p. cm.
Includes bibliographical references.
ISBN 978-1-59629-452-3
1. Saratoga Springs (N.Y.)--History. 2. Saratoga Springs (N.Y.)--Social life and customs. 3. Summer resorts--New York (State)--Saratoga Springs--History. I. Title.
F129.S3H65 2008
974.7'48--dc22
2008008997

Saratoga Springs is an example for a thousand small cities in America.
It has seen many lives, across several eras in its history.

"The City in the Country" grew out of the wilderness, achieved glamorous repute and fell into obsolescence. Then it rose again, against the odds, and once more became a coveted destination.

This is a story of success that owes its history to people who cared.
To those, and to those who follow in the same spirit,
this book is dedicated.

Contents

Acknowledgements

The single best place to find out more about Saratoga Springs is the Saratoga Springs History Museum, located in the Canfield Casino in Congress Park in the heart of Saratoga Springs. The museum's website (saratogahistory.org) provides a sense of the breadth of the collections, the variety of exhibits and the schedule of programs and events.

Like the museum, this book is an introduction to Saratoga Springs and an invitation to explore. Other rich resources are the Saratoga Room at the Saratoga Springs Public Library and the Saratoga Springs city historian, care of the City of Saratoga Springs.

Among the many who have given knowledgeable help with this book are: James Parillo, executive director of the Saratoga Springs History Museum; John Conners, curator of the Bolster Collection, and Doris Lamont, archivist, both at the museum. Thanks are given for the gracious hospitality of the museum and its volunteer Board of Trustees.

Mary Ann Fitzgerald, Saratoga Springs city historian, who gave so generously of her time, knowledge, interest and encouragement.

Geoffrey Bornemann, former city planner; Charles Wait, community leader in a multitude of capacities.

James K. Kettlewell, historian of art and architecture.

Chris Millis, in more ways than one bringing new generations to keep the flame.

The helpful and resourceful staff of the Saratoga Room at the Saratoga Springs Public Library.

In particular, Libby Smith-Holmes, whose tireless efforts for the betterment of Saratoga Springs extended to indispensable help with the content and editing of this book.

Those not named here will be thanked personally.

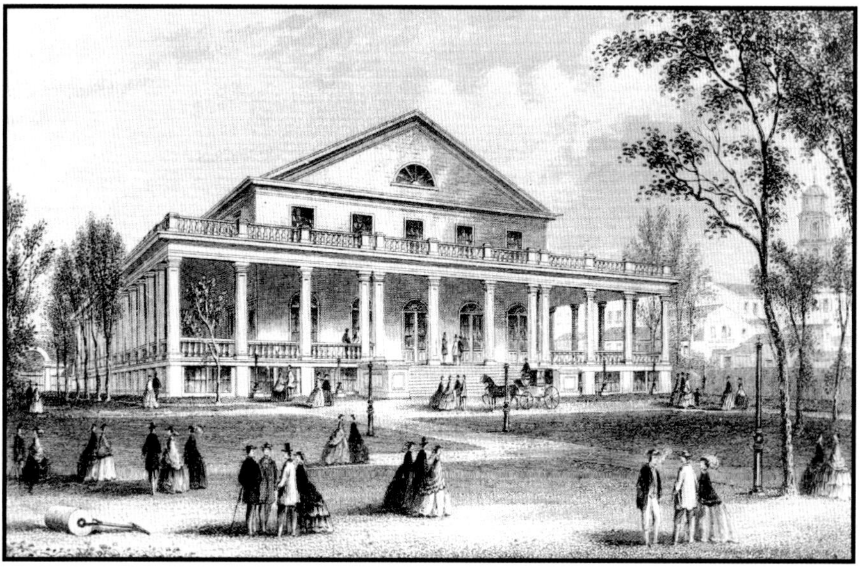

The Leland brothers added a 1,600-seat opera house "chastely elegant in design and luxuriously comfortable" in back of the Grand Union Hotel, according to the *New York Times* of July 10, 1865.

Introduction

Over the course of more than two centuries, thousands of observers have written millions of words about Saratoga Springs. A congruence of ancient geology and modern human enterprise has given it a lasting place in the American story.

In the robust years of the late nineteenth century, *Harper's Weekly* noted, "The curious charm of Saratoga life to a student of human nature is the fact that beyond any other American resort it is a social microcosm in which our distinctive national traits are happily portrayed in miniature." The writer was observing the result of nearly a century's worth of responses to our natural desires for leisure and opportunity.

The story of Saratoga Springs did not stop with the end of the Victorian era. After decades in which economic and societal changes seemed to write the city a death sentence, Saratoga today has recaptured the freshness and verve of the earlier age. Its past reputation for wickedness now seems quaintly interesting. Its mix of old and new residents contribute energy to adapt the community to the needs of a new century while caring deeply about its past. Fortunately, there were avid collectors among the passionate players, and they captured facts and artifacts that tell the stories. Their contemporaries and the great events connect us with the shaping of the country.

This book is published in observance of the Saratoga Springs History Museum's 125th anniversary, to bring the story up to date and to recognize the difference made by caring for our community.

Chapter One
Bedrock and Foundation

The Land and the First People

The landforms in the area of Saratoga Springs are the result of the ongoing process of interactions between climate, rocks, air, water and living things over a very long period of time. Human alterations to the land have also shaped the landscape we see today

Ocean waters that once covered what is now the East Coast withdrew and the land rose up. The bedrock under the Saratoga area is complex, formed of ancient gneiss and granite overlaid by sea bottom deposits of sandstone, limestone and dolostone. The fossil algae seen in the Petrified Gardens at the city's western border are evidence of the warm, shallow sea that once was here. A later layer of mud deposits formed a water-resistant cap of shale over the bedrock. A succession of glaciers twenty-five thousand to twelve thousand years ago shaped ridges and valleys as far south as Long Island.

When the climate changed and the ice gradually melted, the outwash from the retreating glaciers moved large boulders, coarse gravels and fine sediments down the gouged-out valleys, depositing them in layers. The sandy plain between Saratoga Springs and the Hudson River is the legacy of glacial Lake Albany, whose remains persist as Saratoga Lake and Lake Lonely and in small ponds and marshes.

At some ancient time, the deep rocks cracked through the shale layer in a north-south direction for approximately sixty miles through the Saratoga region, forming the MacGregor Fault. The fault allows trapped seawater, charged with carbon dioxide, to bubble to the surface in the mineral springs that give Saratoga its surname. Although diluted by rainwater percolating into the earth, the water's carbonic acid causes minerals to leach out of the limestone layers, creating a great variety of pungently flavored mineral springs.

In the warming climate after the last glacier retreated, mastodons (now extinct) and herds of caribou and elk were gradually replaced by wildlife species we know today, such as deer, bear and beaver. The ridges of the hills offered passage for trails; the valleys of the region's streams, rivers and lakes provided water routes used by Native Americans as they hunted and fished from the land's bounty. While there is no evidence of permanent villages, archaeologists have discovered numerous campsites along the lower portions of the Kayaderosseras Creek and on the shores of Saratoga Lake. Pottery, bone tools and stone arrowheads tell of thousands of years of activity. After AD 1400, the Mohawks, the easternmost tribe of the Iroquois confederacy, began to move into what had been Mohican hunting grounds, finally driving the rival tribe out by 1628. The Mohawks called this area—bounded by the Mohawk and Hudson Rivers, Lake George and the Adirondack Mountains—Kayaderosseras, poetically translated as "land of the beautiful lake of the winding river." Although most of the Mohawk tribe relocated after the 1780s to northern New York and Canada, a few native families remained in the area, and some of their descendants still live here today.

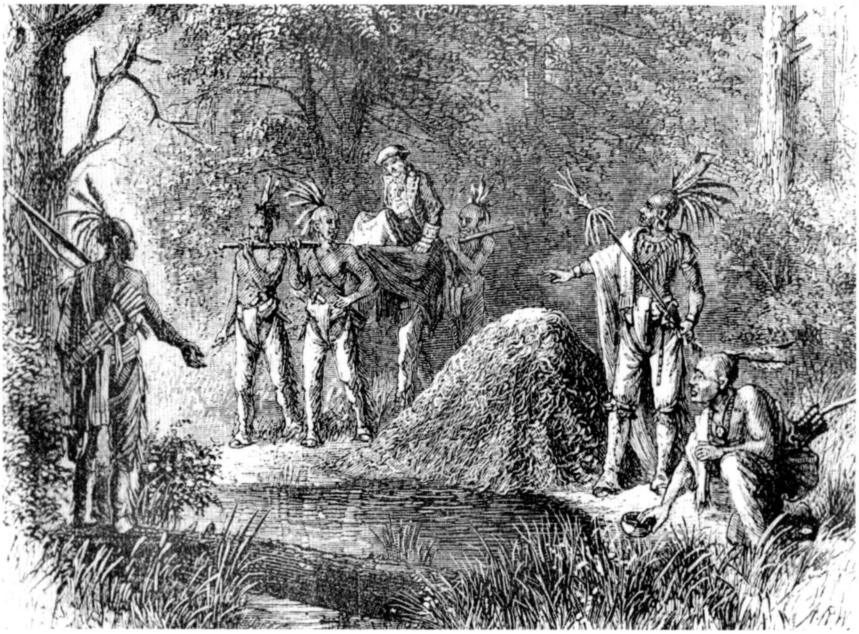

Sir William Johnson's visit to High Rock Spring is identified with the founding of Saratoga Springs. A similar scene with only the Mohawks has been adopted as the city's seal.

When the English took over the colony of New York from the Dutch in 1664, the Mohawks began selling rights to their hunting grounds. They sold a patent for the Kayaderosseras to agents of Queen Anne sometime between 1703 and 1708, but the title was not confirmed until 1768, with the help of Sir William Johnson, superintendent of Indian affairs for the British colonies, who made sure that the Mohawks were dealt with fairly.

Sir William Johnson was a prominent figure in colonial New York. In 1771, feeling the pains of an old war wound, Johnson was taken by his native friends to be healed in the medicinal waters bubbling out of a rock in a swampy area of the Kayaderosseras patent.[1] Although the drinking of and bathing in the waters provided little permanent relief, the superintendent reported the experiment to some of his correspondents, including General Philip Schuyler.

Saratoga

Thirty miles north of Albany—which was originally a trading post established in 1616 by the Dutch as Fort Orange—the first settlers of this region of New York chose the place where Fish Creek, the outlet of Saratoga Lake, empties into the Hudson. It is a natural place of power. In the Hudson-Champlain Valley, a blade of waterways that cuts through the mountains, this point is a crossroads of both land and water, with evidence of use through the entire period of human presence in the region. The place was called Saratoga.[2]

The best understanding we have today of the word "Saratoga" is that it refers to the section of the Hudson River near today's Schuylerville, the swiftness of the rapids now diminished by the power dam and canal. The immediate area took on the name, which was adopted by the settlement and later by the town. Saratoga Springs, ten miles to the west, was an early destination for those who traveled there from the Hudson River settlement.

Battles of the Revolutionary War were waged along the Hudson River Valley, most notably at Saratoga in 1777. General Philip Schuyler, the scion of a prominent Dutch family, held extensive lands along the river near the scene of surrender of British General John Burgoyne, whose defeat at Saratoga had been a pivotal event in the war. In 1783, Schuyler cut a road through the forest to the spring reported by Johnson. That summer some of the newly victorious leaders came to inspect the sites of the Revolution. General George Washington, Alexander Hamilton, Governor

George Clinton and others were guests of Schuyler at his summer home in Saratoga, later called Schuylerville. Washington, interested in the efficacy of water, visited the spring flowing improbably from a cone of rock and inquired about buying it.

The Early Resort

The spring was the touchstone of attraction and development. "The spring near Saratoga" would be known thereafter for its distinction as the first of the springs visited in the community. Dubbed "High Rock," it appeared to flow from the middle of a three-and-a-half-foot-high cone of rock that was twenty-four feet around its base. The cone actually had been formed by minerals settling out of the spring water and solidifying into a porous rock called tufa. On the high ground above the marsh in which it stood, a son of Samuel Norton had come in 1783 and laid claim to the cabin his father had abandoned at the outbreak of the war. Four years later Alexander Bryan, a secret agent for the Patriots during the Revolutionary War, bought the modest abode. Bryan came to stay and began in a rudimentary way a tradition of hostelry that became the community's trademark. His log tavern above the High Rock Spring was the nucleus of what became known as the upper village. By 1793, visitors would have found two frame houses and the log tavern, but they would have had to sleep in the covered wagons in which they traveled. The High Rock Spring had already passed through many owners, from the heirs of Rip Van Dam (an original holder of the Kayaderosseras patent) to Henry Livingston to Henry Walton. One owner, Isaac Low, had lost the title when he was condemned for treason as a Tory during the Revolution. Walton had bought out the Van Dam share by the time the health seekers came in earnest.

The character of a community relies on the mix of personalities that show up, and how they respond to the challenges and opportunities presented by interactions with each other and the environment. The enduring success of Saratoga Springs is the result of extraordinary individuals working at each critical turn in its history. A few of these follow.

After the new republic emerged from the War of Independence in 1783, the first Americans to settle the Saratoga Springs area came from New England and from the southern counties of New York to clear the frontiers and expand the young nation. They bore names such as Arnold, Mosher, Jewel, Taylor, Fitch, Jeffords, Mott, Thorn, Rockwell

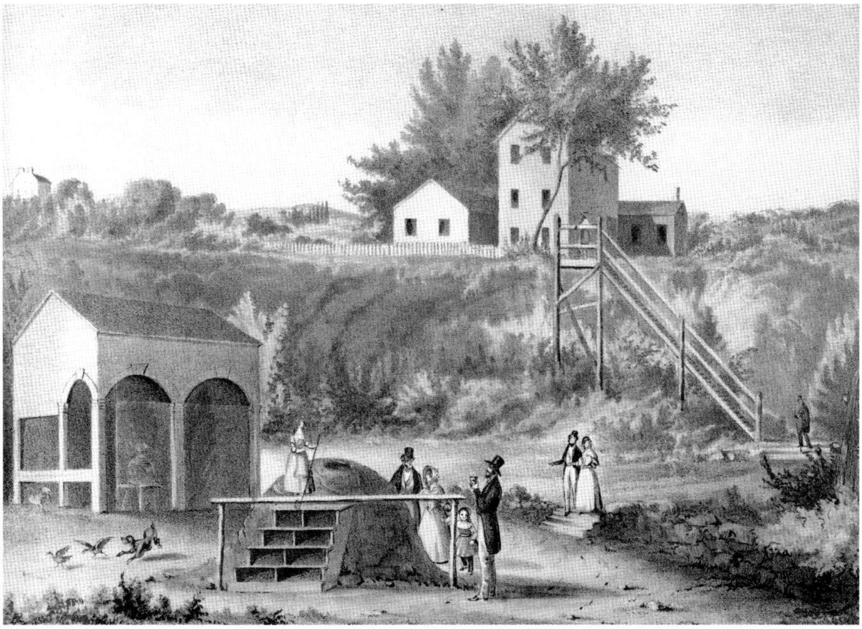

This 1843 lithograph by Endicott depicts a dipper girl serving patrons from the High Rock cone in an earlier time. Behind the partially drained swamp, the embankment marks the great fault line that runs through Saratoga Springs and Ballston Spa.

and Lightfoot. There were Crawfords, as many times as not spelled Crawfoot.[3] These settlers were of rugged stock, bolstered by a strong and sometimes stern faith imbued with a Puritan ethic that extolled hard work, simple living and thrift. They tended to distrust pursuits seen as frivolous, so present from Saratoga's start was an element of opposition to amusements, gambling, drinking and fashionable attire that was soon to be severely tested.

Gideon Putnam came in 1789 at the age of twenty-five. Born in Sutton, Massachusetts, he was a man with energy and entrepreneurial instinct. He established himself just south of the settlement at High Rock, starting the lower village through a lumber business with customers in the growing cities down the Hudson River. Putnam had married into a good Connecticut family, many of whom also came to Saratoga. His wife Doanda's father Benjamin Risley owned the first recorded store in the upper village. Before long, Putnam was able to purchase three hundred acres from Dirck Lefferts, one of the original proprietors of the Kayaderosseras patent.

With the clearing of forest came the discovery of new springs along the fault line. John Taylor Gilman, who had represented New Hampshire

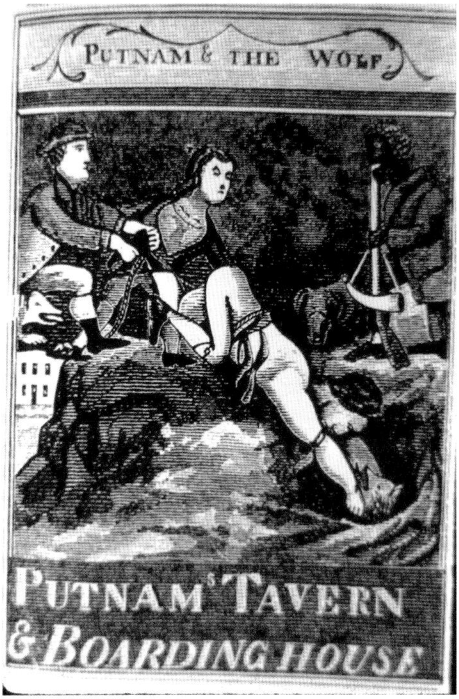

Gideon Putnam's relative, General Israel Putnam, had rid Pomfret, Connecticut, of a marauding wolf. Doanda Putnam used the family legend to create a memorable sign for Putnam's Tavern in 1802. The original sign is in the Saratoga Springs History Museum's collection.

in the Continental Congress, ventured into the marsh near Putnam's lumber operations with a hunting party from the upper village. There he spotted a new mineral spring bubbling up at the edge of a stream. Young Henry Holmes reported that "the congress" had discovered it, and the name stuck. The timing was right for developing this natural resource, coinciding with scientific inquiry into the curative powers of drinking mineral waters and bathing in them.[1]

Putnam seized on the opportunity presented by the Congress Spring. He purchased more adjacent land and, in 1802, put up Putnam's Tavern and Boarding House, a three-story hotel. Greeted with skepticism as overly optimistic, his venture was justified when the number of visitors continued to grow, making his accommodations essential. He reinvested his success, expanding the hotel. Putnam went further in contending for permanence, laying out a broad avenue and donating land for a church, school and cemetery.

Others followed to take advantage of new opportunities. Farther north on what became Broadway, a second hotel proprietor followed with the Columbian Hotel in 1808. Two years later, although there were only thirty houses in the upper village and fewer in the lower village, many more visitors had come to enjoy the springs.

Gideon Putnam excavated, tubed and improved new springs—Columbian, Hamilton and Washington. He planned further expansion of his hostelry, beginning construction of Congress Hall in 1811, across Broadway from his first establishment. His entrepreneurial career was cut short by a fall from scaffolding, incurring lingering injuries. When he died

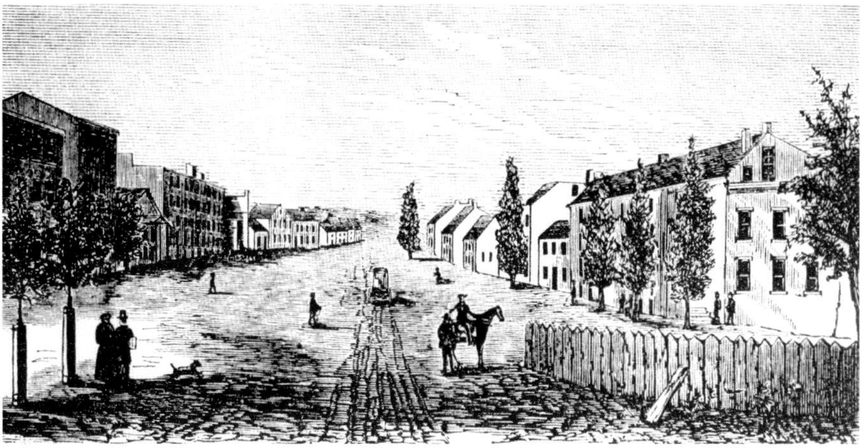

A dependable guide, *The Fashionable Tour*, was published through the 1820s by G.M. Davison of Saratoga Springs, offering travel routes and destination descriptions for *An Excursion to the Springs, Niagara, Quebec and Boston*. It carried this image of Broadway.

the next year, his was the first burial in the cemetery area he had designated. The Congress Hall hotel opened in the next year under the management of Putnam's family members.

Putnam's legacy lives on in the commodious infrastructure of downtown Saratoga Springs, which has accommodated successive generations with their changing needs in transportation and public entertainments. The streets he laid out were Broad (later Broadway), Washington, Congress, Federal, Bath (now Spring) and Putnam.[5]

At first the setting was sufficient. The village was somewhat rough around the edges, the mile of road between the upper and lower villages a sandy track that traversed a ravine. But Gideon Putnam's elementary village layout gave simple structure in the lower village, and the High Rock Spring remained an object of fascination. All was surrounded by pristine forest, increasingly cleared for developing farmland.

This scene suited the up-and-coming gentry of the burgeoning young country. It was a safe place for the first phase of resort growth.[6] But soon facilities for relaxation, recreation and entertainment were added, making a combination of resort amenities that set Saratoga apart from other watering holes. Saratoga Springs, the upstart, soon eclipsed Ballston Spa as a destination of choice. In the hotel parlors and on their vast verandas, visitors from many places could meet, conduct business and, perhaps, flirt. Traveling professionals gave musical performances, although dancing was

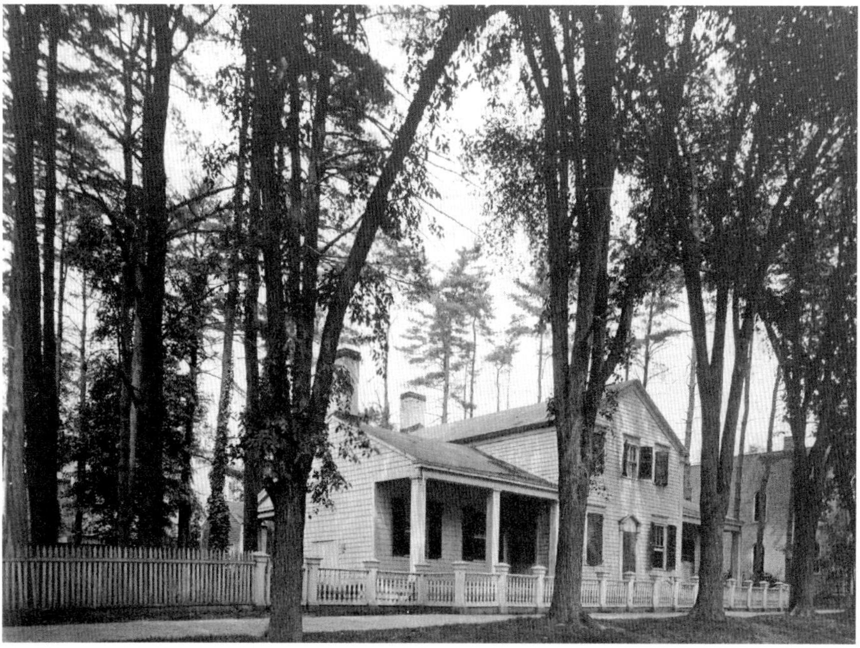

Pine Grove, on Broadway, built in 1815 by Judge Henry Walton, who lived here only for a few years.

in some circles still considered risqué. Card playing, mostly whist, occurred in the evenings, and liquor seemed to be readily available.

However, it happened that a native son of the nearby township of Moreau found his mission in proselytizing for abstinence from intoxicants, part of the growing temperance movement. Dr. Billy J. Clark in 1808 founded the Moreau and Northumberland Temperance Society and brought it to Saratoga Springs. Members pledged not to touch wine except at public dinners, and never distilled spirits except in case of "actual disease." A twenty-five-cent fine was allowed for slippage of one drink, and a fifty-cent fine for actually getting drunk.

The children of Putnam and the settlers who joined them maintained reserve and a canny talent for assuring the customers that they were right. Small industries developed to serve the growing community—a blacksmith shop; stores for groceries, dry goods and hardware; and services for horses and carriages. Although diversions for springs visitors were few at first, comfort was readily accommodated for each taste.

Among the prominent shapers of the community were the landowners, one of whom was Henry Walton.[7] Henry Walton moved to the springs near

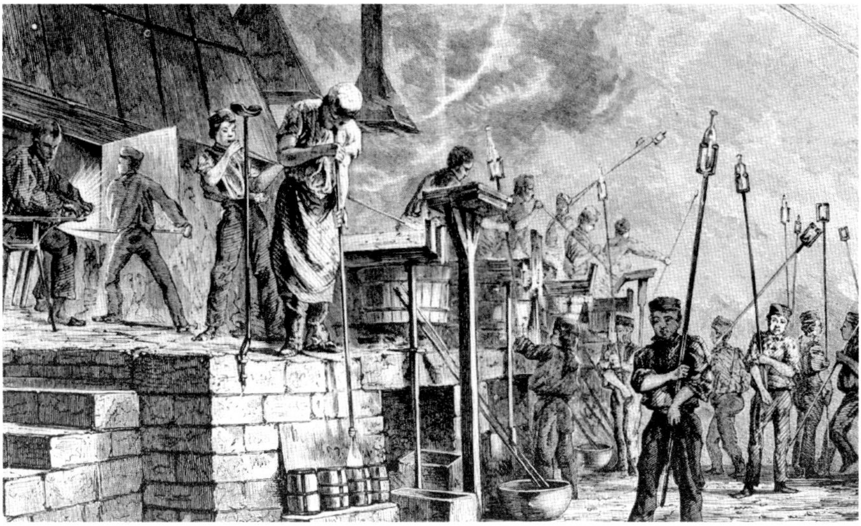

A glass factory owned by Oscar Granger since the mid-1800s was moved, workers' houses and all, from Greenfield to Congressville on the western edge of Saratoga Springs, closer to the springs bottling operations, from 1871 to 1915.

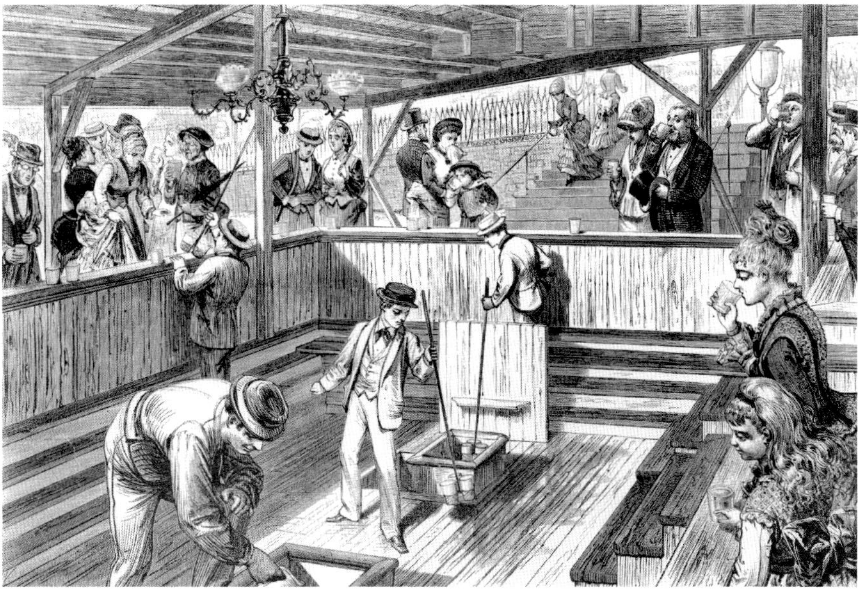

The springs provided employment for enterprising boys and girls who served up mineral water for all comers.

Saratoga in 1816, taking possession of land willed to him by his father and his uncle. Born of a prominent New York City family, Walton had been educated in England and resided previously in New York City, Ballston and Albany. Having studied with Aaron Burr, he practiced law and soon realized the advantages of public enterprise. Walton owned the United States or Magnesia Spring, and in 1819 built the Pavilion Hotel. To the northwest of the village settlements he began the building of an estate, later quite splendid and called Woodlawn, now the site of the Skidmore College campus. An enduring contribution of Henry Walton, and of his second wife Mathilda Cruger Yates, is their son Henry Walton, born in 1806. In the years before daguerreotypes and photography were in widespread application, his drawings, landscapes and portraits provide some of the earliest glimpses of Upstate New York places and people.[8]

John Clarke arrived about 1823. Born in Yorkshire, England, he came to the springs from New York City after operating one of that city's first soda fountains, an innovation of the time.[9] Clarke bought the Congress Spring and started bottling the waters for shipment through Troy downriver to New York City. He improved the grounds around the spring, draining the swampy land and laying the foundation for the park. By 1825, his improved bottling works, operated by a man and a boy, could fill and cork twelve hundred bottles of spring water in a day. He was a skillful promoter of his bottled water, building its reputation as a healthful and stimulating product. He marketed internationally, placing his product in the best hotels, trains and ships.

Clarke savored his life in Saratoga and was fully engaged in the advancement of the community. Among his civic initiatives was a local law that gave back a portion of the road tax for each tree planted by landowners on the roadways. Having bought additional land around the park in Saratoga Springs village, Clarke planned and laid out Circular Street, adding dimension and symmetry to the district. His own house still stands above Congress Park, keeping watch over the heart of the city. Clarke's success inspired others to tube new-found springs and to add bathhouses and more bottling works.

From the beginning there was awareness of and aspiration for life away in larger places. Some of the families went on after a generation to the western parts of the state or farther. Those who stayed brought a steady flow of health seekers, other visitors and enterprising people willing to build a community from the wilderness. And from the beginning, the local residents were close to the hospitality industry. An accommodating friendliness became the cultural finish atop the quiet New England reserve.

The Mineral Springs

The outstanding feature of the springs is their natural carbonation. The waters flow from the earth with carbon dioxide in solution. The nearest carbonated waters to those in Saratoga are found in Colorado. Other springs in the East and South are often sulfurous. Reassurance of the positive attributes of water, and bathing in particular, were an exciting discovery after some centuries of circumspection in Western culture. Famously, Queen Elizabeth is reported to have stated, "[I] bathe once a year whether I need it or not." The seventeenth-century belief that wearing linen had a cleansing effect probably still had adherents a century later.[10]

The tradition of health spas is an ancient one. In earlier civilizations, going to naturally pleasant surroundings where fresh waters are enjoyed for bathing and drinking was a privilege enjoyed by those who could afford it. In 1326, a town in southeast Belgium gave the name to the practice in modern times. A fountain in the woods near Espa gave relief and restoration to an ironmaster who well appreciated its chalybeate (iron) character. On the site he founded a health resort, now one of the most fashionable in the world.

The custom of journeying to healthful spas was taken up in the United States as it was practiced in Europe. Although primarily an activity for the privileged classes, by the 1820s the beginnings of touring and tourism had begun.[11] This purposeful form of leisure also provided opportunity for the young to meet the right sort of people in proper circumstances.

Elsewhere, springs were opening up where they could be found. In northern New York State, there were "mineral springs, oil springs, nitrogen springs, sulfur springs and salt springs."[12] There were springs in Virginia, and there was a class of people who could afford to go to both White Sulphur Springs, Virginia, and Saratoga.[13] Springs of long-standing custom were to be found in many states. Those of Lynn, Massachusetts, had been frequented by the Puritans.

In Saratoga, the springs are charged with carbon dioxide, which enables the water to dissolve the minerals from the rocks through which it passes on its way to the surface. The different springs vary in concentration and proportion of minerals and each was deemed appropriate for different therapeutic applications.

The described characteristics of the springs are antacid (alkaline), iron-rich (chalybeate) or laxative (cathartic). Bicarbonates of calcium and magnesium, along with sodium chloride (table salt) and potassium

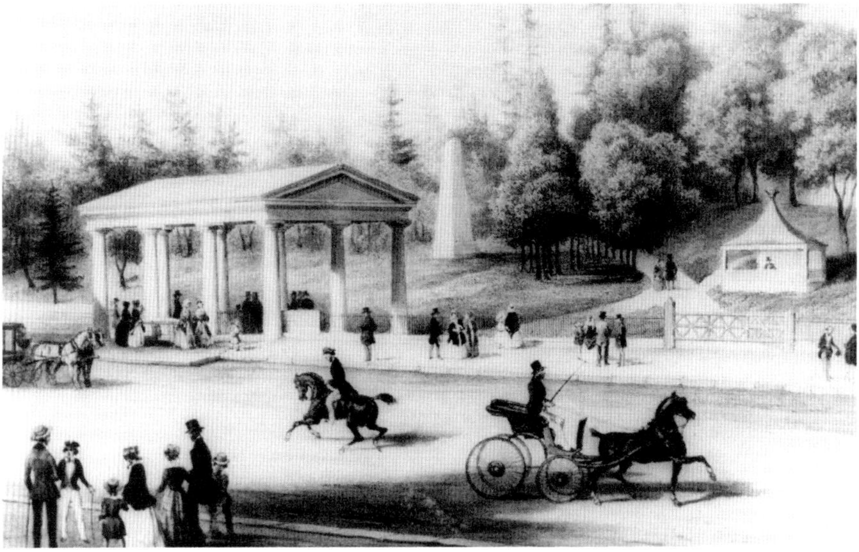

"Doctor" John Clark's improvements to the Congress Spring included a Greek-styled pavilion and landscaping that created Congress Park. The obelisk shaft in the background held the fresh water supply for the growing village.

chloride, form the bulk of the dissolved substances. Iron in this form was considered easily assimilated by the human body and valuable in treating anemia. Lithium was proclaimed to be of medical significance; today its use is considered in the treatment of nervous system disorders. Iodine was detected in several of the springs. Many other trace elements have been recorded.[14]

By 1830, the active springs were the High Rock and the Flat Rock; the Congress, the Columbian and the Hamilton, in the same park; the Washington, the President, the Monroe, the Red and the Ten Springs.[15]

Among the first medical men to endorse the value of the springs at Saratoga was Dr. John H. Steele from Leicester, Massachusetts, who came to this area at an early age. He was a physician, surgeon, chemist, geologist and researcher, and so recognized by eminent societies in North America and Europe. He wrote *An Analysis of the Mineral Waters of Saratoga and Ballston with Practical Remarks on their Medicinal Properties*, published in several editions until 1838. Distinguished physicians followed him, some opening clinics and treatment centers. The vogue for spas continued throughout the nineteenth century, with obvious appeal. The *New York Tribune* carried the advertisement in 1888,

Dr. Strong's Sanatorium
Saratoga Springs, New York
A popular resort for health, change, rest or recreation.
Elevator, electric bells, steam, open fireplaces, sun parlor and promenade on the roof, croquet, lawn tennis. Massage, Turkish, Russian, Roman, electric thermal, all baths and related remedial appliances.
Family prayers daily, no additional charge.[16]

When a spring was detected or found by drilling and was desired to be opened, it was excavated and directed by tubing to ground level, the excavation filled in and leveled off. A structural covering would enhance and dignify the location.

John Clarke set the pattern with Greek temples above the Congress and Columbian Springs in 1830.

The custom was generally followed of allowing free public access to the springs, another aspect of Saratoga that made the visitor welcome. The amenities, usually lodging and dining houses, were closely identified with a particular spring, and on this the fortunes of an establishment might rise or fall. As is always true in promoting real estate, location was the most important factor. An Urban Cultural Park Feasibility in Saratoga Springs proclaimed of the springs on October 31, 1980, "The waters do not cure all diseases, but they very definitely are worthwhile in a large percentage of cases of arthritis, rheumatism, circulatory and skin problems."

A National Leisure Class

From the early days of the republic, trade carried on as in colonial times. Long-established cycles, including long-distance shipping from New England to the South, the Caribbean and Africa, built wealth for the traders. A seasonal migration of Southern planters brought families to Newport, Rhode Island. In springtime the planters' ships would carry them north, along with cargo, to enjoy the summer in Newport's ocean breezes. Their ships would return for them in the fall.

A resort circuit developed. The oceanfront destinations included those in New Jersey, as well as Rhode Island and Massachusetts. In this circuit, the mineral spas held their special place. The natural settings offered strength as the visitors' puritanical fear of nature dissipated. The healthy purpose supplied an environment implying safety and appropriateness for social development. Cool, stately Bostonians met with the languid elegant planters from the South. Of course there were many springs, north and south; Saratoga's could be championed for their nonsulfurous diversity. The resorts in the North took the lead; engaging in the full measure of society called for trips to the springs.

The idea of aristocracy continued in the early republic. The predominance of the landed gentry, particularly in the North, was shrinking in the face of newly prosperous entrepreneurs. Americans were becoming experts in industry and marketing, and the evolution of successful resorts relied on the ability to cater to the newly wealthy.

It was noted with surprise by visitors from Europe and the Southern states that people of different classes were able to mingle freely in Saratoga. Approval of this opportunity was viewed according to the observer's perspective. Those with social aspirations came to see Saratoga as rich with potential for finding illustrious matrimonial matches for their offspring. For the old money, the more relaxed attitudes of Saratoga provided some relief from the stiffer proprieties of other places on the circuit, such as Newport. In Saratoga, these attractions were both available.

Travel

Saratoga is just far enough away from the cities to be an adventurous trip. Entrepreneurial initiative ensured that distances would be manageable. Through the 1820s, the journey was a long one. Almira Reid, the wife of a whaling captain from Fairhaven, Massachusetts, journeyed for eight days in 1826 by sloop, steamer and stage to reach the spa.[17] The overland route was equally difficult. General M. Whitney traveled in July 1827 "seven days over hills and dales, mountains and rivers" from Boston. This was all worthwhile to take in the springs, the changeover of the crowd at Putnam's "monstrous establishment," remains of fortifications and battles at Bemis Heights and the Hudson River and the thriving new Champlain and Erie Canals.[18]

The railroad connection to Saratoga was an early one in the transportation revolution. In September 1831, Albany was connected to Schenectady; in 1832, a rail line reached Saratoga Springs. Horse-drawn cars were soon replaced by steam locomotives, ensuring a novel and thrilling experience at a breathtaking twenty miles an hour.

The first train tracks came right up Broadway. There the passenger disembarked to see the elegant boarding establishments stretching along the

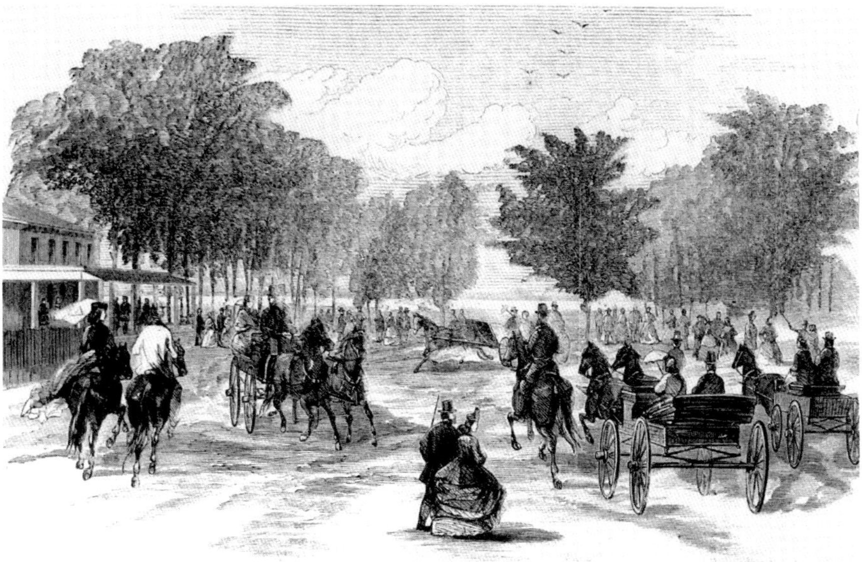

Traffic has always been a problem when events take place. In the early days, the event was carriage rides to Saratoga Lake every afternoon.

street: the United States, Columbian Hotel, Montgomery Hall, Union Hall, Pavilion and Congress Halls. The needs of travelers were arranged for:

> *There is in the village a printing office and book store, with which is connected a reading room, a mineralogical room, and a library...The reading room is ornamented with a variety of maps and charts, and is furnished by the daily mails with about 100 papers, from different parts of the United States and from the Canadas, besides many valuable periodical publications...These rooms afford a pleasant retreat from the poise and bustle of the boarding establishments, and are much frequented by ladies and gentlemen of taste and fashion...*
>
> *The mail arrives at Saratoga Springs, during the months of July, August, and September, every evening, and departs every morning...*
>
> *At both the villages of Ballston and Saratoga Springs, there are always sufficient objects of amusement to render the transient residence of their summer guests pleasant & agreeable. Those whose taste is not gratified at the billiard rooms, which are annexed to most of the boarding establishments, can always enjoy a pleasing recreation at the reading rooms, or in a short excursion in the neighborhood, where sufficient beauty and novelty of scenery are always presented to render*

> *it highly interesting. The amusements of the day are usually crowned with a ball or promenade. The respective apartments appropriated for these occasions, are calculated to accommodate from 150 to 200 guests; but they often contain a much greater number.*
>
> *The spacious areas of the cotillion rooms are between 80 and 90 feet in length, and when enlivened by the associated beauty and gaiety resorting to the springs, present a scene of novelty and fascination seldom equaled.*[19]

Soon to come to spa were inventions and novelties such as daguerreotypes, which were rapidly promulgated after their invention in 1839, and the telegraph that enabled the traveler to keep in touch with the home office after 1840.

Live entertainment had become an attraction from the early years, competing with the prayer sessions and games of whist. A reminiscence published in 1889 included long-remembered amusements. Vilalave, a strolling player who arrived in 1818, specialized in sleight of hand and tightrope exhibitions, and by 1821 he had formed a stock company with a trim little theater on Washington Street. At Broadway and Caroline Street, Walton Hall hosted lectures, debates, magicians and touring dramatic companies. The first music at the hotels is said to have arrived in 1822 with the celebrated black band led by Frank Johnson, whose tunes of the day and original compositions made Saratoga Springs a destination.[20]

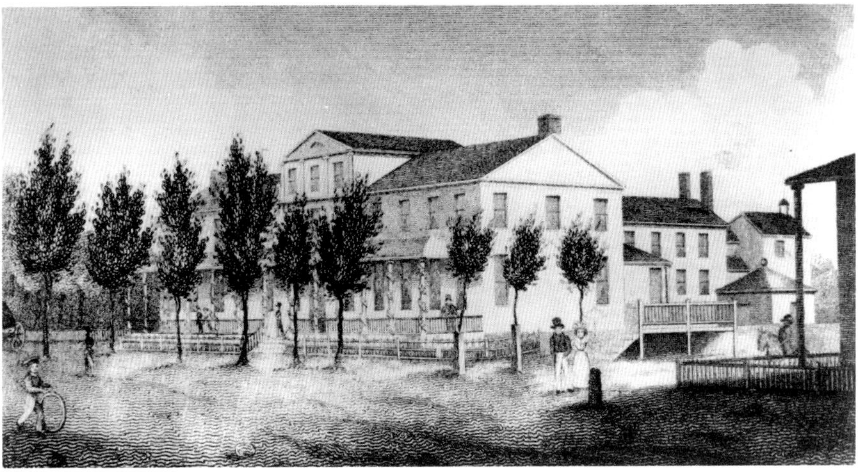

The Pavilion Hotel, one of the early establishments, occupied the area on Broadway where city hall has stood since 1871. The Pavilion's gardens and spring were a feature of the early village.

Several places of entertainment were later taken over by churches. The Elysium was purchased by the Roman Catholic congregation and used for worship while St. Peter's was built over it, after which the little theater was dismantled and removed. Covent Garden was put up by Daniel McLaren, father of celebrated comedian Dan Rice, then removed and the First Presbyterian Church was built in its place. A man named Hysenbottle built the Globe Theater in 1841, which subsequently suited the Methodists for a time.

In the words of the day, adapted from ode to Bath, England:

Of all the gay places the world can afford,
By gentle and simple for pastime adored,
Fine balls and fine singing, fine buildings and springs
Fine rides and fine views, and a thousand fine things
(Not to mention the sweet situation and air),
What place with these springs can ever compare?
First in manners, in dress, and in fashions to shine,
Saratoga, the glory must ever be thine!

The visual evidence of the past in Saratoga Springs is so intertwined with people and events that it is difficult to try to separate them. The people, what they did and what they built are presented in chronological order to the extent possible. Themes that weave in and out of the inevitable passage of time are entrepreneurial enthusiasm, synergy of personalities and an uninhibited expression of individual taste. Although this combination of factors may not be unique to Saratoga, it flourished here and reached its peak at the turn of the twentieth century.

Commerce in Earnest

The Hudson River Valley was a leader in commercial tourism, building on the natural attractions and a ready market in the growing cities. There arose a rivalry in promoting visitation for the waters. Ballston Spa, six miles south of Saratoga Springs, shared the same fault line whose gift was the mineral springs. In the beginning, Saratoga Springs was the more somber and strait-laced place, governed by the large township surrounding it. Ballston Spa had its advantages as the principal town, having been made the county seat in 1794.[21] Embellishments of entertainment and gaiety were added first at Ballston Spa. The opening of the elegant Sans Souci Hotel in 1803 put that village ahead of the spare accommodations at Saratoga Springs.

Wrote the Reverend Elkaneh Watson of Ballston Spa,

> *This is the most splendid watering place in America and scarcely surpassed in Europe in its dimensions and the taste and elegance of it arrangements…Here was congregated a fine exhibition of the beau monde. A large proportion of the assembly was from the Southern States, and distinguished by their elegant and polished manners. In the place of the old-fashioned country dances and four-handed reels of Revolutionary days, I was pleased to notice the advance of refined customs, and the introduction of the graces of Paris in the elegant cotillion and quadrille.*

Saratoga Springs responded in kind, hosting in its expanding accommodations the diversions and entertainments needed to gain preeminence. As Cleveland Amory wrote in *The Last Resorts*, Saratoga became known "if not for home society and the *haut monde*, then at least for hotel society and the *beau monde*. Newport, with its ocean and its palaces, was the Queen of Watering Places, but Saratoga, with its springs and its horses, was the King of Spas."[22]

Famed Newport habitué Henry Clews was able to confirm,

> *The ladies of the West have heard of Saratoga, the far-famed spa of America, and as fortunes of their husbands mount higher and higher into the millions, they become more and more anxious to see this great summer resort of wealth and fashion. Their influence prevails, and at the height of the gay season they may be seen at the United States or the Grand Union. They are in practically a new world. There is the rustle and perfume, the glitter and show, the pomp and circumstance of the more advanced civilization of the East, and the ladies, with innate keenness, are quick to perceive a marked difference between this gorgeous panorama and the more prosaic surroundings to which they have been accustomed.*[23]

In 1819, Saratoga Springs was separated as a town from the original larger town of Saratoga, and a Board of Excise formed; in 1826, the village of Saratoga Springs was incorporated and chartered within the town of Saratoga Springs. Now, with its own governance, the community could shape itself and better serve its purposes. It undertook the requirements of a village with an identity distinct from the surrounding farms and woodlands. Before long, Saratoga Springs caught up with Ballston Spa and soon eclipsed it as a resort.

The transformation was described first in personal correspondence, as Elihu Hoyt, of Deerfield, Massachusetts, wrote.

> *Monday August 6th, 1827: We begin to see the fashionable world as it displays itself at this place. We see here some of every condition in life. One would suppose that we should find everybody here on the sick list but it is far from the case. Many of the visitors come here probably in good sound health, for amusement and for the sake of spending a week or two among the fashionable to see and to be seen. Here we see all the latest fashions of the cities intermixed with the more plain fashions of the country. We have fashionable balls, concerts, and all descriptions of amusements. Many matches have been negotiated here which have eventuated in wedlock.*[24]

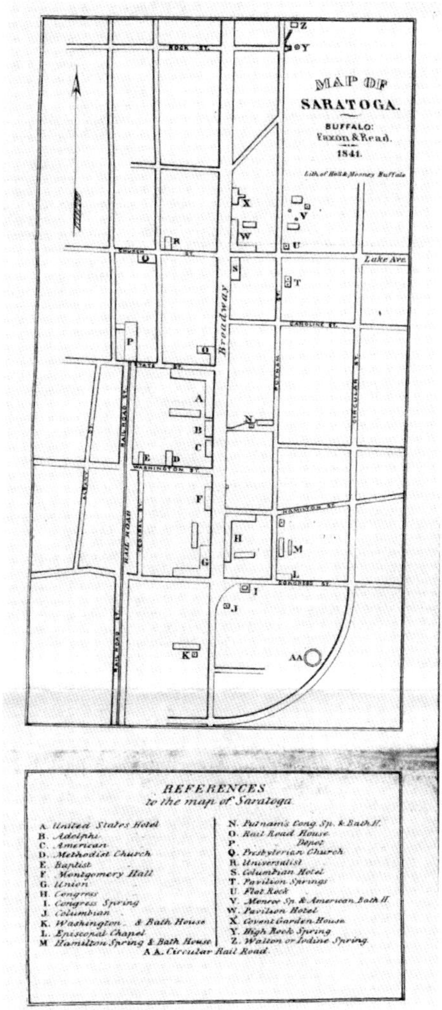

1841 map, Hall & Mooney. The hotel district was concentrated on Broadway, with all attractions at hand. Development followed social activity, closer to the springs in the lower village.

When the railroad reached Saratoga Springs in 1832, it brought convenience for the travelers. Yet there still was significant expense involved in such travel, and it inclined to attract only the more "substantial" class of persons.

The recorded history is inclined to give emphasis to "the right people." Yet what distinguishes Saratoga is that it represents the opening up of leisure to broader classes of people. Beneficially, the year-round residents acquired a quite sufficient worldliness and ease of exchange with those who came from away, such that they became able to enjoy the sophistication of the wider world from their exceptional seat between the city and the mountains. Most of the permanent residents and some of the dignitaries among the seasonal crowd would continue to influence the community with a calm and moderating restraint. Nevertheless, the ebullience of summer life inevitably generated legendary escapades and excesses.

Chapter Two

What They Built

An Architectural Landscape Develops

The most evocative evidence of the past stands in the built landscapes left to us. Thanks to its early start, Saratoga retained preeminence among the "watering places" in America through the nineteenth century. Due to the prosperity that came, the character of the built city kept pace with the development of American epochal styles. The sense of history and pride of place allowed much of it to be preserved and maintained. Of course, the pioneer shelters that preceded "design by architect" were basic cabins engineered by expediency.

Saratoga was emerging from the wilderness when the Federal style appeared in America about 1790.[25] Federal style is an English architectural form, carried on in America after the Revolution. There are a few examples extant in Saratoga Springs.

The Olde Bryan Inn (123 Maple Avenue, the John Bryan House), important to Saratoga for its location and connection to the earliest settlement, dates from the 1820s. In it are found some features of the Federal style, including a low pitched roof, the plain façade and slender window sidelights flanking the doors. In the Federal style, the effect of Robert Adam emphasizes a refinement of bulk, decorative richness of color and ornamental detail.

Two styles that lend importance to Saratoga Springs' visual character are Greek Revival (about 1820 to 1840) and the various modes classified as Victorian (1840 through the rest of the nineteenth century).

There are several examples of the Greek Revival style in Saratoga Springs. This important American style is characterized by its symmetry and the raising of the first floor as on a platform or podium, in the pattern of Greek (then Roman) temples of antiquity. Neoclassical design

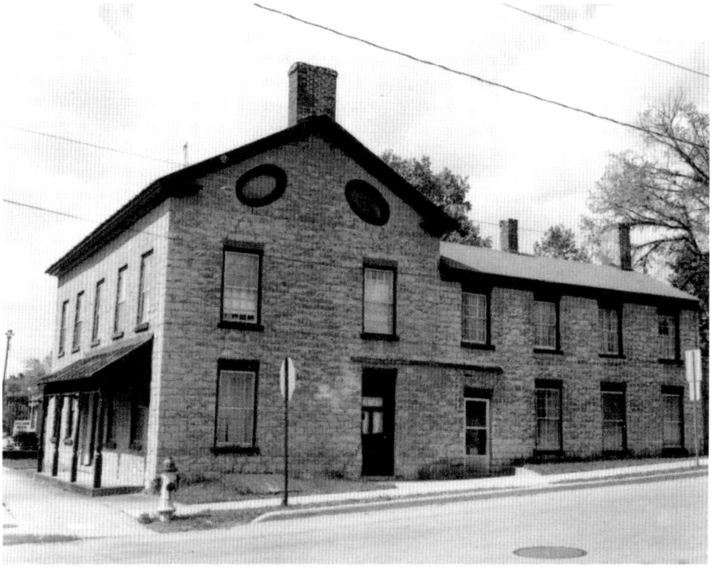

The Olde Bryan Inn, standing at the Upper Village site, was built about 1826, its features characteristic of the Federal style. Its predecessor is seen in the lithograph of High Rock Spring.

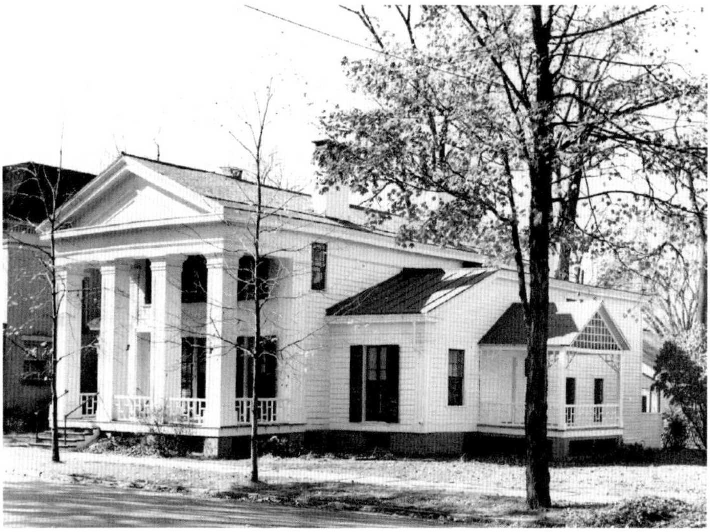

Built probably by John Hodgman along with the Clarke house, the Jumel house's square wooden columns are distinctive. The wings were added later, but in keeping with the style.

tends to the massive, plain and austere, with white surfaces preferred. The triangular pediment and an entablature band above the porch are distinctive features. Surfaces are generally left plain without enrichment and are painted white.

The earliest documented Greek Revival building in Saratoga Springs is the Jumel house at 129 Circular Street. It was built in 1832. Madame Eliza Bowen Jumel (1775–1865), one of the most colorful characters in all of the spa's history, purchased the house in 1839. By this time, many of her tumultuous life events were behind her—the unsuccessful attempts at acceptance into New York society, the death of her wealthy husband Stephen Jumel, adventures in Napoleonic France and her brief marriage to Aaron Burr. She purchased the house from John Hodgman and named it Les Tuileries, after the palace connected to the Louvre in Paris. Her conspicuous summers in Saratoga followed. She boldly had her carriage driven to the head of the line in the afternoon parade from downtown to Saratoga Lake, and for a while was queen of the day. Her tenure of the house, marked in the last year by loneliness, lasted until 1864.

The first designed structures in Congress Park, erected by Dr. John Clarke, included the temple over the Congress Spring. This set the tone for

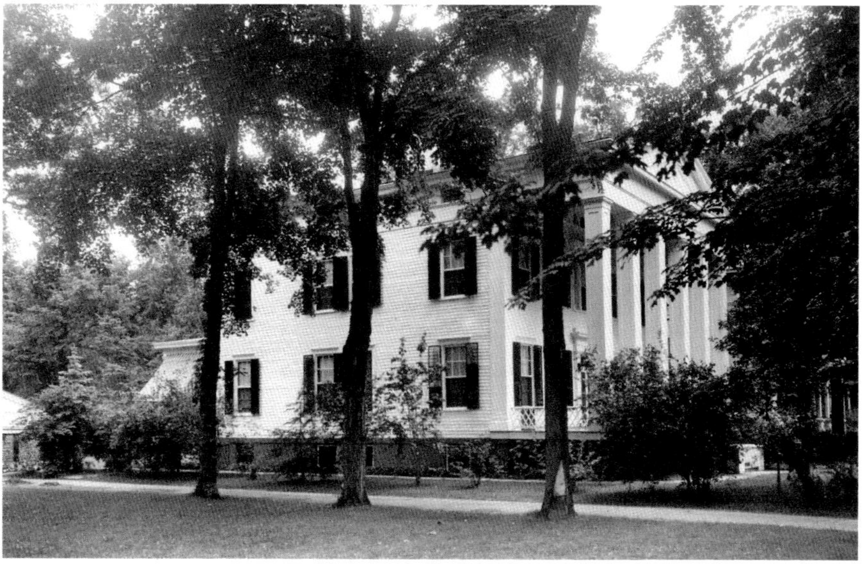

In 1832 John Clarke placed his temple-like house in a classical position on heights overlooking his spring and park. Correct in Neoclassical style, a complete entablature runs around the top of the wall below the eaves.

similarly emphasizing the importance of the springs elsewhere in the city for some time to come.

The classical period for Saratoga Springs lasted until the Civil War. During this time the aspect of the village was distinguished by the dignity and regularity provided to the streetscape by such architecture. The standard color scheme for this style is white or muted ochre.[26] It suited the quality of people who came to attend court or to visit Chancellor Reuben Walworth, as well as the genteel nature of taking the healing waters.

Showman that he was, John Clarke knew that the satisfaction of visitors to the springs would be enhanced by the architecture of the stately Greek Revival style. His residence at 46 Circular Street was in keeping with this fashion. It sits above Congress Park grandly and serenely. For years its magisterial presence stood alone on the horizon it dominated. The house follows the form of a six-columned Greek temple.

A notable feature of the Clarke and Jumel houses is that the columns on the front porch are flat and square rather than round. This characteristic was made popular by George Washington at his home Mount Vernon, and has been regarded as an example of his practicality

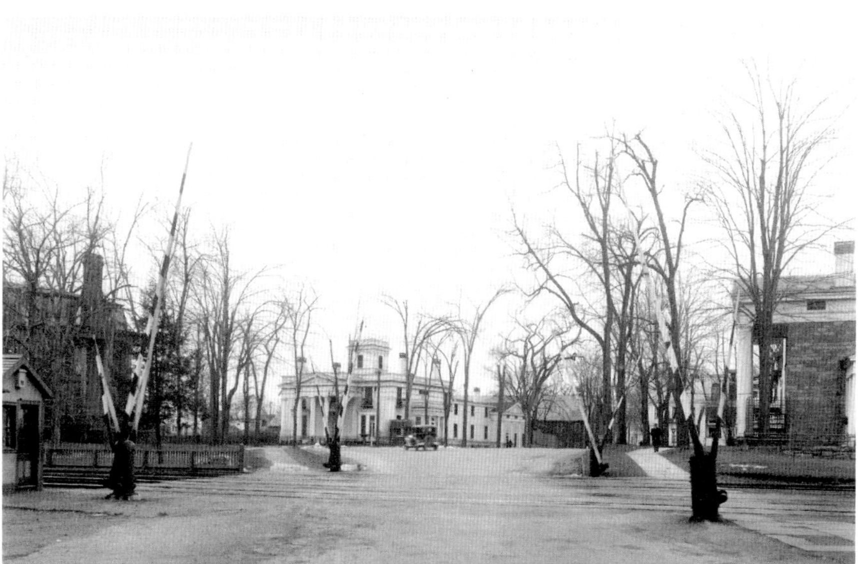

The house at 4 Franklin Square was built by Judge Thomas Marvin in 1832, after he had purchased the United States Hotel and property on the square, which lay beyond the railroad tracks separating it from the hotel district. It has the greatest mass, proportion and architectural features of the surviving Neoclassical buildings in the city.

The building at 1 Franklin Square, built circa 1834, achieves a dramatic effect contrasting the Doric porch with the yellow stone body of the building. The side wings resemble those on the Bower House of Northampton, Massachusetts, the model Greek Revival house in America, built in 1828. As elsewhere in Saratoga Springs, some later modification occurred, in this case to the windows in the 1870s.

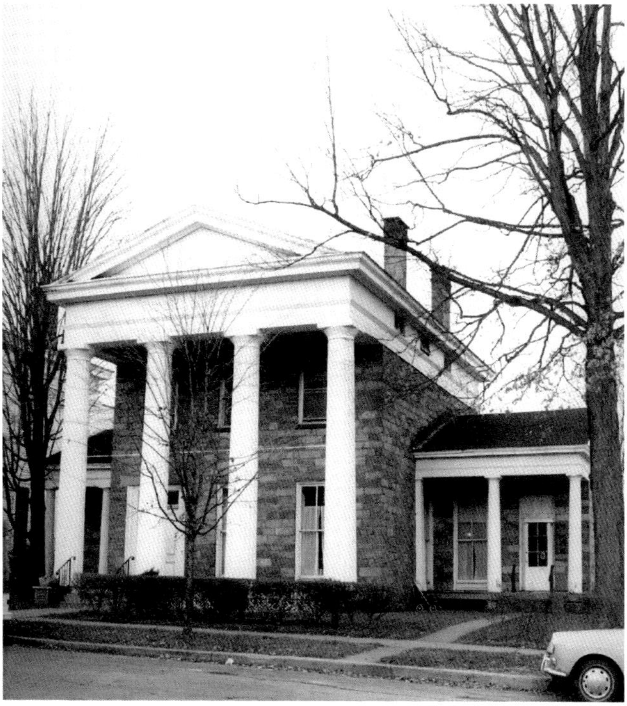

in retaining good form. The column style was also incorporated into the house of Philip Schuyler, Washington's host in Saratoga (now Schuylerville), in a porch that no longer exists.

Queen Victoria reigned in England from 1837 to 1901. The predominant taste of the times featured ornate display, technical invention and complexity, and this culture significantly influenced the living styles of the United States.

Saratoga Springs today is identified strongly with the Victorian era. Along with the building booms that occurred during this time, the prodigious output of printed images was spurred by evolving technical capability. From engraved images appearing in widely circulating newspapers and periodicals, photography came to memorialize both fleeting experiences and the more lasting built landscape.

At least three distinctive facets of accessing nature appear prominently in Saratoga's Victorian architecture: the FRONT PORCH creates a transition from interior to exterior; BAY WINDOWS and OBSERVATORY TOWERS thrust the indoors occupant safely into the greenery of shrubs or treetops.

Early Victorian Styles

Bethesda Episcopal Church represents the Gothic Revival, a phenomenon of the early Victorian years. In this country the Gothic style of pointed, arched windows and steeply pitched roofs was considered suitable primarily for churches. It was closely identified with England, where it was taken up widely and considered something of a national style.

It took years for the Episcopal Church in the United States to regain strength after the War of Independence, as this branch of faith had originated in the Church of England. John Clarke, the Lancashireman who built up much of the village, had provided a chapel near the Congress Spring for worship along these lines. With Victorian culture becoming predominant and fashionable, the Episcopal Church rebounded successfully.

The Saratoga Springs congregation contacted architect Richard Upjohn, who had just gained national recognition for his Trinity Church on Wall

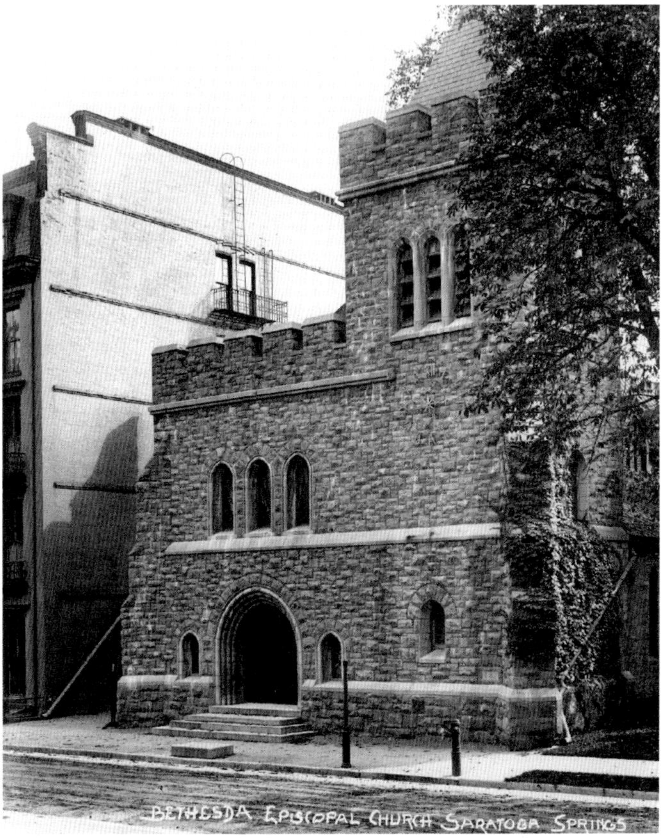

The exterior of Bethesda Episcopal Church was altered twice, with side aisles added in 1858 and an expanded and remodeled front added in 1887, changing Upjohn's original Gothic design.

Street in New York City. Upjohn came to the springs, met with the vestry in Judge Thomas Marvin's house on Franklin Square and then provided full working documents for the building. Gideon Putnam's son Rockwell gave the land, tearing down his own house for the site. Opened for worship in 1844, Bethesda is considered important as an example of English Gothic church style in this country.[27]

The church was remodeled twice, in 1858 and in 1887, when Tiffany windows of angels were added to the front façade, which was changed to more of a Norman Romanesque style.

The Italian Style

Shortly after 1840, a distinctive vogue for Italian culture expressed itself in this architectural style. It is distinguished by low or flat rooflines and much wooden bracketing with window ornamentation, preferably arched, and often a tower on the roof. One of the examples in Saratoga Springs is the school built in 1856 at Circular and Spring Streets by the Reverend Dr. Beecher. Two years later it was purchased by Reverend Charles F.

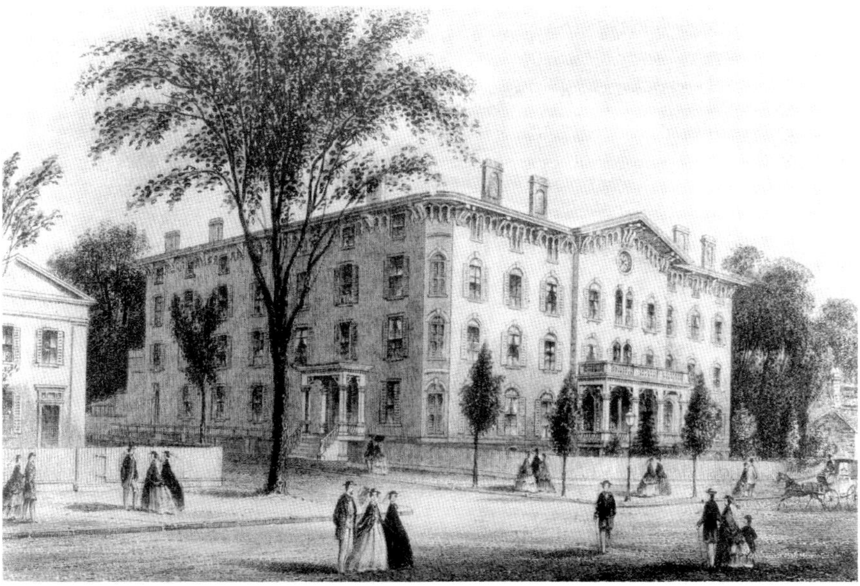

Temple Grove, built in 1856 in the Italianate style as a school, has seen successive lives as part of Skidmore College and an apartment complex.

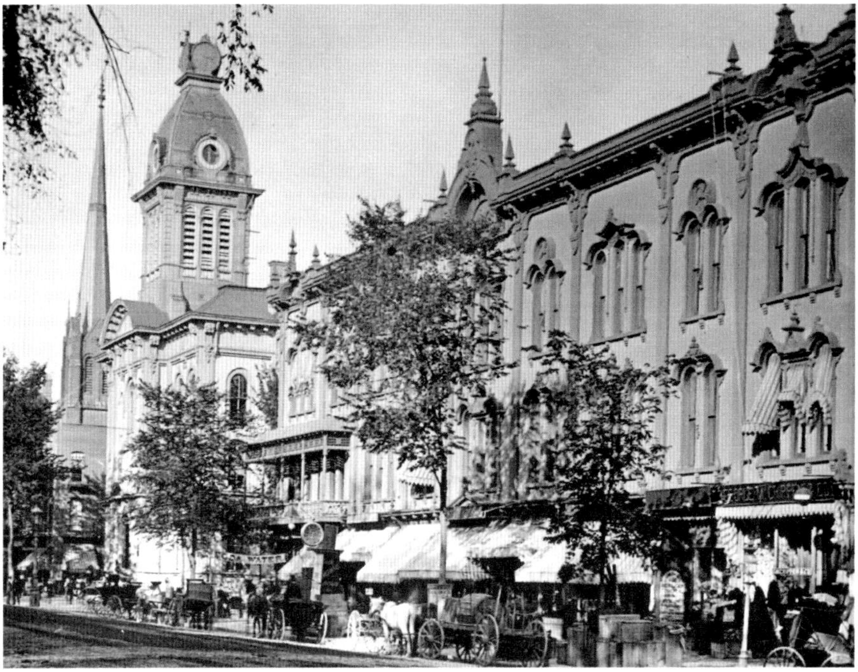

The Ainsworth Building, city hall and the Presbyterian church are here seen at the heart of the city on Broadway.

Dowd and made into a first-class ladies' seminary. Dowd so improved the facility that the building itself still serves into present times. Dowd is remembered for his scientific studies that resulted in the establishment of standardized time zones. The Ainsworth Building (456–470 Broadway in Saratoga Springs) is an unusual variation on the Italian style, which was significant from 1840 to 1875.

Italian style was the first of the Victorian styles to become widely popularized in the United States. Building on the importance of classical references, the political emergence of Italy in the 1840s made some familiarity with Italian culture almost mandatory.

In the photograph, both the Ainsworth Building of 1871 and the town (later city) hall behind it show characteristically round arches and ornaments. The Casino in Congress Park and the Adelphi Hotel on Broadway all belong to this distinctive style.

The Hotels

The hotels left the most durable impression of Saratoga Springs. They provided a sort of stage set for the city and were written about, drawn and then photographed copiously. They were places for observing people and being seen from the immense piazzas fronting the hotels; for departing and arriving in carriages; and for dancing in the evenings. In addition, they provided restaurants for eating, a principal resort activity.

After Gideon Putnam's success with his tavern and boardinghouse, others followed in similar enterprises. On the next major intersection, the Columbian Hotel went up in 1808; Putnam's own Congress Hall, nearest the spring, was opened in 1812 by his heirs. The Pavilion Hotel of 1819 stood across Lake Avenue from the Columbian, where city hall now stands.

After 1830, American hotel design was profoundly changed from the boardinghouse type of building. The best accommodations were to become great public spaces, grand in scale and with salons, dining rooms and ballrooms to detain and entertain large crowds of visitors. Hotels were intended to attract social organizations to assemble and meet. According to the new design principles, light and air should be made available to as many

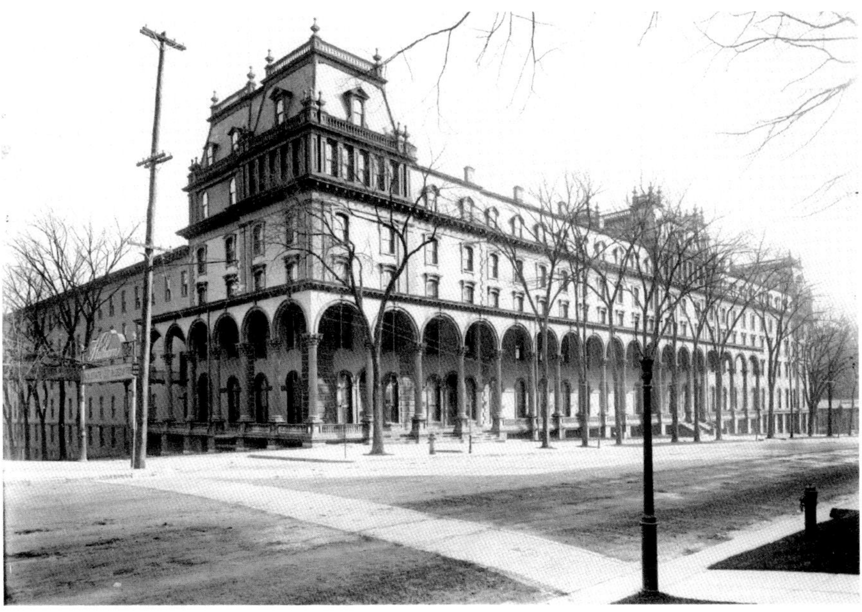

The Congress Hall Hotel covered the expanse between Congress and Spring Streets at the northwest corner of Congress Park.

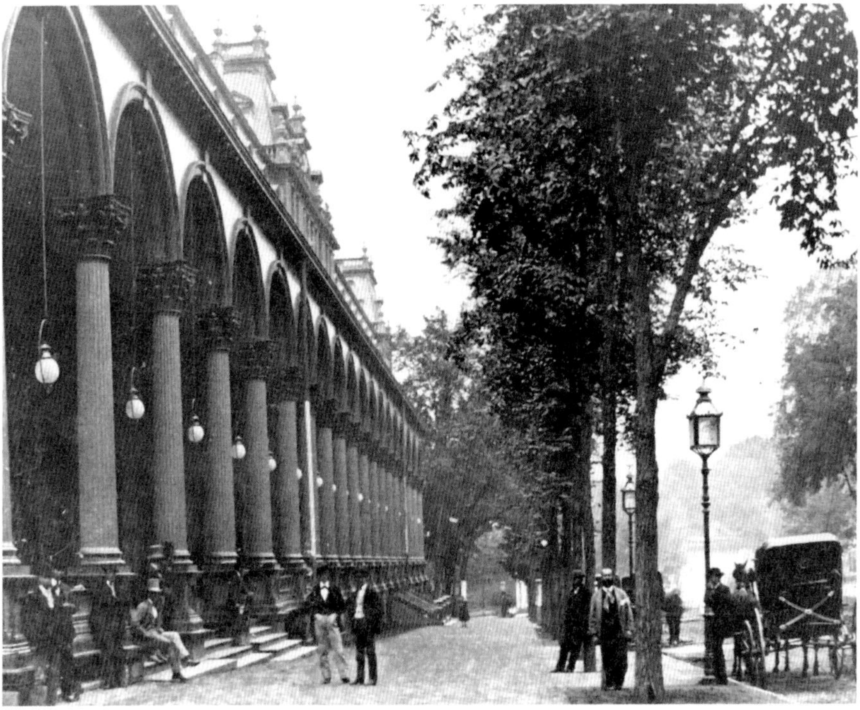

Location and the imposing front on Broadway gave a strong claim on the tourist trade.

rooms as possible. Long, narrow wings around a central courtyard achieved this purpose.[28] The hotels were remodeled to keep up with stylistic changes.

Congress Hall was one of the first to adopt the Tremont House innovations. It also had been one of the first hotels in Saratoga Springs to extend a great porch or piazza along the entire front of the building, at a height of two stories. Congress Hall was to burn down in 1866. It was rebuilt and fully appointed by one of the vigorous Saratogans, H.H. Hathorn, in 1868. The wings extended back three hundred feet, a promenade on the roof gave guests a superlative view and an elevator ("vertical railroad") carried guests effortlessly to the upper floors. Music for the Friday night balls was provided by the unparalleled Bernstein's Orchestra. A bridge over Spring Street carried visitors into the second-floor ballroom in the building that still stands on the northeast corner of Spring and Broadway.

Union Hall, originally started by Gideon Putnam, was purchased in 1864 by the Leland brothers, William, Charles and Warren. They built an opera house at the rear of their courtyard and added cottages in the courtyard as luxury accommodations for those who could afford a bit more privacy. They

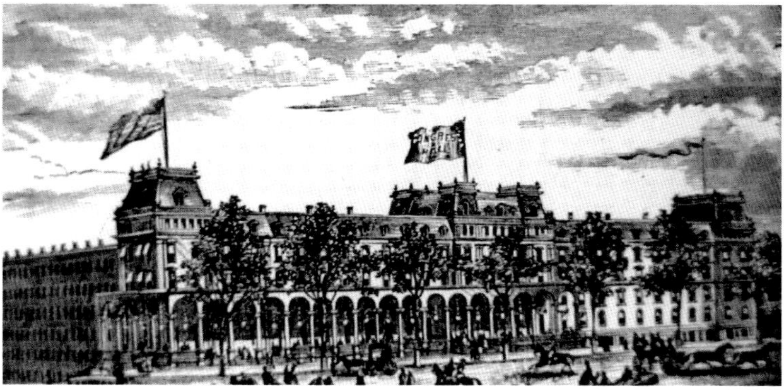

Advertising cuts in the big-city newspapers were a key to remaining competitive.

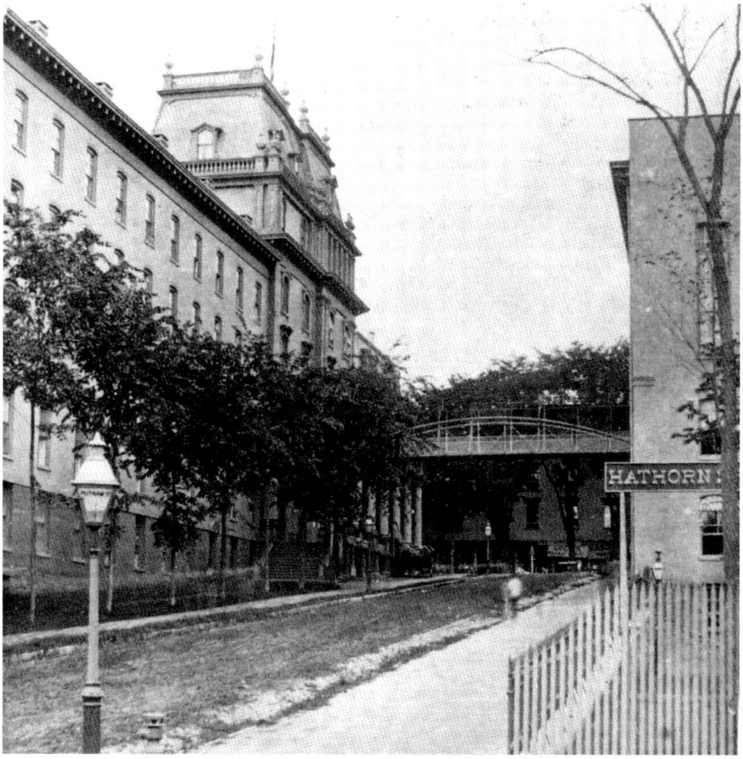

Looking toward Broadway from the corner of Putnam and Spring Streets, a footbridge crosses from the Congress Hall Hotel to its second-floor ballroom in the building across the street. Congress Hall, built by Gideon Putnam, was remodeled after a fire in the Second Empire style and later razed in 1912–13.

expanded the building and renamed it the Grand Union in 1869. The Grand Union pushed the limits of sustainability. It was promoted as the largest hotel in the world, with 825 rooms connected by two miles of hallways, one mile of piazzas and a dining room that could hold twelve hundred people. By 1871, with financial obligations in New York City complicating their holdings, the Lelands were bankrupt. The hotel was bought at auction by A.T. Stewart, the department store magnate, who was actively buying up the block. After even further expanding the hotel, Stewart died in 1876.

Judge Henry Hilton, executor of Stewart's estate, was an old-time judge who had learned well and done well in the business of politics. He had no scruples about duping the widow Stewart out of almost all of her inheritance. He proceeded to run down Stewart's various enterprises and, cut away from New York society, he lived out his life improving Woodlawn, the old Walton parkland estate, with Mrs. Stewart held close by as his permanent guest.

The original part of the UNITED STATES HOTEL was built in 1823. It was an impressive three-story brick structure, with a two-story colonnade in front covering a piazza raised far above the street. The United States became the contender against the Grand Union, and after complete refashioning following fire in 1865, was drawing the most elegant guests by the end of the century. The hotel was a draw from its early years for visitors to the Walworths and other celebrities of the day. Among the authors who through its long run made the United States a landmark were Washington Irving, Edgar Allen Poe, Nathaniel Hawthorne and James Fenimore Cooper.

Postwar Exuberance and the Empire Style

The newly rediscovered love of nature—as a Victorian sensibility—translated into architecture, within the strictures of the times. The main thoroughfare of Saratoga Springs had been made an exhilarating portrait

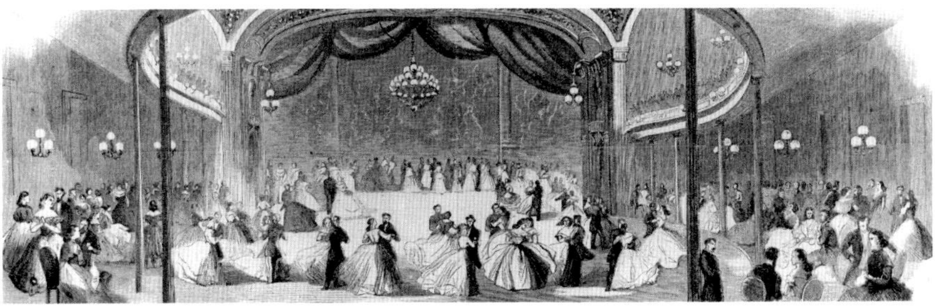

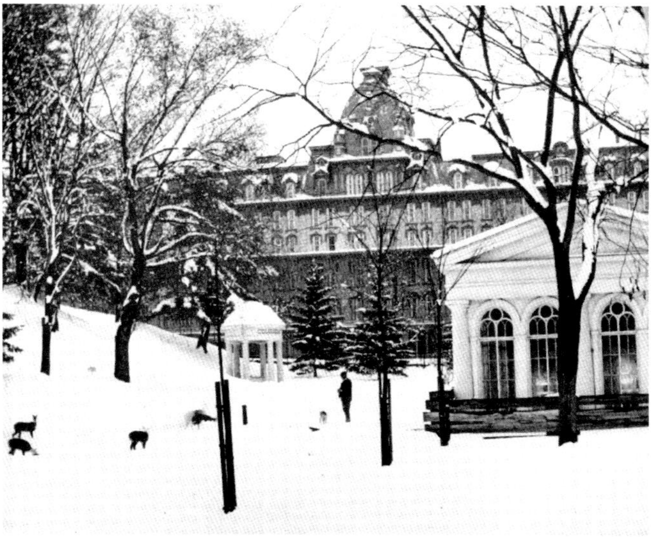

Victorian taste added arches and winter enclosure to Congress Spring's Greek pavilion. The Grand Central Hotel in the background lasted only two years, burning in 1874, dating this photograph to the winter of 1873–74.

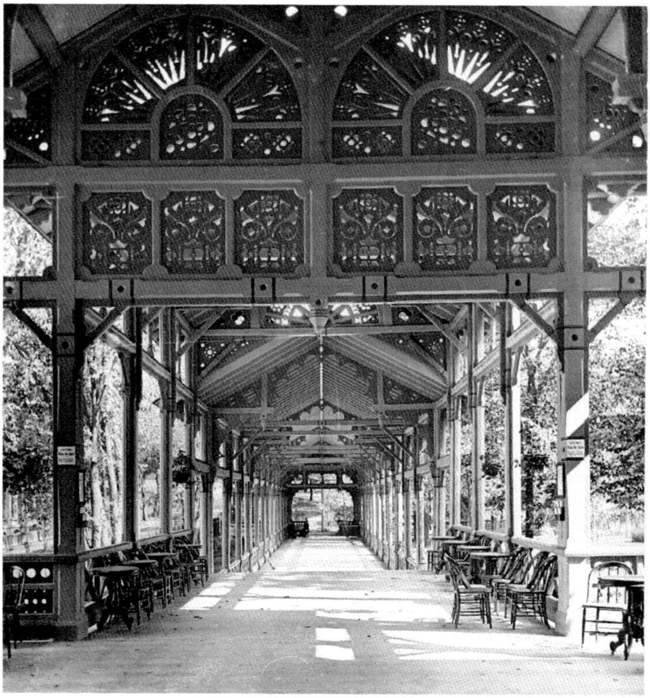

Throngs of visitors could "take the waters" in all kinds of weather under the protecting roof of the Congress Park pavilion. Mineral waters were dispensed from elegant bars.

Opposite: Leland's Opera House hosted musical, variety and dramatic productions, dances and conventions as the resort blossomed with racing and post–Civil War prosperity.

of success into which the summer visitor could step. The high Victorian style known as Second Empire swept into Saratoga Springs with the summer patrons' good fortune accompanying and following the Civil War.

The summer guests prior to the war represented the political, social and sometimes intellectual elite of the country. After the war, the cream of Southern society was gone, replaced by the industrial buccaneers who were igniting new financial horizons. The Second Empire style, whose heyday was roughly 1865 to 1875, was suited for them. The grandeur and mass of buildings such as the Grand Union Hotel or the United States expressed mountainous power, while the controlled order suggested adherence to conservative values. The distinctive mansard roof and other Second Empire features came along following the Civil War.

Many houses in Saratoga Springs were built by local residents, successful merchants and industrialists from nearby, often Albany or Troy. Up to this time the glamorous summer residents had stayed at the hotels. Even those in the perpetual resort circuit chose to build their "cottages" in places like Newport, Rhode Island. During this epoch, some chose to make a statement in Saratoga instead.

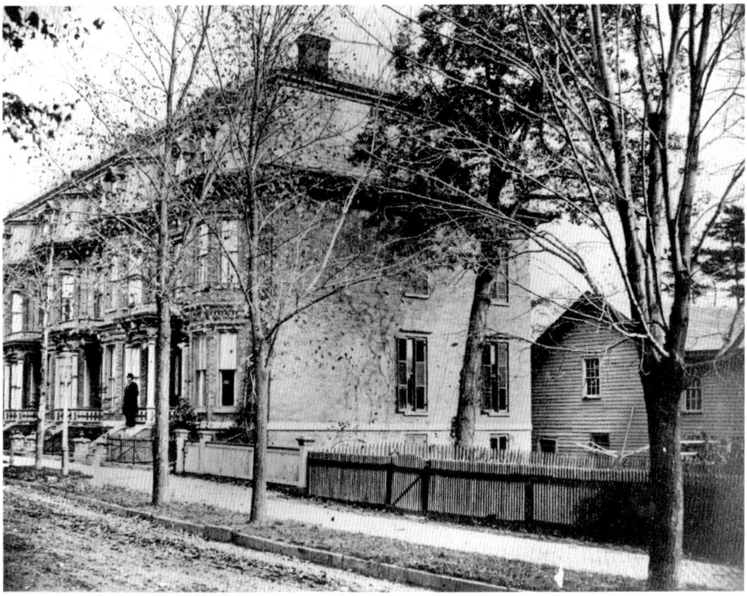

The Holmes block of town houses on Woodlawn Street remains a good example of the Second Empire style, characterized by usable space on the top floor due to the nearly vertical front roofline.

Queen Anne and Romanesque

Probably more surviving buildings than of any other type in Saratoga Springs belong to the Queen Anne style, which dominated from 1880 to about 1895. Features described as Romanesque are often included in this style group. Shingle style is a treatment popular in America that is part of this overall fashion.

Romanesque features are displayed on the Algonquin Building on Broadway. Built in 1892–93, the Algonquin anticipated what would one hundred years later be recognized as a key to successful downtowns: the inclusion of spacious apartments on several floors above fine stores at street level. These were equipped with decorative fireplaces and were lighted with large windows. Lasting appeal was assured with sturdy construction, and the stonework was superbly finished in time-proven motifs. The checkerboard pattern is borrowed from French Romanesque architecture of seven centuries earlier.

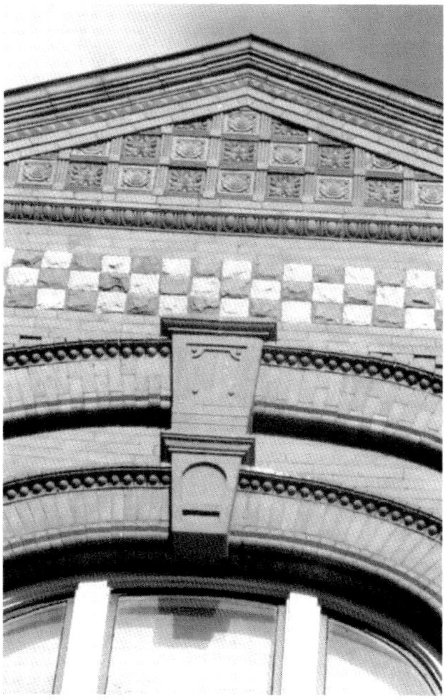

The Algonquin Building at Broadway and Grove Street survives as a massive Romanesque Revival structure with natural light provided to upper-floor apartments through central stairwells.

The Lucy Skidmore Scribner House on North Broadway was built in 1898. It was constructed under her supervision and she elected to apply styling of the late Queen Anne genre, including an English gambrel roof facing the street. Combining elements of several historic periods, the house is considered an elegant understatement of Mrs. Scribner's worldly travels with the Victorian penchant for openness to nature.

Many residences in Saratoga Springs were designed by R. Newton Brezee. He opened his Saratoga office in 1884 after apprenticing in Garden City, Long Island, with the architect A.T. Stewart, and at the dawn of the Queen Anne vogue. S. Gifford Slocum is the other architect who made a substantial lasting impact in Saratoga Springs.

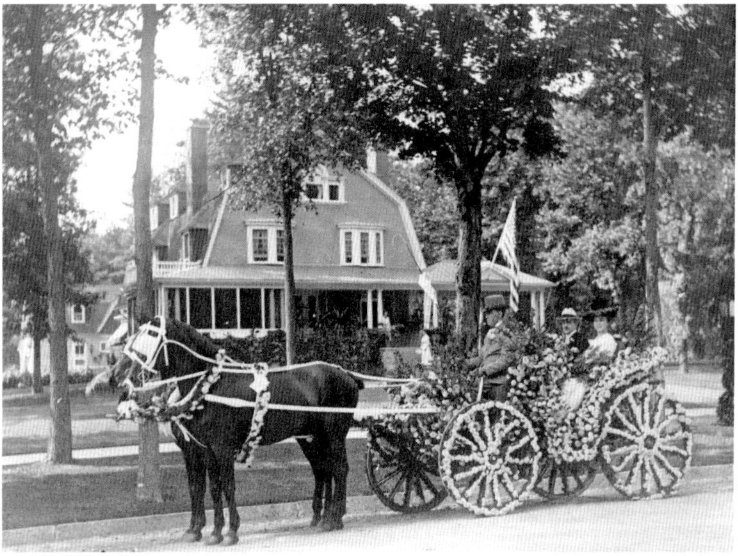

Combining elements of several historic periods, the North Broadway house built by Lucy Skidmore Scribner in 1898 is now home to Skidmore College's presidents. The horse and cart were bedecked for the Floral Fête parade.

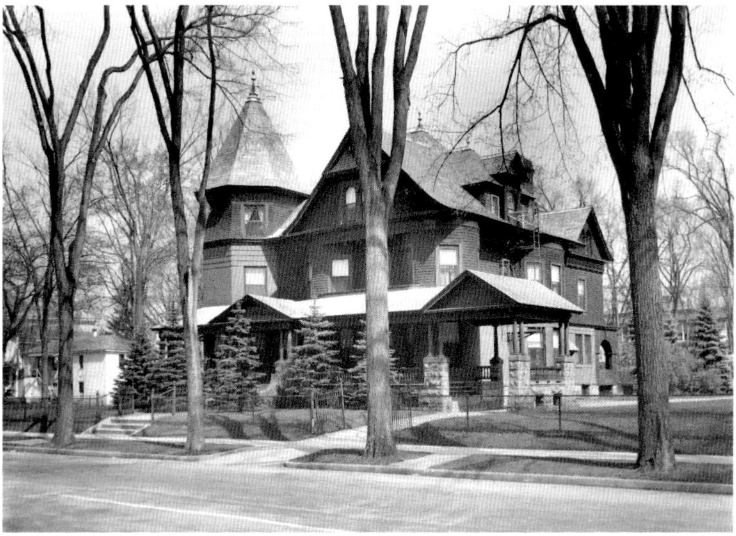

Furness House, once a Skidmore College freshmen dormitory, is a masterpiece of late Queen Anne style designed by Newton Brezee for George Crippen and later owned by Charles Furness. In 1992, it opened as the Union Gables Bed and Breakfast.

Pine Grove and the Walworth Family

An example of a house changing over time is Pine Grove. The house was built in 1815 by Henry Walton. It sat in pine woods, split by Broadway and not far from High Rock Spring. Reuben Hyde Walworth bought the property after military service and a term in the United States Congress. He was a distinguished jurist. Originating from Connecticut, he spent his professional and political life in New York State. In 1828 he was appointed the state's highest judge as chancellor. He would be its last, as the Court of Chancery was abolished in 1848. He commanded the respect of his peers and served well the application and improvement of equity law.

When possible, he convened the court in a small office at Pine Grove. This was a drawing card for residents as well as for the legal professionals. Among the personalities coming to visit Judge Walworth—and Saratoga Springs—were national opinion shapers of the day, writers and political figures, joined by the new industrial wealthy. In the drawing room of Pine Grove and at the big hotels met such prominent thinkers as Daniel Webster, Henry Clay, Martin Van Buren and others, advancing their views on the issues that bound America.

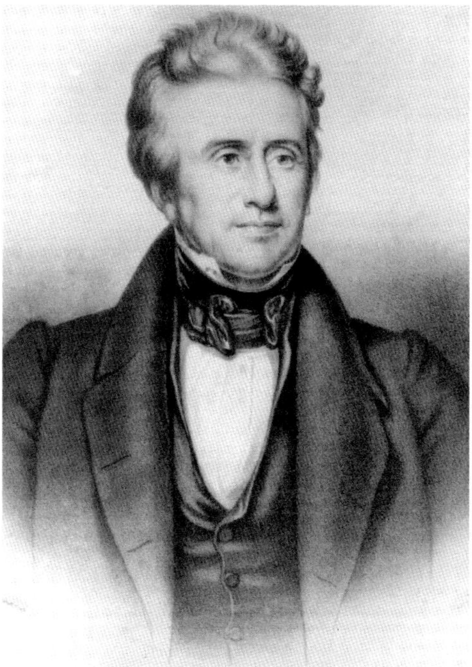

Chancellor Walworth was known both for his genteel hospitality and the insight embodied in his legal rulings. His opinions contributed significantly to equity law.

The house was expanded with a second story in 1860 to contain the large Walworth clan, which included Mrs. Walworth's children by her first marriage. Chancellor Walworth devoted his life to building the framework of law. The daughter of his second wife was a leader in the movement to preserve American history. Ellen Hardin Walworth expanded the

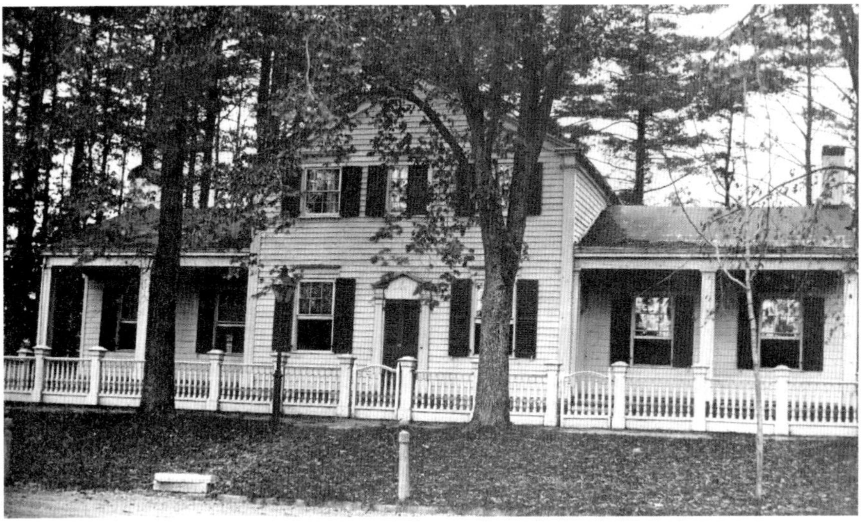

Pine Grove, the home the Walworths bought from Henry Walton in 1823, was on Broadway (across from today's City Center), seen here before 1885. After Chancellor Reuben Hyde Walworth's death in 1867, Ellen Hardin Walworth conducted a school here.

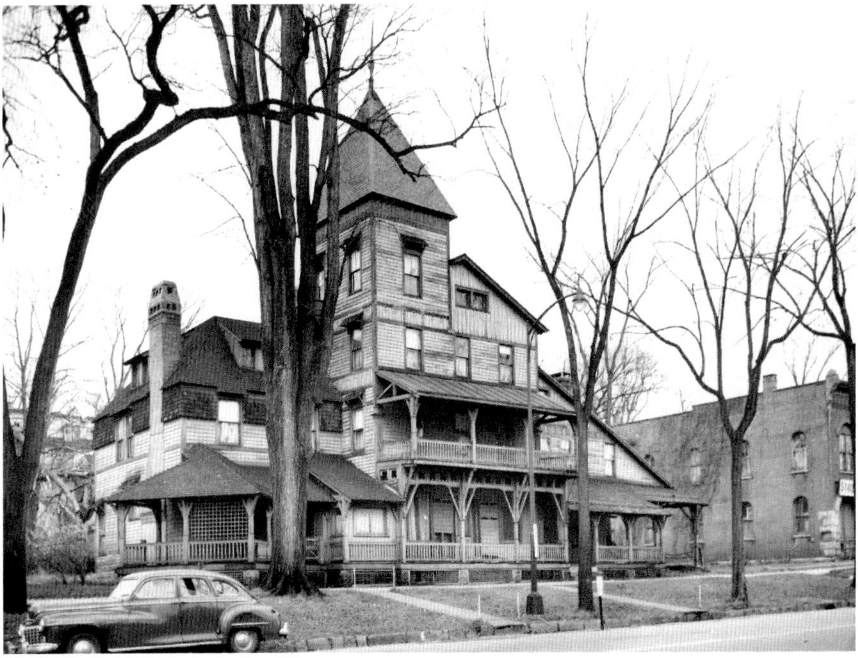

Pine Grove was expanded by Ellen Hardin Walworth in 1885. It became an unwieldy building with fifty-five rooms, serving for a while as a boardinghouse. By the time Mrs. Walworth's granddaughter willed its contents to the city, the house was no longer usable.

building to fifty-five rooms in a Queen Anne mode in 1885, engulfing the original house. Unwieldy and ungainly, it lasted until the 1950s. Interiors were moved with care and installed in the History Museum.

The Trasks

In rolling parkland to the east of the Saratoga Race Course, in 1891 the Trasks built a mansion styled after Haddon Hall manor in Derbyshire, England. Their preferences created a building that is strikingly unique.

Spencer and Katrina Trask were born and bred New Yorkers. His career was brilliant, making the most of the financial industries of the late nineteenth century as a prosperous Wall Street broker. His firm, Trask and Company, led the Street. He invested in hopeful inventors such as Thomas Edison. He was at the forefront of introducing technologies that transformed America through the growth of those years—electricity, newspapers, railroads and real estate.

Spencer Trask supported the arts and intellectual disciplines. He served on the boards of numerous institutions, including the Metropolitan Museum of Arts, the National Arts Club and the American Teachers College. In Saratoga, he worked to turn the city from a gambling center

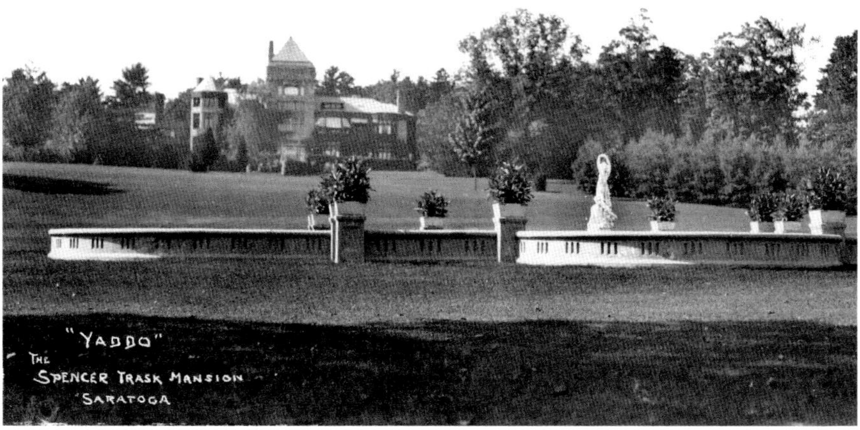

Since 1922, Yaddo has nurtured the creative process, providing an opportunity for artists to work without interruption in a supportive environment in residencies of two weeks to two months.

to a spa in the European tradition. Katrina honed her considerable artistic capabilities and expanded the social universe wherever she stayed. With Spencer she enjoyed the metropolitan life when in New York City; in Saratoga Springs she created a milieu that would draw creative talent from many different quarters.

The Trasks had bought an Italianate villa on the handsomely wooded site in 1881. It stood just to the east of Saratoga Race Course. The location earlier was that of Barhydt's pond and inn. The villa had been built by Dr. Richard Childs in 1854, before the racetrack's era. Spencer and Katrina Trask set about rebuilding the villa in a large but unpretentious contemporary Queen Anne form. In 1891, their work was undone when the house burned to the ground. The mansion that stands today is the replacement, started the same year.

The woodland setting endures, enclosing the estate. The strong but unconventional building's exterior denotes some imposition of the owners' opinions in the design process while the architect, William Halsey Wood, did his work. It has been suggested that Katrina's interest in British romantic literature and her instinctive response to what she felt were psychic inspirations imposed some features that cause imbalance of design. The house commands a perfect view of the large expanse of lawn that reaches down to a broad fountain, a screen of pines and the rose garden. Inside the house, a two-story great hall forms the centerpiece. Interior spaces are richly enrobed in wood paneling.

As Spencer and Katrina Trask worked on their mansion, their lives had already been touched by sorrow. Their first child, son Alanson, had died in 1880, before they came to build in Saratoga Springs. Their daughter Christina, who had playfully named the estate Yaddo as a rhyme for the shadows of the tall pines, died of diphtheria in 1888. The contagion took Spencer Junior at the same time. Their last child, Katrina, was born in 1889 and lived only twelve days.

In the aftermath of losing all of their children, the Trasks continued. Katrina found spiritual renewal in improving the estate. Spencer continued successfully in financing and building the innovative enterprises that were transforming the country. Yaddo fulfilled its design, becoming the center of their social world. In addition to the progressive industrial players naturally drawn to Spencer, both of the Trasks took profound pleasure in the creative arts and their entertaining inclined toward creative artists. They determined to perpetuate the estate for the sustenance of artistic creativity, and founded the Yaddo

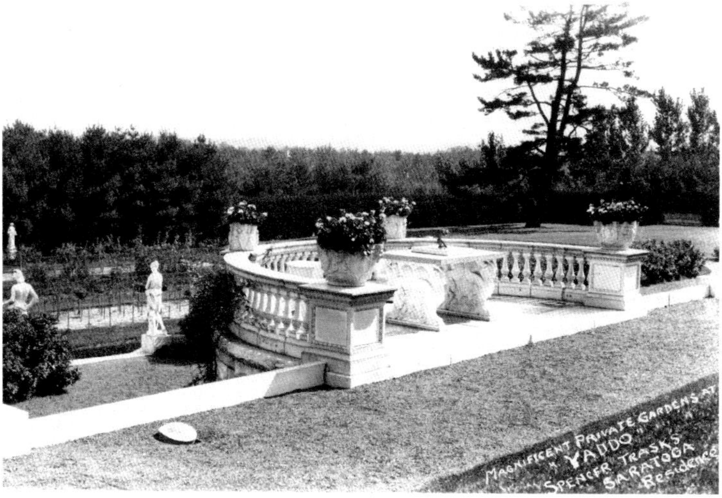

The balustrade overlooking the lawns and rose garden.

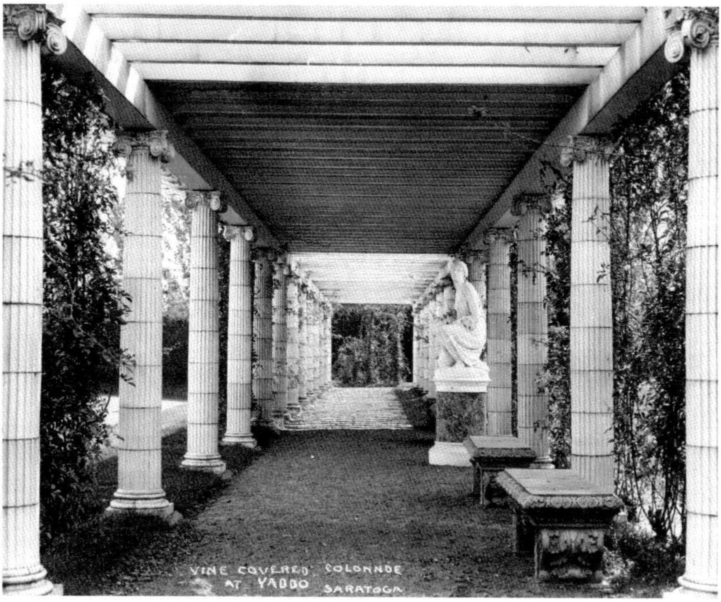

The 180-foot-long pergola on the Yaddo grounds is being rebuilt with private contributions through the Yaddo Garden Association, founded in 1991 by Jane Wait. It is a favorite place for wedding photos, overlooking the rose garden maintained by volunteers.

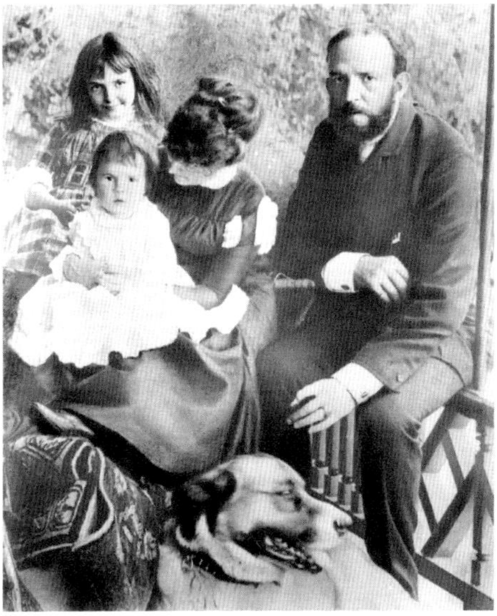

Left: The sense of comradeship and affection evident in the Trasks' family portrait at Yaddo sustained them through personal tragedies and helped direct their energies to a noble purpose

Below: Spencer and Katrina Trask really knew how to put on a party. Their Twelfth Night revels at Yaddo were legendary for highbrow fun, lavish costumes and brilliant society.

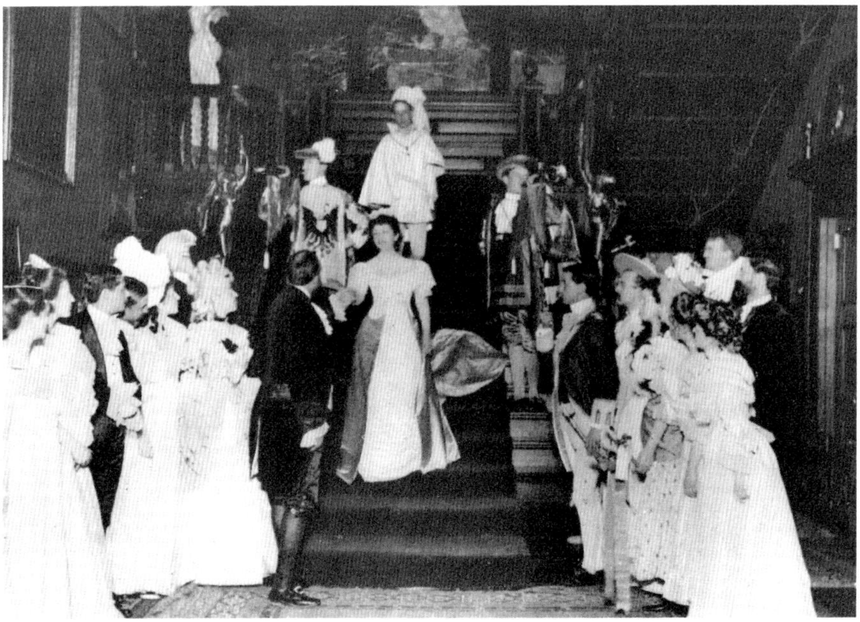

Corporation in 1900. In business and socially, George Foster Peabody was loyal to them both.

The evolution of architectural styles continued to be represented in Saratoga Springs, with fine examples to be seen today.[29]

Chapter Three

The Life

THE GRAND SHOW

Immortal Thoroughbreds

Horse racing in America followed on from the venerable pastime and sport in England. The British settlers brought horses and horse racing with them to the New World, with the first racetrack laid out on Long Island as early as 1665. The competitive side of breeding and racing was carried on privately among those who could afford it. Match races were arranged on a challenge basis between leading breeders and owners. American leaders in colonial days included George Washington and other Virginia gentlemen.

The quality of thoroughbred stock had been depleted in the Revolutionary War, but by the mid-nineteenth century was well on its way to being restored by the new generation of enthusiasts.

Founding of the Saratoga Race Course

Saratoga Springs was the anomaly that inspires the betting spirit. Founded on a hunch by Gideon Putnam, the resort had maintained a winning formula by repeatedly finding the choicest entertainments to stay ahead of competing destinations. The spa city filled itself on a season twelve weeks long at best, returning to the quiet life through bracing winters. It shrugged off financial crises such as the Panic of 1837. When the country was torn by the Civil War, Saratoga Springs flourished. The new millionaires came to play.

With the prosperity that accompanied the Civil War for those who seized opportunities, organized gaming was on its way. The ubiquitous pastime of

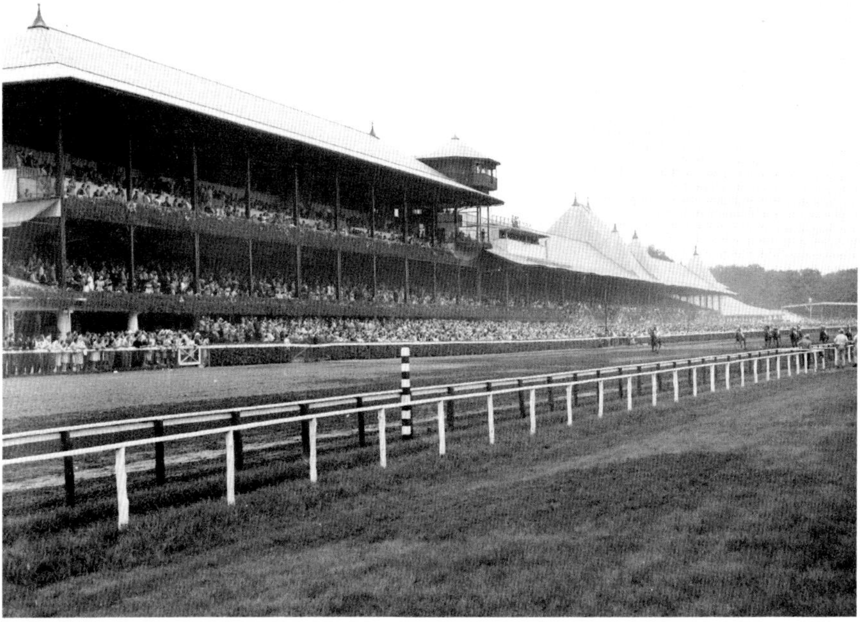

From the first years in the 1860s, the sweep of the vast grandstand's roof has been a distinctive feature of the Saratoga Race Course.

gambling had undoubtedly made its way early and informally to the springs with the military passersby and some of the settlers. The first gaming house on record was set up by Ben Scribner in 1842, around the corner from the United States Hotel.[30] A half-mile trotting track was opened a few years later with casual betting practices by spectators.

William R. Travers was a noted Wall Street man, a success in the market and society and a member of the best clubs of New York City. He bought his seat on the New York Stock Exchange in 1854 and was the founder of several successful brokerage firms, the first of which was Travers & Jerome with his lifelong friend and business partner Leonard.[31] Leonard W. Jerome was himself prominent in the social scene, being a self-sufficient man in the flourishing industrial society of nineteenth-century America. Known as a premier yachtsman, he cultivated the advantage of his relationship with "Commodore" Cornelius Vanderbilt and enjoyed the company of the resorts and centers of leisure. One of his legacies is his daughter Jenny Jerome, whose marriage to Lord Randolph Churchill produced Winston Churchill.

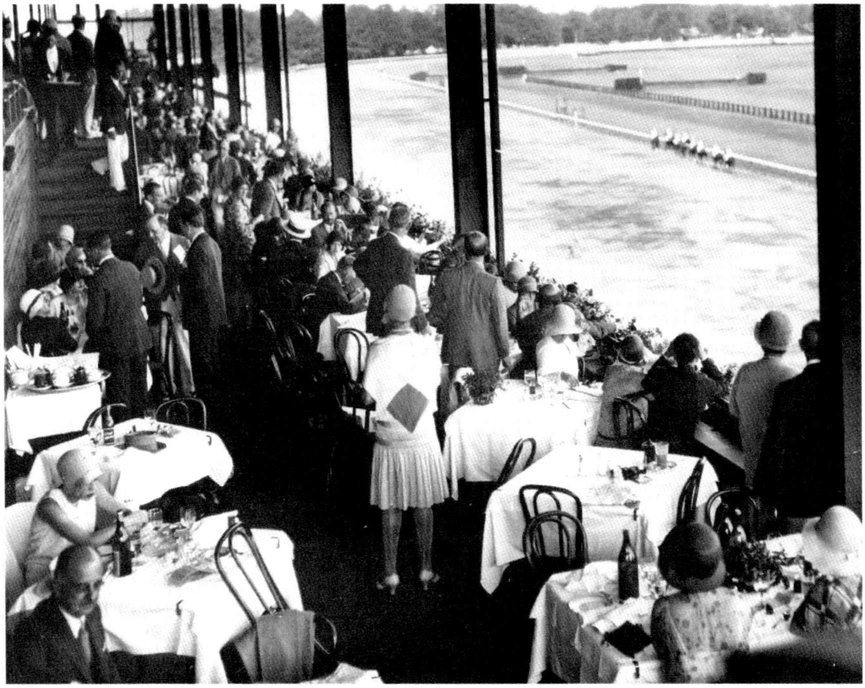

Fashionably garbed racing fans lunched in style at the clubhouse in 1929, enjoying the scene that remains remarkably unchanged today. The clubhouse still maintains standards of dress, while the grandstand and grounds allow much more casual wear.

John R. Hunter was an expert horseman, advisor and co-owner of bloodstock with William R. Travers. In 1863 these men convened to form an association to organize racing in Saratoga. They gathered twenty-six horses for an initial season of four days at a track they called Horse Haven, less than a mile east of Broadway. Lizzie W. won the first race at Saratoga before a crowd of five hundred spectators, kicking off a tradition that persists to this day. Responding to the welcoming success, Travers and Hunter realized that an expanded facility might appeal broadly to the summer crowd. They determined to create an environment for thoroughbred horse racing that would rival the best of entertainment venues.

August 2, 1864, saw the opening of the larger Saratoga Race Course on 125 acres, across the street on the south side of Union Avenue. A new prize race, the Travers Stakes, was introduced in honor of the racing association's president. At the same time, a steeplechase was introduced and became a favorite event. Great horses and great races were to follow, with names such as Kentucky and Longfellow setting high standards. The Travers Stakes came to be regarded as "the fourth jewel in the Triple Crown" of racing, and Saratoga went on to eventually become the oldest racecourse in the country in nearly continuous operation.

The Saratoga Race Course was remodeled in 1902 in late Victorian style. The architect was Charles Leavitt of New York City, hired in the firm determination of William Collins Whitney to restore the track to preeminence and appeal.

The Casino

Joining the social leaders in promoting the racecourse was John Morrissey, a product of the new urban society. Brought from Ireland to Troy, New York, in 1833 in his infancy, he became streetwise early. He learned how to use his fists, but his assertiveness went too far and landed him in jail several times for small crimes and assault.

He moved to New York City to try wider horizons and found himself at home with the street life. He traveled to San Francisco in the clamor of the gold rush. There he became proficient at the gaming tables. Morrissey turned his hard-won skills to advantage by entering the fight game, taking on a boxer named George Thompson and winning a $4,000 purse and a side bet as well. On returning to New York, he was able to arrange a match with James Ambrose Sullivan, which he won in the thirty-seventh round when Sullivan distractedly went after Morrissey's seconds outside the ring. Morrissey won the match, title and prize money.

After earning political savvy in New York City by becoming useful to Tammany Hall, in 1861 Morrissey established his first gambling room on Matilda Street in Saratoga Springs, beginning a successful career in the resort town.[32] Morrissey joined with the respectable gentlemen establishing the racecourse. He added boat racing as an attraction on Saratoga Lake, bringing top teams and crowds of spectators. College rowing teams followed and began the championship tradition that continues to this day.

Although the pugilist entrepreneur turned his political acumen to good use and gained election both to the U.S. Congress and the New York State Senate, business proved more to his liking. Perhaps modeling from a recently successful establishment in Monaco, Morrissey purchased roughly thirty acres lying below the Greek Revival mansion left by Dr. John Clarke, groomed the property and in 1867 built an impressive red brick clubhouse

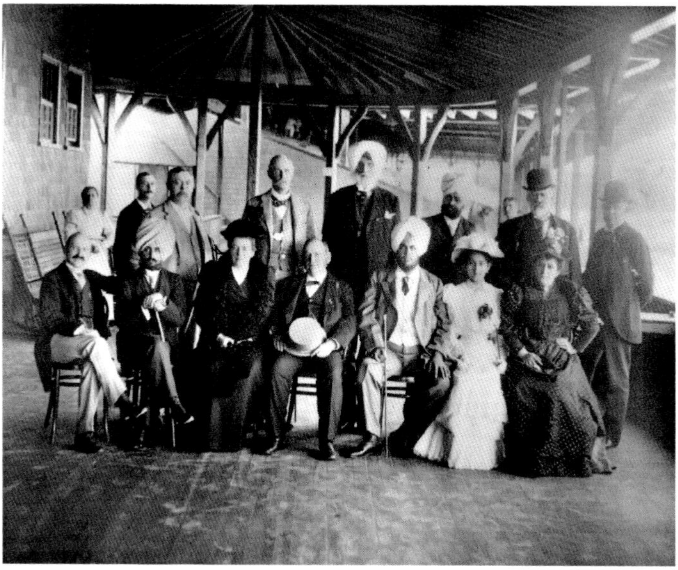

Saratoga has always catered to a diverse public, as evidenced by these race visitors of 1893.

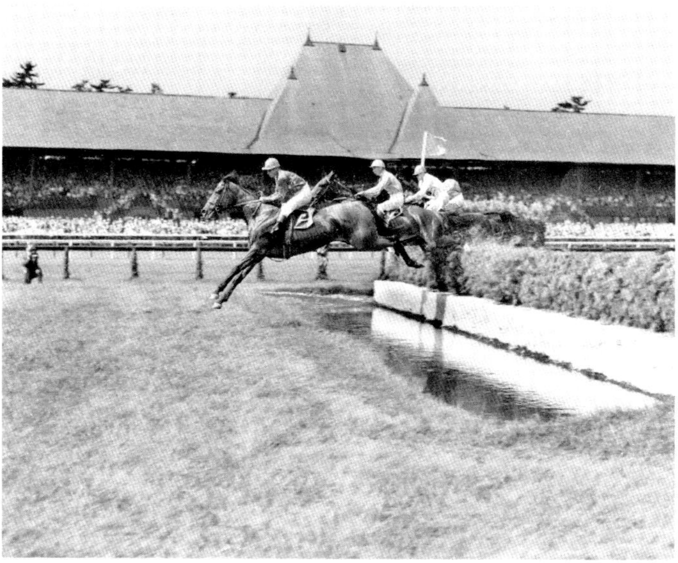

On the racecourse's two inner turf tracks, approximately six steeplechase races are held each racing season, including two graded stakes races. The horse must jump fence and ditch obstacles in addition to racing on the grass.

in the center. The crowds that had begun to convene in Saratoga with a taste for wagering were ready. The Morrisseys' Club House Casino was an immediate success.

Morrissey publicized his charitable donations throughout the community, but his gaming house stirred concern among the local residents and other observers of the scene. When Morrissey died in 1878 at the Adelphi Hotel at the age of forty-seven, he had gained such great popularity that more than twenty thousand people attended his funeral, yet he never attained the hoped-for level of respectability.

After interim ownership, the Casino's next successful proprietor was Richard Canfield. He was born in New Bedford, Massachusetts, but unlike his predecessors who had founded Saratoga Springs, he was far from puritanical. Canfield had developed successful, though illegal, gambling centers in Rhode Island and New York before settling on the Club House in 1893. Canfield brought back glamour and success to the Casino. He installed a world-class chef, Jean Columbin, detailed the furnishings and service extravagantly and, most unusually, extended credit to the players. The Casino was a terrific success and a top attraction.

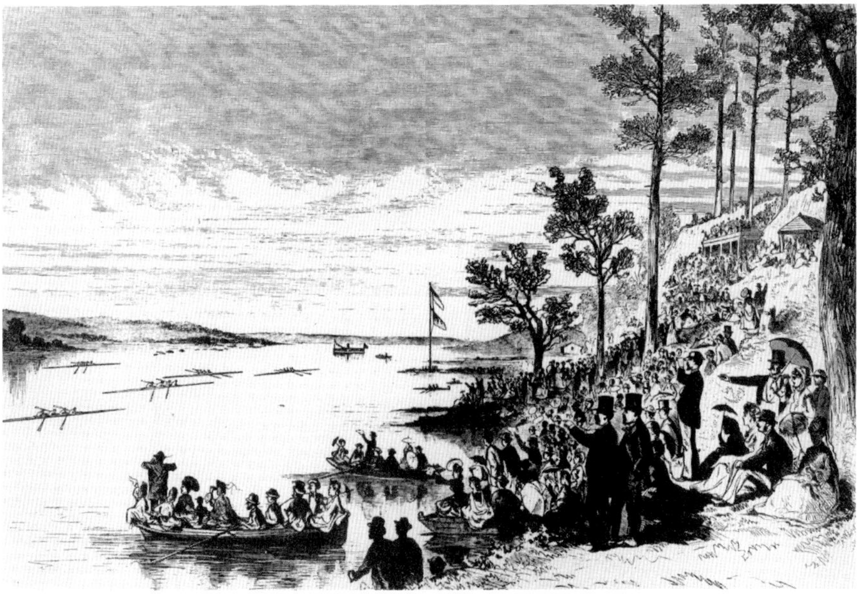

Intercollegiate rowing races were extremely popular on Saratoga Lake in the last half of the nineteenth century. The regatta tradition has been revived, with the Head of the Fish (Creek) regatta hosting 1,200 boats each October.

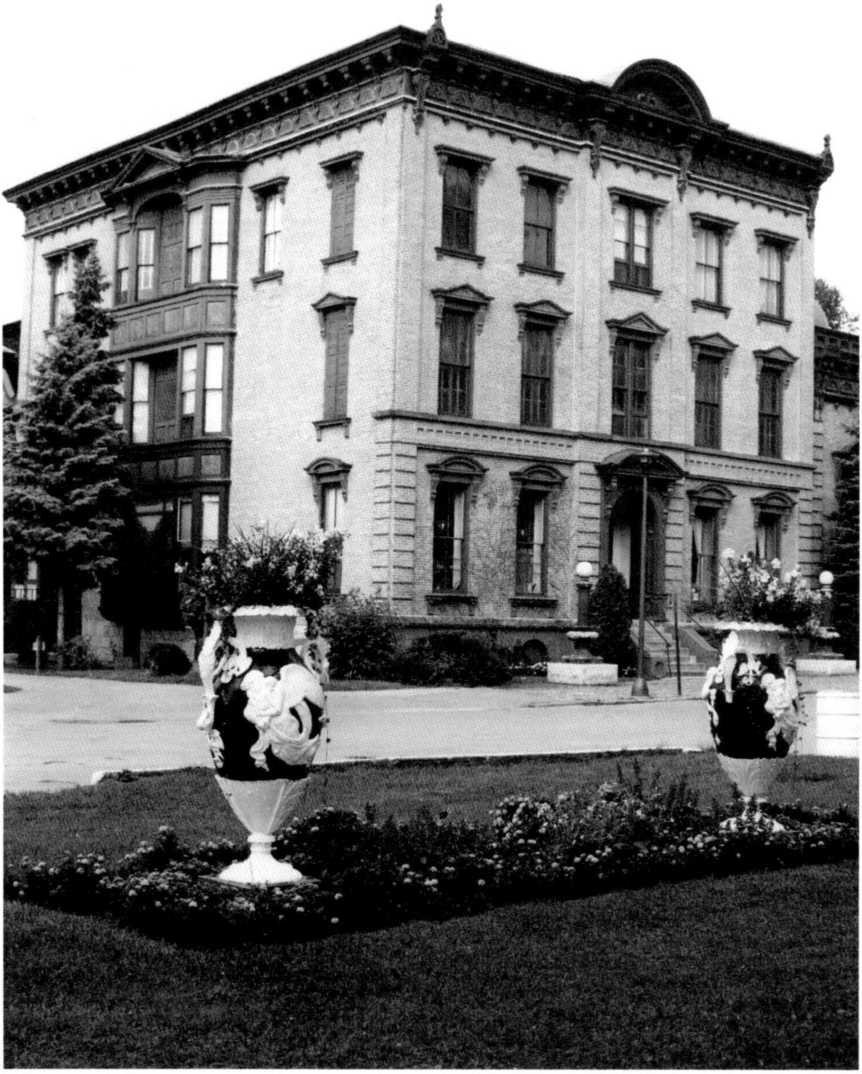

The Historical Society urged the City of Saratoga Springs in 1965 to restore the building and its furnishings, which started in time for its one hundredth birthday in 1967. Its success spurred the gradual restoration of Congress Park. The vases, by Bertel Thorvaldsen (1770–1844), were brought from Denmark by Dr. John Clarke.

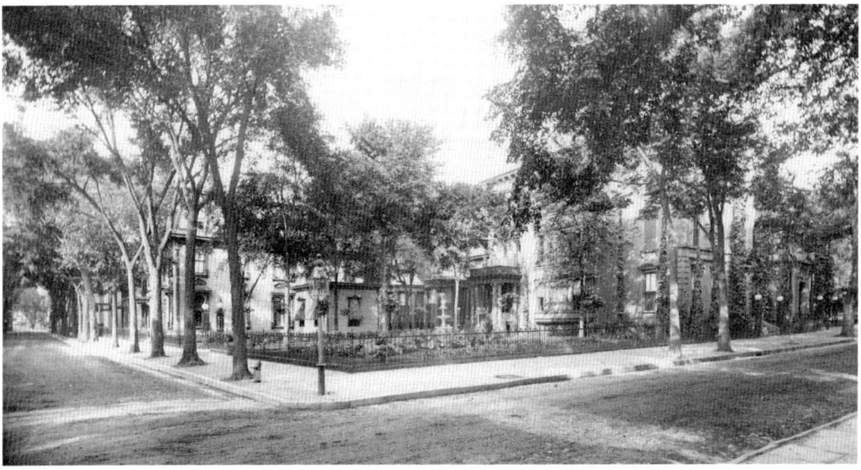

Now a tranquil part of Congress Park, there was once a busy city intersection of Putnam and Congress Streets adjacent to the Canfield Casino.

Among the noted personalities to wind up near the springs was Ulysses S. Grant, Civil War general and president of the United States. In the summer of 1885 he was in dire financial straits. Suffering from throat cancer, he was determined to complete his memoirs in the hope that their publication might yield income to sustain his wife. Stepping up to help him was Samuel Clemens (Mark Twain), who favored Saratoga for its ambiance and a bit of gambling. The famed author saw Grant through his last days and assisted with the publishing project. Grant's memoirs were a bestseller and achieved their intended result. The cottage where he died just north of Saratoga Springs was loaned to him by Philadelphian Joseph Drexel, who among other accomplishments served as the first president of the Saratoga Springs Historical Society. It is maintained as a state historical site, complete with the original funereal floral tributes.

The Height of the Gilded Age

The year 1894 was perhaps most emblematic of the Gilded Age. It was the most profitable year to date for Saratoga and began a dazzling ten-year stretch. Richard Canfield went all out to make his Casino irresistible to the high rollers. He presided in tails and a white tie and did not hesitate to raise the betting limit for big spenders who were known to him.

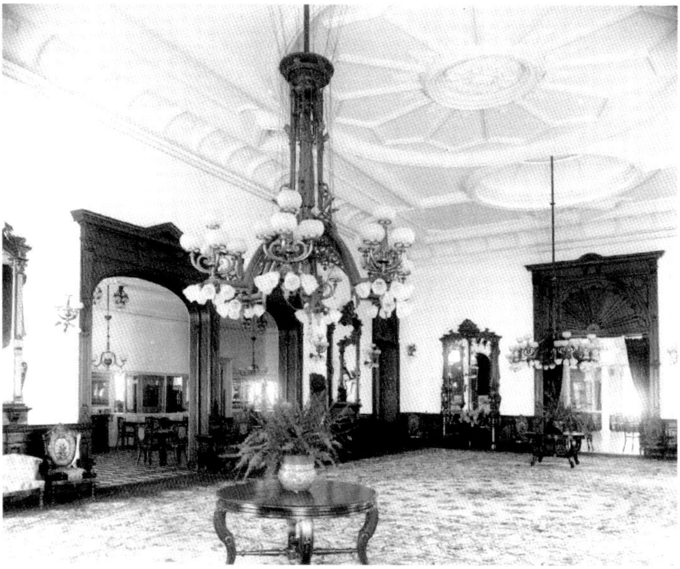

The grand parlor of Morrissey's Club House was added in 1870 to house gambling games in an elegant setting. The parlor and adjacent ballroom can be rented for civic events and weddings.

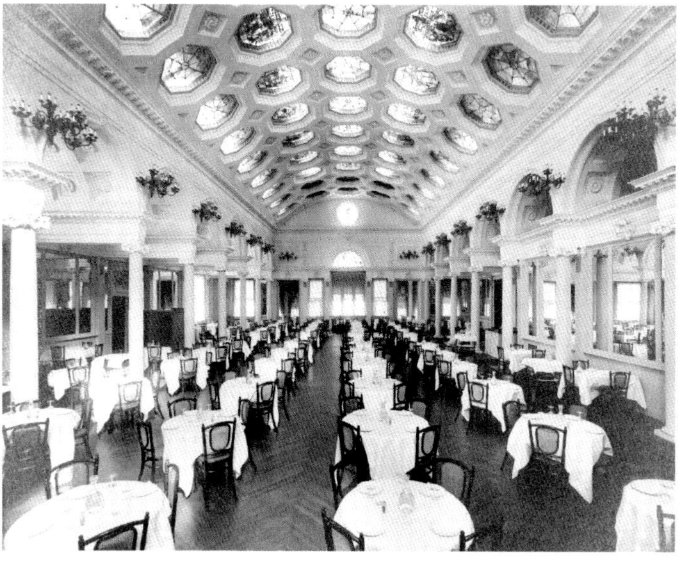

Richard Canfield added the ballroom to the back of the Casino in 1905 for dining and dancing, functions it still fills today.

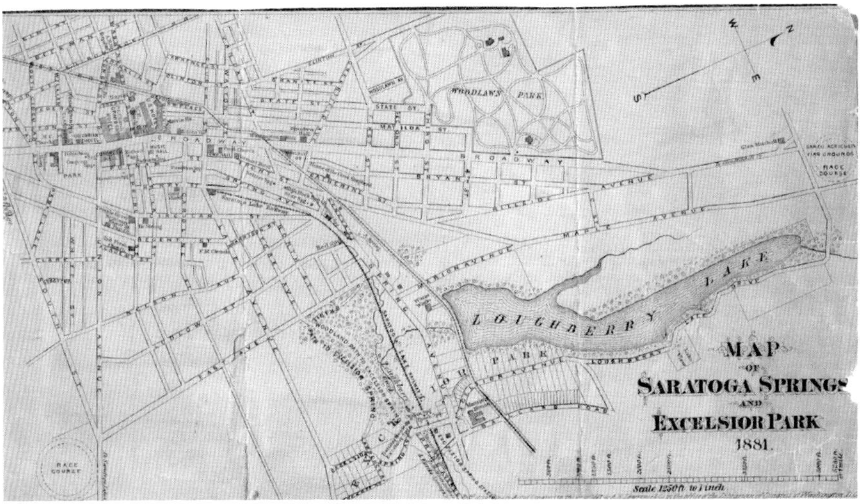

1881 map.

Providers of staple product and services formed the bedrock business community and were prosperous if the season was good. The hotels were open from late June until October 1. It was reported that the People's Party, an agrarian movement, mirrored the major political parties in holding a convention. The first of the Floral Fêtes was held. Frank James, brother of recently deceased Jesse James, came to the racecourse.

Diamond Jim Brady and Lillian Russell were two stars in the public eye who never disappointed their public. Miss Russell would drive through the streets in a carriage drawn by black horses trimmed out in white doeskin harnesses. Diamond Jim lived up to his name. It was given on good authority that he owned thirty sets of jewels, more than twenty thousand diamonds in all. His fortune was made selling railroad equipment. At the spa he held his own with the tycoons who were his customers.

Society editors for the newspapers sent cards to those who had been invited to the important events, requesting details of the ladies' titles, complexion and jewels worn for the evening.[33]

The world's best—and some of the worst—gamblers moved between the track and Canfield's Casino. Political luminaries were present, including past and present leaders of Tammany Hall; the village president, Caleb Mitchell, operated his own gaming house on Broadway. It was a time of exuberance, excitement and excess.

One of the most colorful characters to grace the Saratoga scene was E. (for Evander) Berry Wall, who earned the title "King of the Dudes" through

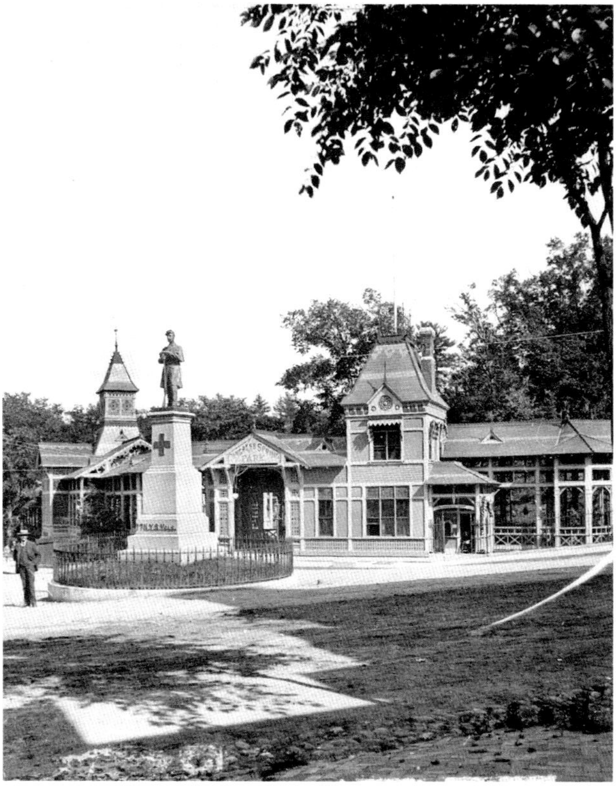

A new Victorian pavilion replaced Clarke's Grecian temples for the nation's centennial in 1876, connecting the Congress and Columbian Springs under one elaborate roof and making a grand entrance to the park.

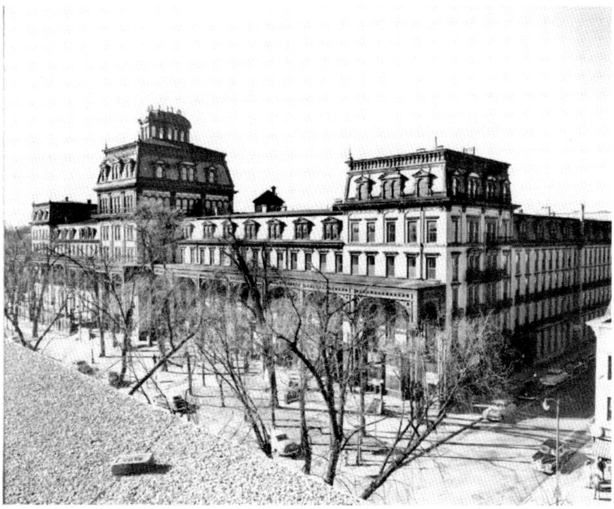

The Grand Union Hotel, starting humbly as Putnam's Boardinghouse, had grown by 1876 to claim the title of the world's largest hotel, embracing the block between Congress and Washington Streets.

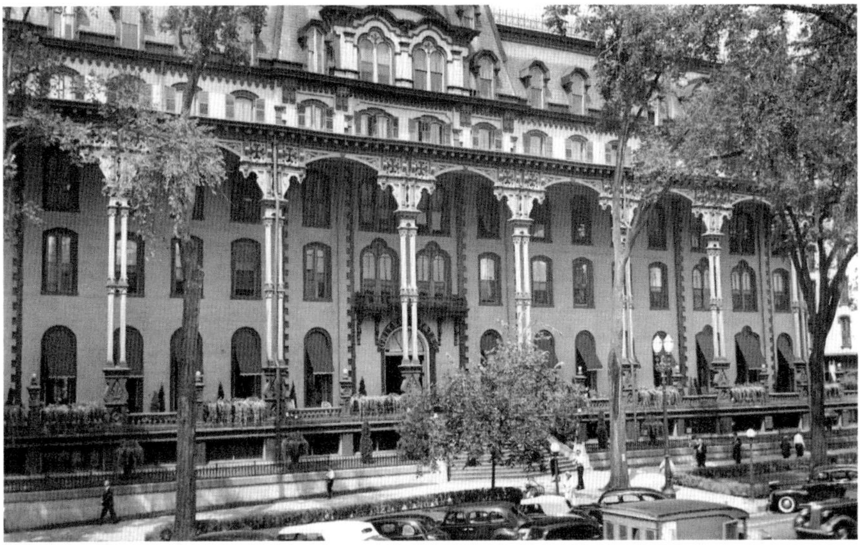

The United States Hotel, along with the Grand Union and Congress Hall, were fine examples of the Second Empire style and provided luxury accommodations, some even with private bathrooms.

a single-minded pursuit of fashion. Perhaps it was a genetic trait—after all, it was his Aunt Celia who had introduced to Saratoga the "Grecian Bend" fad of tortuous posture and extravagant dress a generation earlier. Berry Wall's distinction was earned the day in 1888 he emerged from the Grand Union Hotel attired in no less than forty complete changes of costume. With the help of his valet, his final transformation was to appear in evening clothes to a musical tribute by the hotel's orchestra and the shouts of an admiring crowd. John L. Sullivan, the heavyweight champion, collected thousands of dollars in wagers by betting on Wall's success.[34]

COMMUNITY NOTES

The primary factors that make a community were present from the start in Saratoga Springs, developing in parallel with the tourist businesses and racing. While the young United States was just pushing off the East Coast into the continent, these industries in the Northern wilderness had been perhaps long shot prospects. Gideon Putnam's provision of the staples of community life included church and cemetery. He and those who followed added essentials of a functioning community.

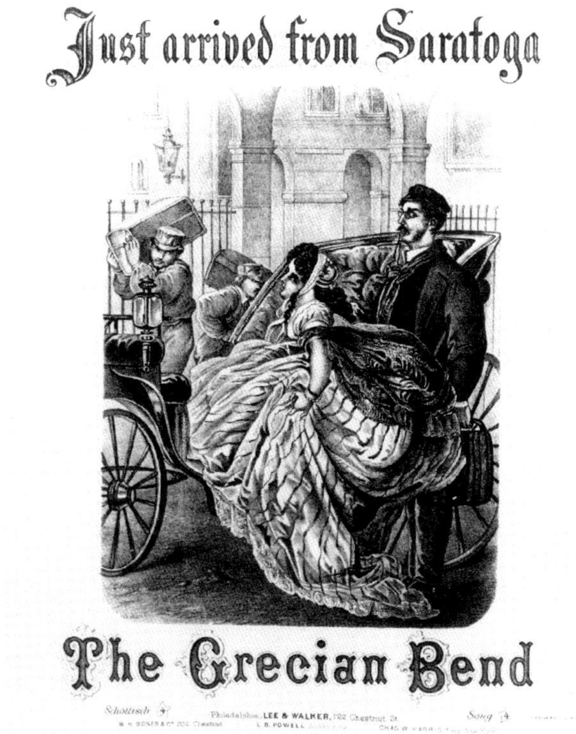

The Grecian Bend was a short-lived fad introduced to Saratoga by Celia Wall (*New York Times*, August 16, 1868). The exaggerated bustle and cinched waist combined with stooped posture to give the wearer an "S" shape, ridiculed by society and disparaged by doctors.

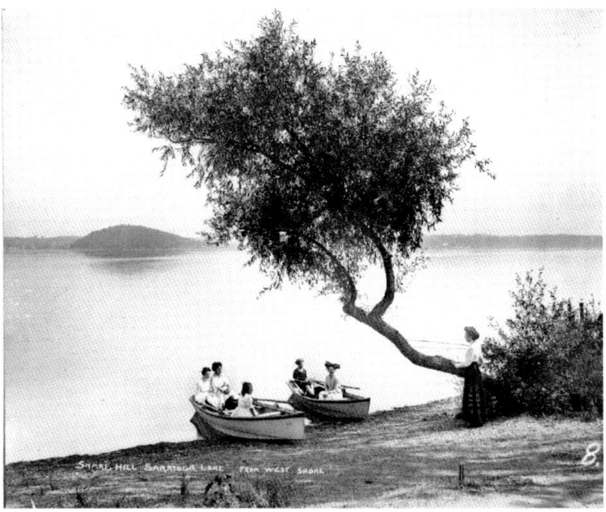

Saratoga Lake has been a destination for adventurous picnickers, sailors and rowers for generations. The City of Saratoga Springs recently bought a site for public access on the western shore.

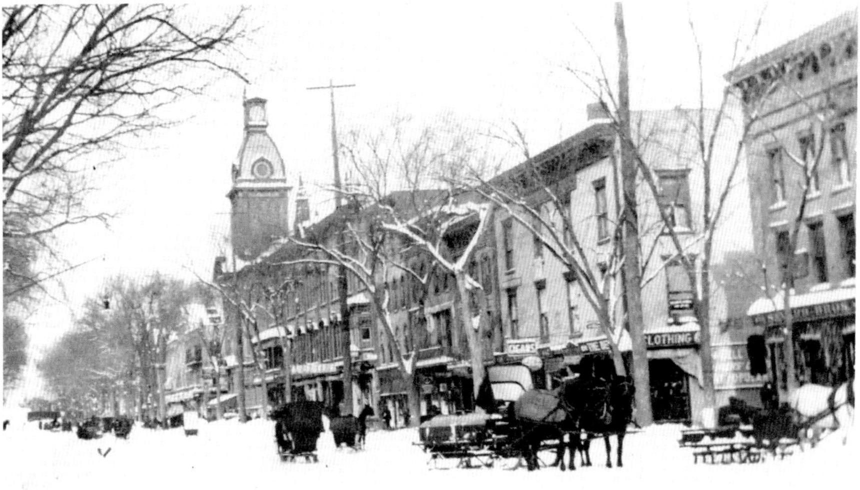

The local traffic is undaunted by winter conditions on Broadway, here looking north toward city hall.

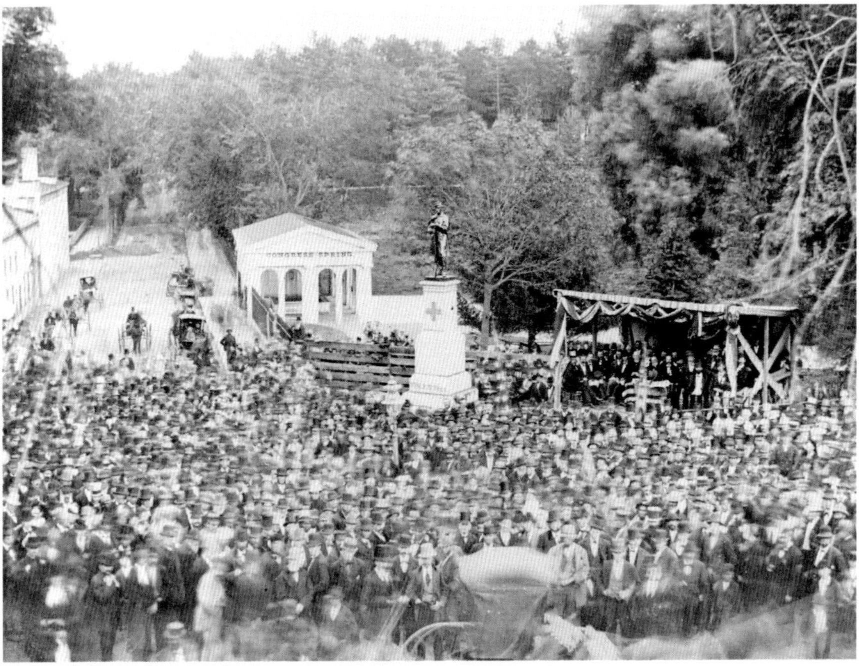

In 1875, Saratogians dedicated a memorial to soldiers of the New York Seventy-seventh Infantry Regiment who served in the Civil War. The monument has been moved several times and now stands guard to the left inside the Congress Park entrance.

National Service

Most men from Saratoga Springs enlisting in the Civil War joined the Seventy-seventh Infantry Regiment. This was in keeping with the proud family histories of the community's original settlers in the Revolutionary War. It is a tradition of service continued in the North country.[35]

Schools

In 1812, a meeting was held to organize the building of a schoolhouse, to be paid for by subscription. Arrangements were made and funds were raised. By the following year, the general school system of the state took effect, and organizers became trustees under the new system. In 1814, Saratoga Springs was in district number fifteen in the town of Saratoga, with seventy-eight students enrolled.

Private schools followed, including a boarding and day school for young ladies conducted by the Misses Wayland in 1831 and a school for boys in 1836. Dowd's Temple Grove Ladies Seminary was granted supervision by the State Board of Regents.

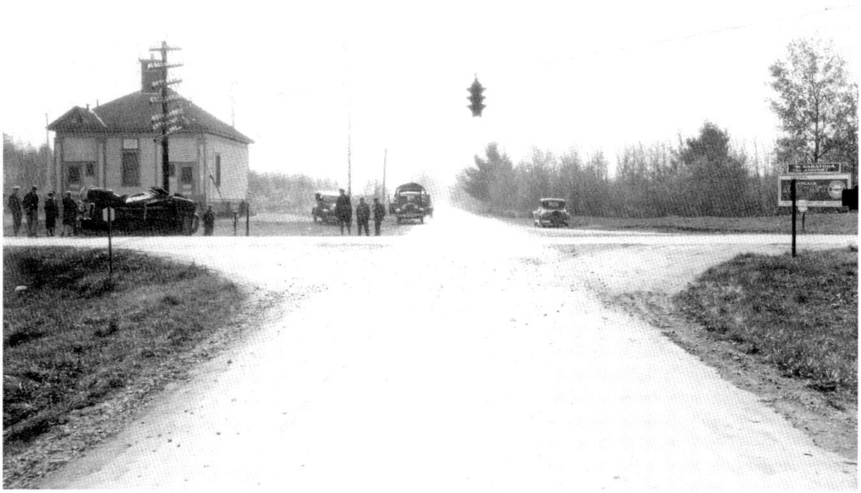

A schoolhouse now housing a business still stands on West Avenue, once open land with the Pitney Farm on the right, still in evidence. The area's first airport used the farm's flat field.

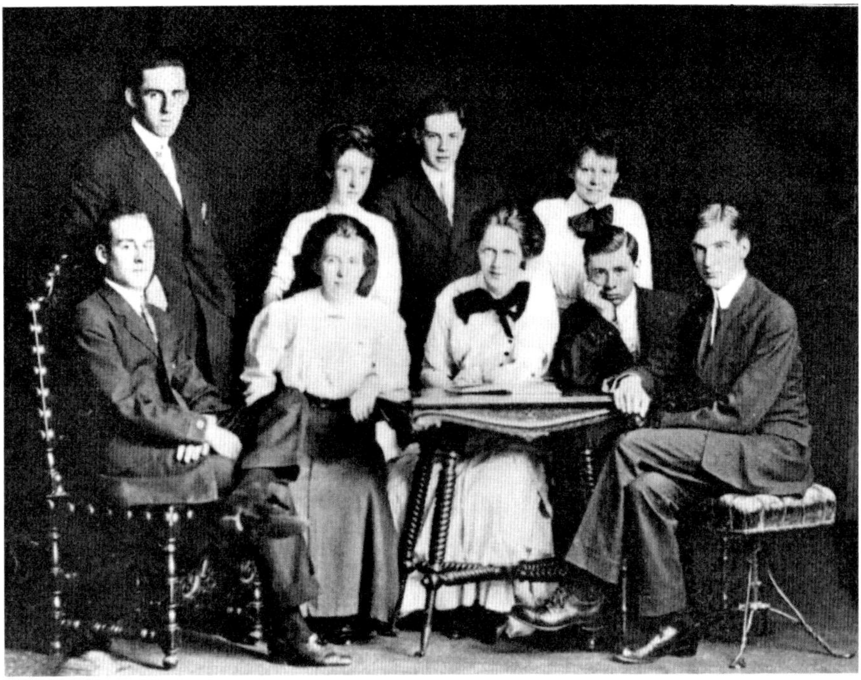

The Saratoga Springs High School class of 1910 yearbook staff contained future luminaries like Frank Sullivan, seated second from the right, and Evelyn Barrett, standing behind him.

Public and parochial schools were established, grew and relocated over the decades. The high school on Lake Avenue now serves as an elementary school. In the past, as now, graduates gained admission to top colleges. Practical vocational training was an option for many through the regional Board of Cooperative Educational Services (BOCES).

Churches

Members of the First Baptist Church in Saratoga Springs met in private homes and schoolhouses from an early time until a church house was built on Washington Street in 1822. Its successor was dedicated in 1856 and was still standing at the end of the twentieth century. The First Presbyterian Church followed in 1816, ultimately residing in a fine edifice on Broadway north of city hall.

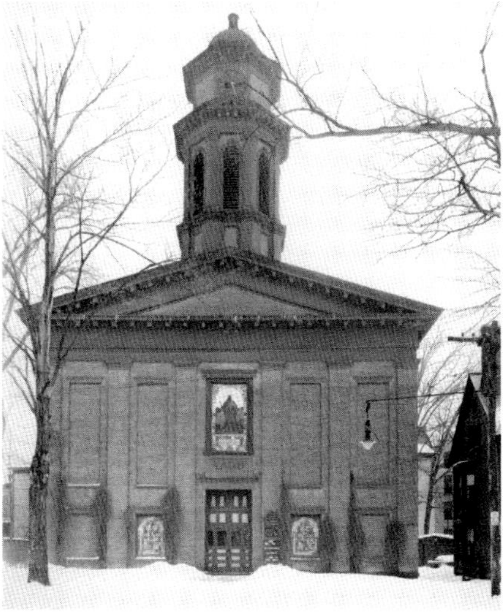

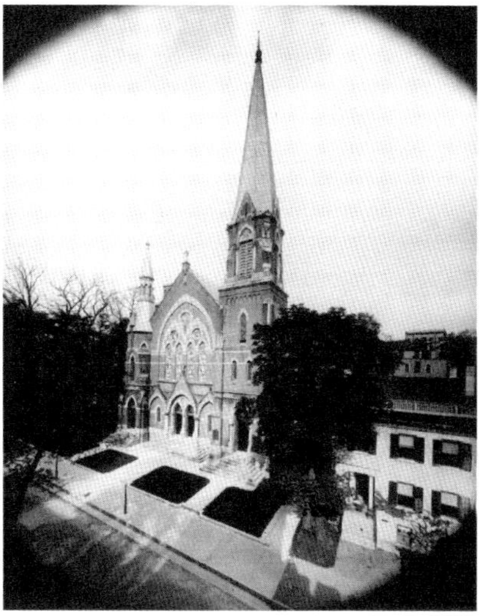

Left: Baptist church.

Right: The former Methodist church has recently undergone transformation into Universal Preservation Hall, a performance space that provides a medium-sized auditorium in the center of the city. A Baptist congregation still meets in the chapel.

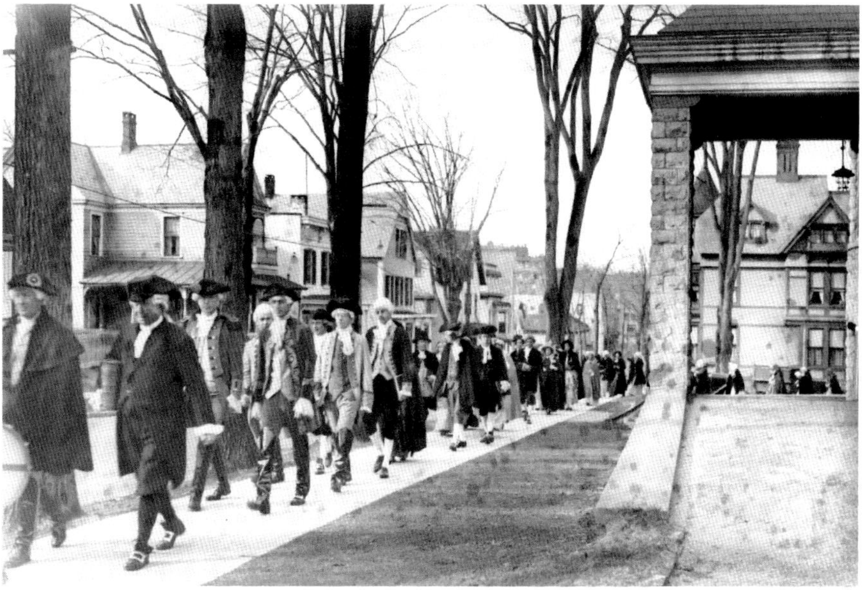

Congregational church members recalling colonial heritage for a city parade.

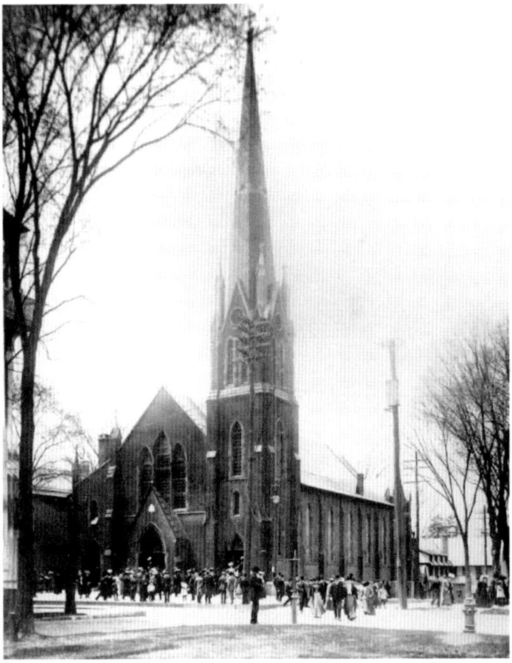

St. Peter's Roman Catholic Church on South Broadway.

The Methodists began, as elsewhere, with a circuit-riding preacher in 1829. Eventually they contributed to the streetscape one of the most impressive of buildings, now the Universal Preservation Hall. The Congregationalist Church, the strong institution from New England, was well represented.

Bethesda Protestant Episcopal Church formed from a small group originally meeting in a chapel provided by John Clarke at the corner of Congress and Putnam Streets, later the center of Congress Park. The group included several community leaders such as Henry Walton, Wallace Crawford, John H. Steel, Joel Clement and Rockwell Putnam. After a studied search for the right architecture and architect, the church edifice was built on Washington Street and first occupied in 1844. This church had a strong role to play in the years to come, and marked the comeback of "the English Church" in America. The distinguished features of the church were somewhat overshadowed by the Grand Union Hotel after the hotel's expansion to its ultimate size, but were revealed after the hotel's demise.

The Pansa building served as the Jewish community center, serving the congregation that had prominence in the portion of the village between Phila and Caroline Streets. Congregation Sha'ari Tefila was established in 1912.[36]

Neighborhoods

The Irish came to Saratoga Springs beginning in the 1830s and 1840s to work on the railroads and canals, among other emerging industries. They settled in the region west of Broadway, which came to be known as Dublin. In the 1870s, Italian families came to the same section. Many were artisans and craftsmen valuable for their skill in producing fine masonry and finishing work on the great hotels. The two groups merged well, and provided staunch support for St. Peter's Church on Broadway. Later, many families moved to the east side of the city, prompting the foundation of St. Clement's Church on Lake Avenue.

After the first generation of settlers, a free African American population was established, from which workers in many disciplines were to develop. Businesses and boardinghouses bloomed to serve black summer workers, such as members of visiting orchestras and restaurant staff. Descendants of those early year-round black residents moved into the middle class, attaining advanced education and recognition. One was Lieutenant Colonel Clarence Dart, who received the Congressional Medal of Honor in 2007 for his World War II service as a Tuskegee Airman.

Hattie's Chicken Shack became a community institution, drawing diners from a wide area. Members of the West Side black community were not discouraged for long when rebuffed by the Elks organization, whose rules barred nonwhite memberships. With initiative and courage they incorporated as the Improved Benevolent and Protective Order of Elks of the World and went on to conduct a lively and effective organization.

The West Side was touched by the fast times of the 1930s and 1940s, with a few nightlife enterprises earning the sobriquet "the sporting district." Today the streetscape is being restored and the remaining buildings have found new uses, following urban renewal and the city's revival.

"The Gut"

The valley lying to the east of Broadway went through several transitions. It forms a natural drainage basin from Congress Park through the Village Brook to High Rock Spring, joining the Spring Run, which flows into Lake Lonely. At one time it hosted the somewhat elaborate Pavilion Spring development of Daniel McLaren, who in 1841 caused a near riot by imposing a small charge for use of the waters.

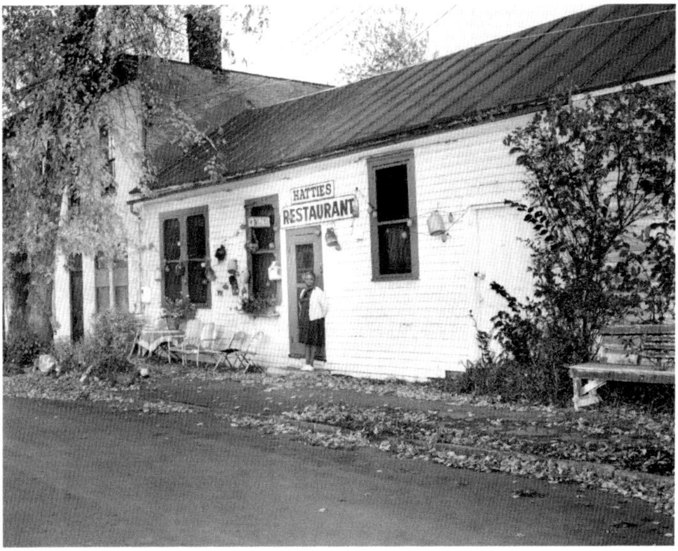

Hattie Mosely Austin was the proprietor of Hattie's on Congress Street from the 1930s until urban renewal swept most of the buildings away. Reestablished on Phila Street, the restaurant retains her name and reputation for the best fried chicken anywhere.

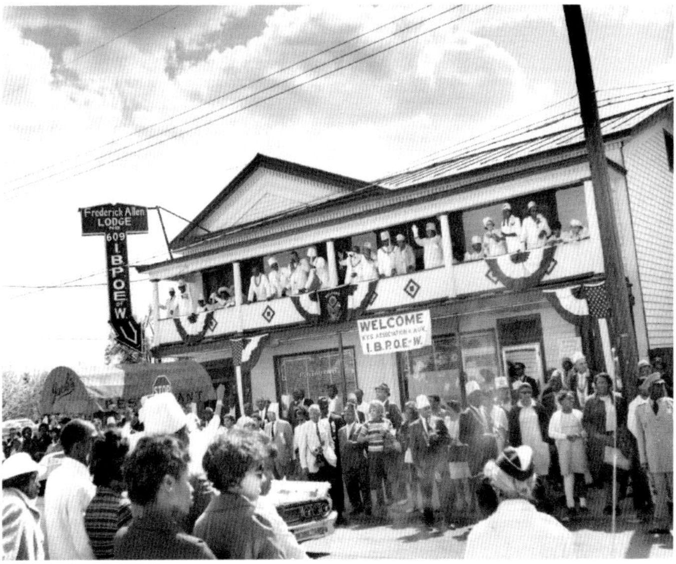

The "Black Elks" held legendary conventions that drew national participation, with lavish parades and festivities at the Canfield Casino.

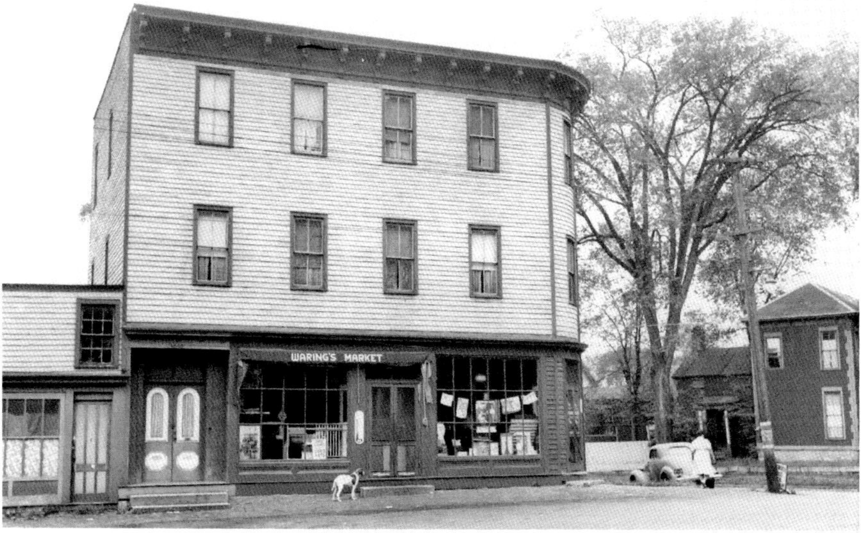

Waring's market on the corner of Franklin and Congress Streets was typical of neighborhood grocery stores that conveniently dotted the city. The building was recently restored as a sports bar.

Recent additions to the city's history recall a tradition of both full-time residents and seasonal visitors of Jewish faith and traditions in the part of Saratoga Springs between Phila and Caroline Streets.

Twentieth-century Saratoga Springs

The *New York to Montreal Guidebook* of 1873 contained an observation that rings true for all of Saratoga Springs' history:

> *There is an inner and an outer life in Saratoga. The inner life is made up of the resident population, whose homes are the abodes of refinement, taste and elegance, which are not surpassed by any inland town in the State. The outer life is the summer fashionable life, which centers around the great hotels, where the wealth, beauty, fashion, wit, wisdom and aristocracy of the continent assemble, with such additions as may drift from foreign parts to our republican shores.*

As the page was turned on the nineteenth century and the gilded Victorian age, there was little foretelling of the changes to come. The season forecast for 1903 was typical. As usual a large number of conventions would occur that year, including the New York State Bankers Association; the American Car Builders Association and the American Master Mechanics' Association; the American Street Railway Association; the Imperial Council of the Mystic Shrine; the Appellate Division of the Supreme Court, Third Judicial Department; and the New York State Undertakers Association.[37]

The Saratoga Golf Club, situated northwest of the village, had greatly improved its links. Nearby, the Saratoga Polo Club would attract top players from across the country. William C. Whitney was president of the Saratoga Racing Association, which anticipated another strong meeting in the month of August. Richard Canfield was reported to be planning $200,000 in improvements to his ten-acre parcel by the Congress Spring Park.

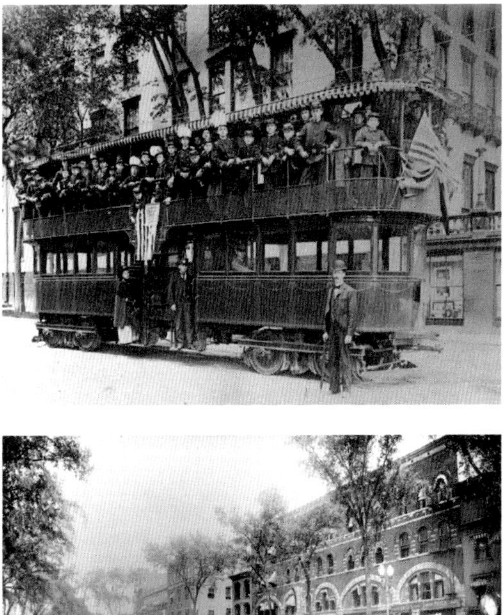

Social organizations held conventions in Saratoga Springs. Here, the Masons try out the latest in transportation.

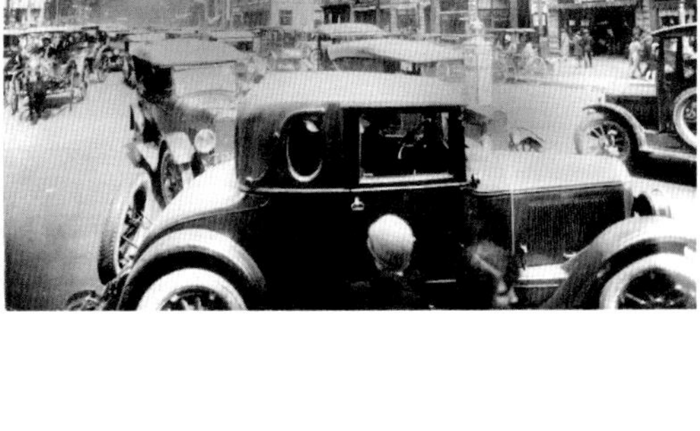

By 1929, cars had become the dominant mode of transportation. Although this stretch of Broadway is 120 feet wide, traffic and parking were already problems.

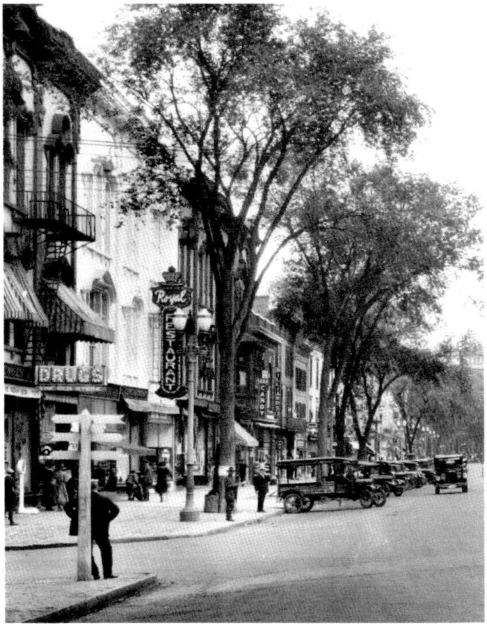

Broadway street life; staple products are continuously successful, despite changing styles.

Road improvements were being kept up. The *New York Times* reported,

> *As substantially all the Summer cottages and many of the hotel guests bring their turnouts with them, the local authorities recognize the prime importance of maintaining the drives at a high standard of excellence. The owners of fine turnouts and speedy roadsters fully appreciate what is done for their pleasure and comfort.*
>
> *While automobiles and similar horseless vehicles each year are becoming more numerous, the number of thoroughbred horses for driving purposes seem to increase rather than decrease each recurring season. The horse will always be in evidence in this horse-loving spot.*

Casino

Canfield added to his improvement of the Club House, which he renamed the Casino. In 1902 he purchased additional acreage north and east of the building. A beautiful Italian garden was laid out with statuary of Carrera marble, including two Tritons trumpeting water at one another from opposite ends of a reflecting pool. Canfield added a wing to the building

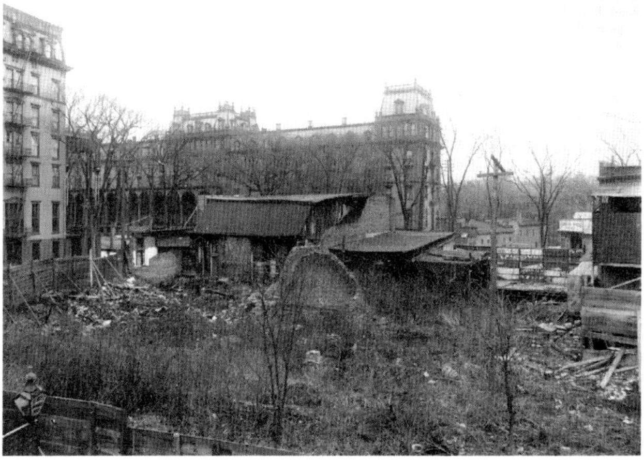

The loss of buildings by fire and demolition also provided opportunity for new sites and uses, as was the case when the vacant Grand Central hotel site allowed for construction of a trolley station in 1915.

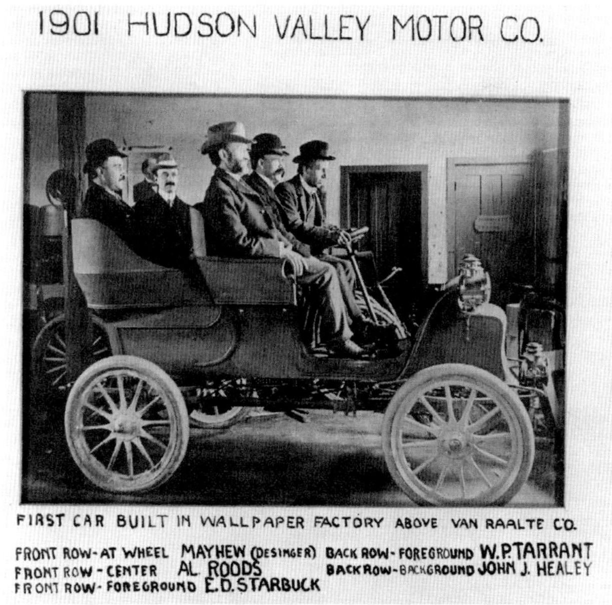

One of more than one hundred automobile manufacturing works in New York State, the Hudson Gas Motor and Vehicle Manufacturing Company in Saratoga Springs produced only two cars around 1901. Not yet road-ready, the car holds local businessmen.

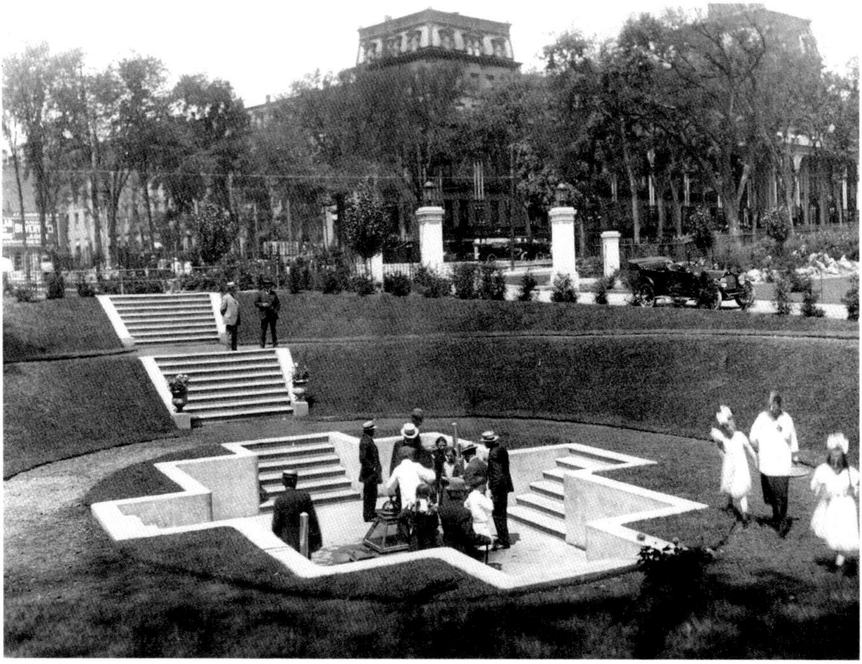

When New York State took over the springs, the large pavilion in Congress Park was taken down, replaced by 1915 with a stark cement slab and steps.

with a spectacular dining room covered by a vaulted ceiling of stained-glass windows.

In 1908 activity at the racecourse was ruffled by official warnings about wagering. Oral betting was strictly prohibited. In 1911, there was serious disruption when the track was closed under the Agnew-Hart antiwagering bill from the state legislature in Albany. The perpetual debate about what constitutes fair gambling was in the public eye.

In June 1908, the *New York Times* was able to report in the "Resort and Fashion" section,

> *The week's visitors have been largely leaders among temperance workers, brought here by the World's Temperance Congress, which will continue in session until Tuesday. Meetings of the Congress, together with that of individual temperance organizations, have been held here all the week. These included the Sons of Temperance, Woman's Christian Temperance Union, Anti-Saloon League, Independent Order of Good Templars, and the International Reform Bureau…Among the week's features at the*

> *Temperance Congress were the unveiling of a monument to Dr. Billy J. Clark, the founder of the world's first temperance society, at his old home in Moreau, and the services at his grave. On Thursday a banquet was served to the foreign delegates, at which the only beverage was Saratoga spring water.*

When pressure eased and modified regulation took effect, another epoch of high living commenced. During the 1910s, the Roaring Twenties and the 1930s, much that happened in Saratoga did not stay in Saratoga by any means. Fortunes were made in running liquor from Canada during Prohibition. New ways of playing long stakes were improvised. One of the costs of doing business for nightclubs was the size of the unofficial payroll for city officials. Boxing great Jack Dempsey trained at Tommy Luther's camp at Saratoga Lake.

Lake Houses

About twenty years after the epic battles of Saratoga during the Revolutionary War, an extravagant character had taken up residence and become Saratoga's first renowned lakeside host. Jacobus Barhydt and his wife mostly kept to themselves. Every few years they would make the journey back to Albany to visit old friends and family. They were otherwise content, having an abundance of resources in their marshy habitat, with several small lakes and ponds and woods still populated with bear, deer, moose and beaver. As their area became more frequently visited by curiosity seekers, Barhydt accepted visits from strangers. He let hopeful anglers try the fishing in his pond. Until 1840 it had an excellent reputation for the fat trout its owner could pull out. His meals were legendary, and he could provide liquor if needed.

Barhydt's visitors included many of the national and international figures coming to the spa. The ex-king of Spain and brother of Napoleon, Joseph Bonaparte, was charmed by the site and made an offer for the property. Faced with the owner's dour silence, the ex-king negotiated himself up to $20,000. After another puff on his pipe, Barhydt is said to have responded, "Sir, if it's worth that to you, it's worth that to me."[38]

In 1825, the same year as Joseph Bonaparte's visit, the Marquis de Lafayette was another of the Revolutionary War heroes to stop at the springs. He was greeted and celebrated at a grand reception on this first visit to the United States since the Revolution.

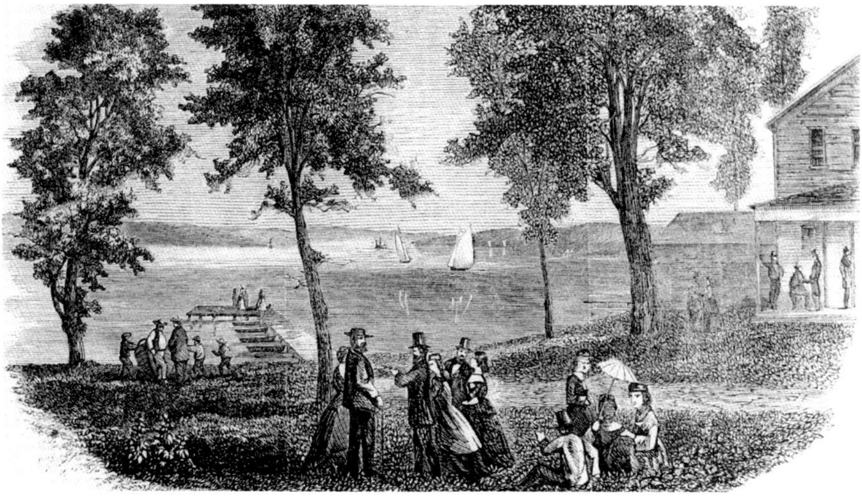

The family prepares for an outing on Saratoga Lake.

With the peculiar magnetism of Barhydt, Saratoga's waterside attractions were established as fresh places to restore one's flagging health or spirits. Other lake houses followed. So did personalities of distinction, enjoying the opportunities for pleasant, relaxing experiences.

A more organized approach to bringing the tourist trade was to be found at Riley's, as early as 1821 reported in the series of *Fashionable Tour* books published by G.M. Davison of Saratoga Springs. Riley's resort, on the western shore of Saratoga Lake, featured a deck built over the water from the shore, suitable for bathers and fishermen alike. Visitors flocked from the hotels of Saratoga Springs and Ballston Spa.

A century later, a different Riley's Lake House overlooking nearby Lake Lonely was one of Saratoga's most famous historical spots. Built by champion rower James H. Riley in 1886, the quaint hideaway served as the Lake Side House until 1931, when it burned to the ground. The house was rebuilt by Louis J. "Doc" Farone in 1934 in the most lavish manner possible. Fountains containing statues of dolphins in the front and nothing but the best furniture and interior decorating would turn this nightclub into a place of excitement and entertainment. If all this relaxation and pampering seemed too tame for the rich, then the back room casino would probably fit their style. Big-time gangsters were attracted to Saratoga for the gaming, and Riley's was no different. Meyer Lansky and Lucky Luciano had a piece of the gambling operations, which were run by a man from Troy by the name of Peter Sullivan.

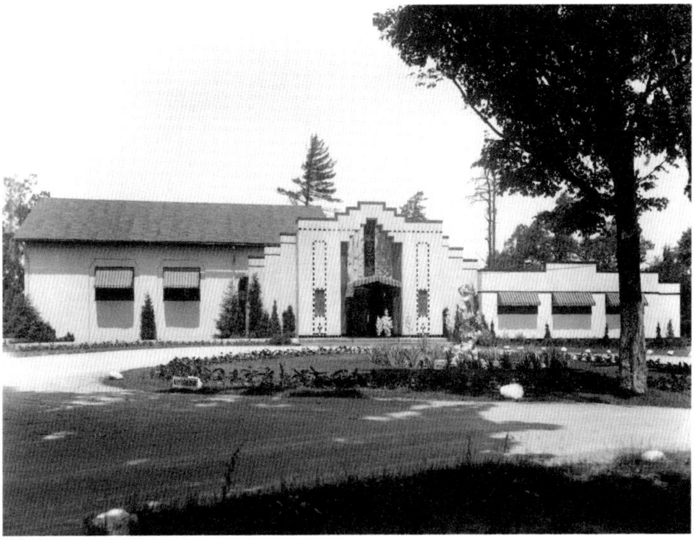

The 1934 rebuilt Riley's Lake House on the ridge above Lake Lonely was the scene of gambling and big-name entertainment in the 1930s and '40s. Its neon sign is in the collection of the History Museum.

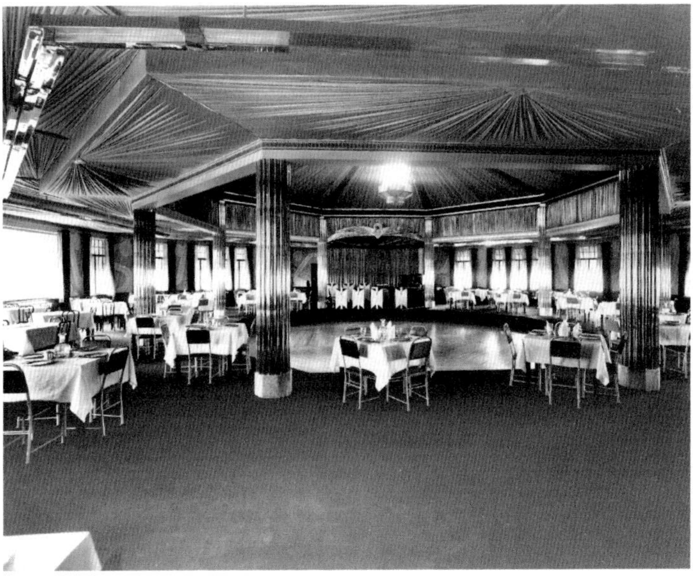

Sophie Tucker and the Minsky Follies were some of the entertainment draws for Riley's. It finally closed in 1956 after the state and national gambling crackdown. High-stakes gamblers transferred the action to Las Vegas.

The casino was run only in the month of August and contained six roulette tables, two craps tables, two card tables and one bird cage. One of the most intriguing aspects of the casino was its version of the "eye in the sky." During restorations of the house, the workers uncovered stairs behind a wall. They led to a chair that was bolted to the ceiling. Sitting in the chair, one could see the entire casino through a grate and watch the patrons and dealers. Further inspection found another of these chairs on the other side of the casino.

Riley's Lake House was not without its problems, however. The managers kept officials on the payroll (estimated at $8,000 a week) and had to contend with occasional harassment from do-good police. In 1942, Riley's closed its doors due to the slowdown caused by World War II. It reopened in 1948 but was again forced to close its doors because of the intense heat of the Kefauver campaigns against illegal gambling. In 1953, the owner, Doc Farone, was convicted of illegal gambling. Without its leader, Riley's survived a timid three years before closing down for good in 1956, ending the story of one of Saratoga's most famous casinos.[39]

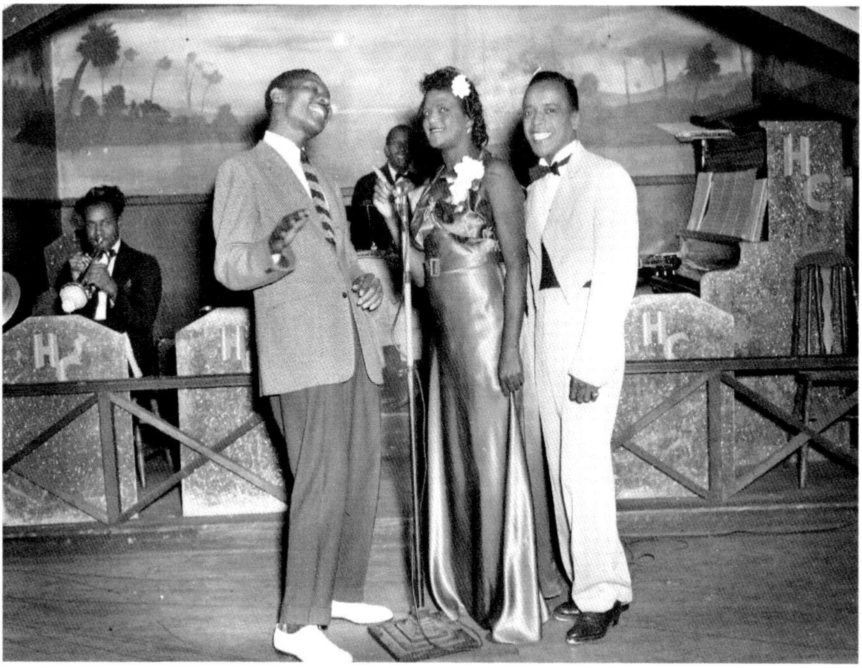

Entertainment was available in many of the bars and clubs. Jack's was a popular spot on the West Side.

The gaming business was catering to sophisticates when the lake houses drew stars of stage and screen and offered an entertainment package that would become an important industry standard—celebrity stage show, fine dining and gambling.

There were other lake houses, all with expertly prepared fresh fish dinners as the main attraction. Avery's and Meyers were on the east side of the lake. Perhaps the most renowned was Moon's, justly famous for its chief cook, George Crum. Like his right-hand assistant Mrs. Catherine ("Aunt Katie") Weeks, Crum was of thoroughly mixed American blood and drew his expertise from various cuisines. A loyal following found its way to Crum's establishment year after year. Summer visitors—including a string of state governors and congressmen, William H. Vanderbilt and other financial superstars—all treasured these jaunts to the crisp lake environment. It was early documented that the Saratoga Chip gained its ascendancy at Moon's Lake House when a fussy diner—perhaps Vanderbilt—sent back his potatoes, complaining they were undercooked. George Crum cut a batch of paper-thin slices, tossed them into boiling fat and sent them back out tastily crisped. It was quickly recognized that a new food group of epicurean delight had just been invented.

There actually were bookies named Gloomy Gus, Rags and the Dancer. Writer Damon Runyon did not need to embellish extravagantly to illuminate the scene that played between Broadway, New York, and Broadway, Saratoga Springs. Action was brisk enough that, for the lucky ones, the Depression was merely a bad rumor.

In addition to the writers and other creative artists unobtrusively coming and going from Yaddo, Saratoga was producing talent as well. Senator Edgar T. Brackett's son Charles hit the top in Hollywood, working on screenplays such as *Ninotchka*, *Lost Weekend* and *Sunset Boulevard*. Monty Woolley, son of the Grand Union manager who gained fame for *The Man Who Came to Dinner*, was part of a small Saratoga circle of friends that included Mayor Clarence Knapp and *New Yorker* writer Frank Sullivan.

At the same time, the instinct for sober living and moral restraint was never far away. There was continuing activity at installations such as the Camp Meeting at Round Lake, just south of Saratoga Springs.[40] This spur for recreation and vacationing was as popular as the gambling.

The Waters

At the end of the nineteenth century it was discovered that carbonic acid gas existed both in a pure state and dissolved in the spring waters. The gas was valuable, as it was the delightful ingredient in soda fountains and carbonated sodas, which were all the rage, as well as in new industrial applications such as refrigeration. Before long, operations were set up at several of the springs to organize extraction and transportation of the gas. To expedite increased volume, techniques were applied to strip the gas from the spring water and then to pressure pump the waters from the ground.

Up to that time, springs had been regarded as entities independent of one another. Private owners had been content with this; the mineral waters had been used simply as they emerged from the ground. An important shift in perception was embodied in *Hathorn v. Dr. Strong's Saratoga Springs Sanitarium*, a Supreme Court case in 1907. At issue was damage to the Hathorn Spring, effected from Dr. Strong's sanitarium via the underground waters. The decision recognized that the springs and wells relied on a common source, and that there must be mutual accountability among the users.

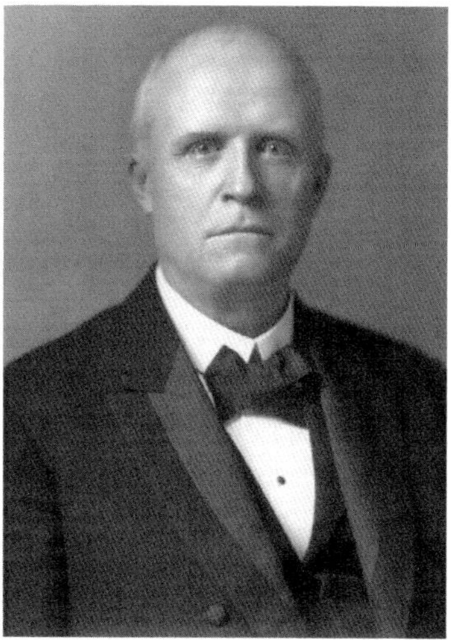

Saratogian Edgar Truman Brackett (1853–1924) was a founder of the Adirondack Trust Company bank in 1902 and also its first president. A driving force in outlawing gambling, he was an influential state senator who sponsored the 1909 bill to protect the mineral springs.

A widespread deleterious effect occurred from the extensive pumping operations. Action was taken by leading citizens and by the legislature. A state bill in 1908 prohibited pumping the mineral waters or their gases. The gas companies' rejection of the legislation caused further concern. They accompanied prolonged appeals and delays with a wasting of the springs, dumping the water that they maintained as their right. Spencer Trask stepped forward and worked with the state legislature. Senator Edgar Truman Brackett, at first retained by the embattled gas strippers, soon was acting on legislation to protect and preserve the springs.[41]

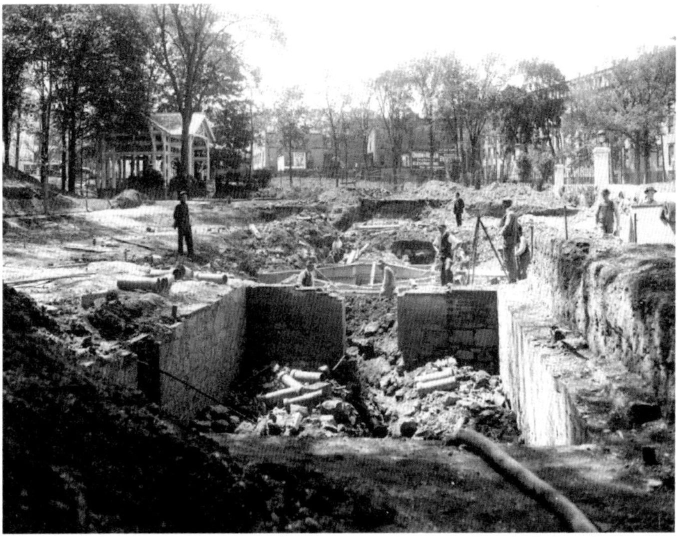

After the springs were closed down to protect the water flow in 1909, the remnants of the Victorian pavilion were removed. Congress Spring was excavated, retubed and returned to service.

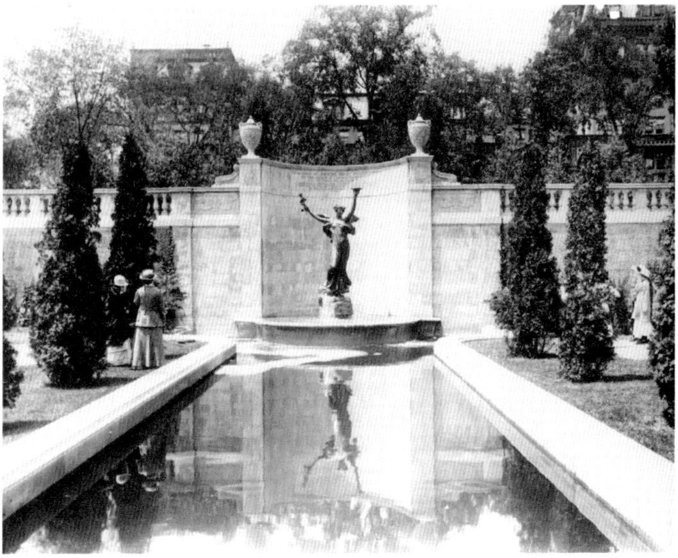

The Spirit of Life, a statue, fountain and reflecting pool in Congress Park, was dedicated in 1914 as a memorial to philanthropist Spencer Trask. Sculptor Daniel Chester French also created the Lincoln Memorial in Washington.

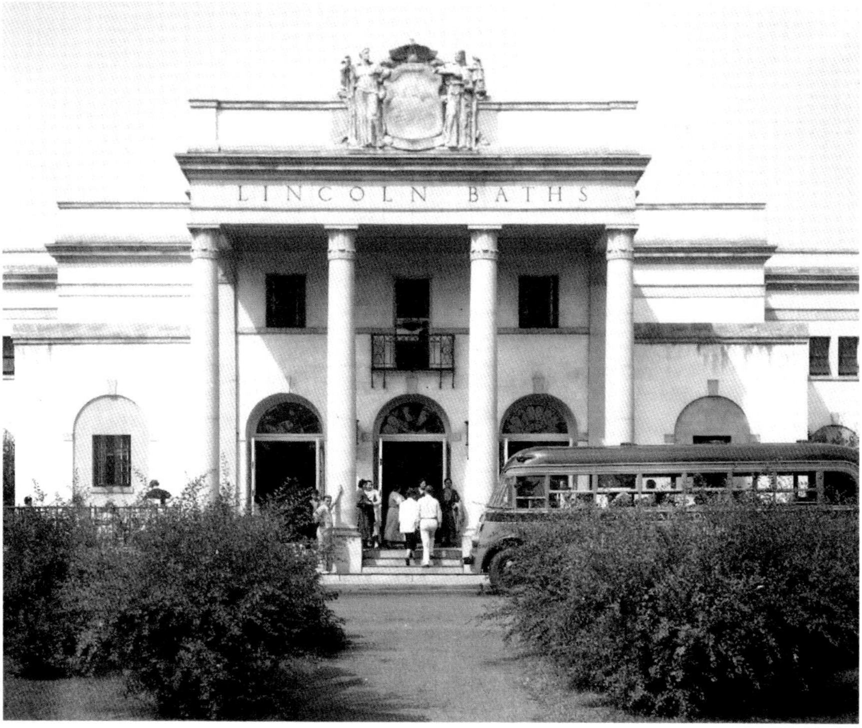

The Lincoln (1930) and Washington (1919) bathhouses at the Saratoga Spa State Park are now adapted for other uses. The park police occupy the Lincoln, while the National Museum of Dance exhibits fill the Washington bathhouse.

A Conservation Commission was established. In 1909, it was finalizing deliberations on actions the commission might take to protect the springs. It was in carrying the final revisions on the report to New York City that Spencer Trask lost his life in a railway crash at Croton-on-Hudson on December 30, 1909. For his constant work to bring out the best in Saratoga Springs, and as a respected leader in the world of finance, he was widely mourned.

In the years that followed, principal springs were taken under ownership and administration of New York State, creating the State Reservation. Under the Works Progress Administration of the Roosevelt presidency, the Saratoga Spa was developed as a medical and educational campus. A new hotel was appropriately named the Gideon Putnam. Splendid bathhouses were built to house hydrotherapy treatment regimens on a European model under leading physicians of this approach, including Dr. Simon Baruch.

Chapter Four

Decline and Rejuvenation

New Community

Postwar Blues

> *"I remember when my father came back from World War II, and the racetrack hadn't run for three years and not one downtown building had been painted during that period. My father said it was the most depressing time in his life; he had returned with a tremendous sense of elation after being victorious in the war, and he was coming back to a turn-down city where he was going to spend the rest of his life. So he banded together with others and said, we've got to do something about this."*
> *–Charles Wait, CEO of Adirondack Trust Company*[42]

Saratoga Springs gave as deeply and dearly as any community after December 7, 1941. While families watched and waited through the long years of World War II, changes were happening in the community. In 1941, trolley service was abandoned and the racecourse went dark as the summer racing action moved to Belmont on Long Island for three seasons. "Standard bred" or harness racing was introduced. Saratoga Springs was faced with an aging infrastructure. The huge hotels that had been built for mass occupancy were falling into extreme stylistic and functional obsolescence. Victorian architecture and design, having prevailed and then hung on for several generations, was rejected by the younger generation, who preferred simpler styles.

After the war, the prospects for Saratoga Springs had changed, as was true for most of the nation. The industrial strength of the nation, emerging from wartime production modes, opened a boom for business, creating new opportunities for personal consumption, mobility and entertainment. On the individual tourist's level, the country was also speeding up. The recreational dream now was becoming freedom to travel, to see fresh vistas each time out. For those born in small cities or large towns, the draw was to the big cities, where opportunity was more powerful and diverse. Resort life for the traditional privileged was fading along with the class that sustained it. But there were now durable community leaders here as well as the traditional visitors who preferred to see Saratoga as it had been.

In 1946, the United States Hotel suffered a fire and was torn down. The same year, the city council established a planning board whose survey, "Saratoga Springs Looks to the Future," constituted the city's first master plan.[43] Mayor Addison Mallery sought the basis for a further planning document in collaboration between the city and Skidmore

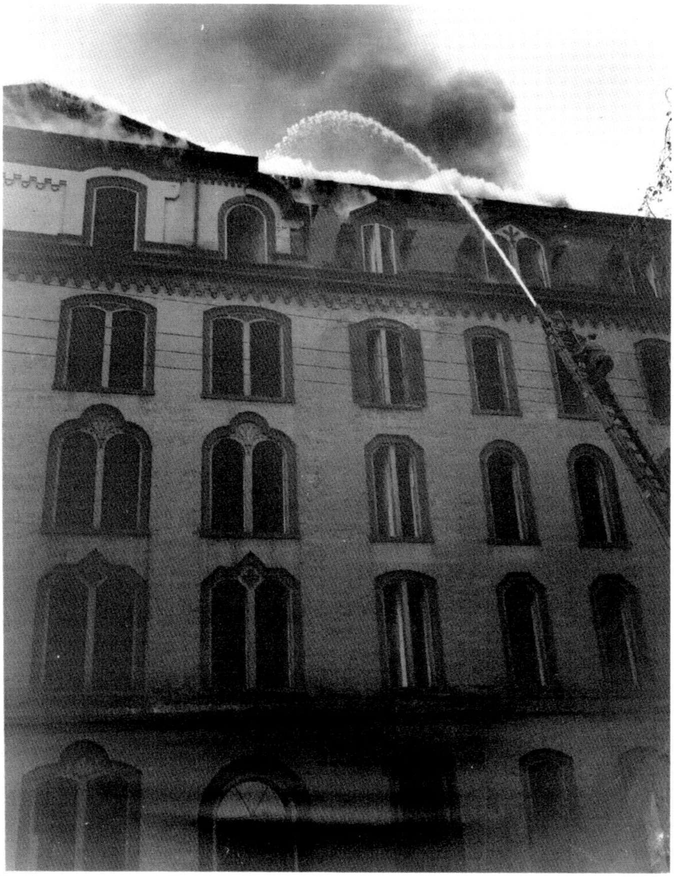

The United States Hotel was so damaged by fire in 1946 that its demolition was inevitable. Over its lifetime, Saratoga Springs has been redesigned many times by devastating fire that left gaping wounds in the streetscape.

College, which produced an insightful and useful analysis. Skidmore students interviewed 2,000 of the city's 4,500 families over a span of three years. Sociology professor Dr. Everett Stonequist summarized the results in a document providing an approach toward a balanced community life. The *Saratogian* newspaper brought questions to the public, with articles elucidating objectives shared by residents; more stable year-round sources of income; less dependence on visitors: diversified local economic, cultural, educational and recreational activities; and a better balance of age and gender. It was determined that residents, working cooperatively, could combine the best features from the traditional past with changing needs of the present and future.

A certain nostalgia was identified. Older citizens could remember the good old days of high Victorian times, a marked contrast to the present scene with the loss of the United States Hotel and the run-down appearance of other landmarks.

Local facilities were lacking: a free library was wanting, and public buildings including schools were becoming outmoded. Passenger traffic on the railroads continued to decline and plans were made to move the rail lines out of the city. (In 1959, a depot was built on the outskirts beyond

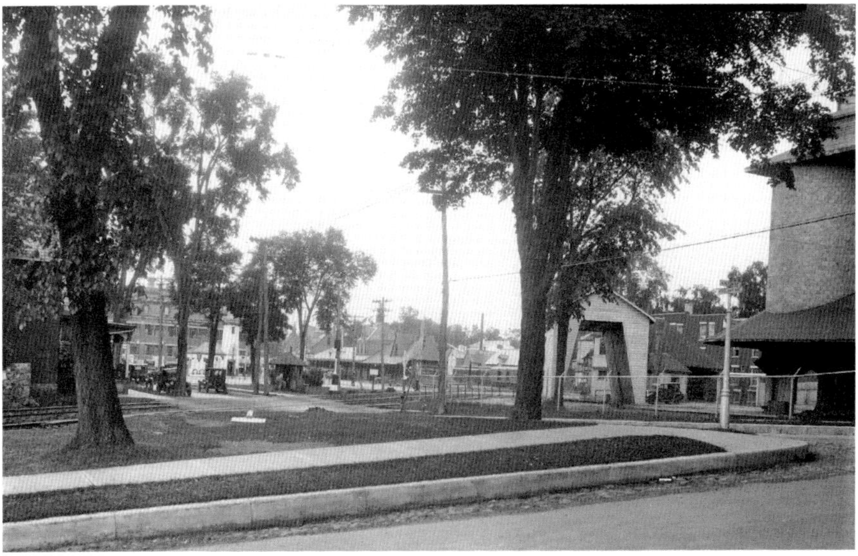

Passengers and freight arrived just one block from Broadway until the rails were moved to the west side of the city in 1959. The coal yard supplied both the locomotives and furnaces in homes and commercial buildings.

West Avenue and the tracks were moved out of the downtown, leaving a strip called "Railroad Place.")

Urban Renewal, a federal program operating in broadly engineered clearing of blighted areas, eliminated historic sites and small businesses on side streets but left much of Broadway intact. Improvements to infrastructure were brought in, including better handling of storm water and sewage. Although the city's center was now much less densely populated than in the era of great hotels, residents were willing to accept a "normal" downtown, without the former glamour. As a small city, Saratoga Springs was still better than most. In 1948, the average family income of $3,500 was above the national level and most amenities were readily available. But the twelve-week summer economy had diminished and new jobs were scarce.

Saratoga Springs had fostered advantages in its evolution from town to village to city, encompassing a substantial area with inside and outside taxing districts, encouraging diversity of development and use. Originally the inside and outside districts had been set up to accommodate moving the gambling out of town. An unplanned benefit, once the gambling had gone, was that there would remain farms within city limits through the end of the century, and expanses remained to develop residential uses for all income levels.

Although "taking the waters" had given way to more complex sciences of healing, physicians and patients still recognized some therapeutic value in the mineral baths. However, the subtle and introspective pleasures of the spa were no longer predominant in mid-twentieth-century America.

In the sphere of entertainment, it was no longer necessary to actually be there to see top name performers. The new medium of television transformed such experiences, making them suddenly accessible to all. Soon the ability and expectation to replay events would take the luster from witnessing events firsthand, including horse racing, which was itself being upstaged by professionally designed and promoted league sports.

In the first half of the 1950s, the Senate Special Committee to Investigate Crime in Interstate Commerce, popularly known as the Kefauver Committee, scrutinized gambling in Saratoga Springs, resulting in the closure of all gaming locations.

The Grand Union Hotel was taken down in 1952, its replacement a strip mall with a Grand Union grocery store and a vast parking lot fronting on Broadway.[44] The passing of the hotels, which had served as icons of a flourishing past, caused a sense of loss and uncertainty.

The 1950s and '60s also saw several proposals to put hotels in Congress Park. These were encouraged by the city council under the philosophy that any economic development was better than stagnation. The opening of the Pyramid Mall in the neighboring town of Wilton represented a tangible threat that propelled Saratogians into action. The downtown vacancy rate reached 50 percent in 1973.

Community Leaders Step Forward

New leadership coalesced to give the city a new perspective and new life. A combination of private resources and public action fused a number of single initiatives befitting the vision to restore Saratoga Springs as a tourist destination.

Among the accomplishments of Edgar Truman Brackett had been the founding of the Adirondack Trust Company in 1901. The leaders of this bank maintained a focus on the success of local enterprise through the twentieth century. In 1964, Newman E. "Pete" Wait became president of the company. Several other community leaders shared his concern that it was time for decisive action to restore economic vitality to Saratoga Springs. They included businessmen such as Fred Eaton, publisher of the *Saratogian* newspaper, and Tom Ashton, who was also a board member of Adirondack Trust. They knew that the city's location was a natural attribute, its history was unparalleled and the tourism tradition continued unbroken. The bank assumed an integral role with its immersion in projects large and small, support for imaginative entrepreneurs and investors and a determination to keep payrolls and business ownership in the community.[45]

Pete Wait and other attentive planners heard of performing arts center proposals, including one for a location in a nearby state. A committee organized to devise the basis for a major cultural attraction in Saratoga Springs. This coincided with initiatives in state government under the Rockefeller administration, which had a forward policy for city planning, construction and modernization.

In spite of the tangible evidence of renewed public and private enterprise, there were no modern hotels or motels, and no national chains were attracted to Saratoga Springs. The community's prime movers took up this lack and launched the Community Hotel Corporation. The Adirondack Trust Company pledged to purchase the first $25,000 of

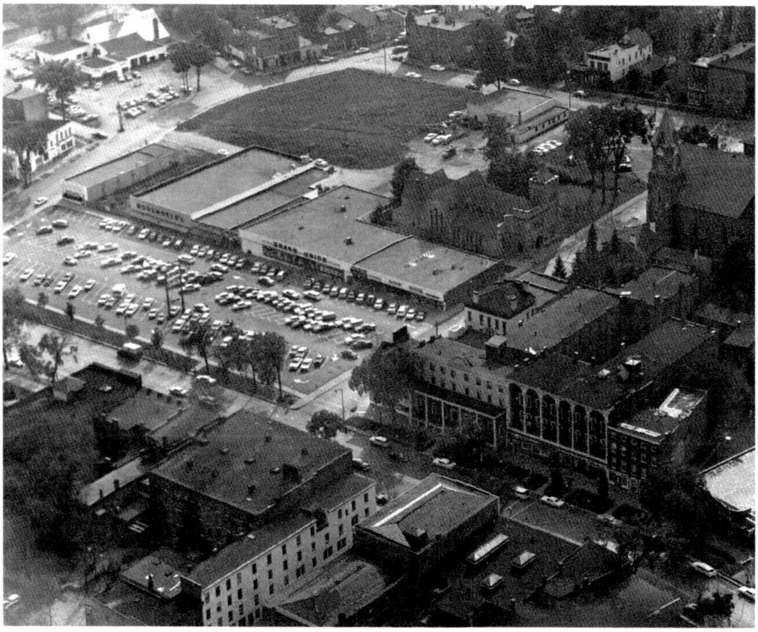

In one of history's great ironies, the Grand Union Hotel site was filled by a strip mall that featured a Grand Union grocery store, demolished in the late 1990s. The hotel's footprint is being gradually filled in.

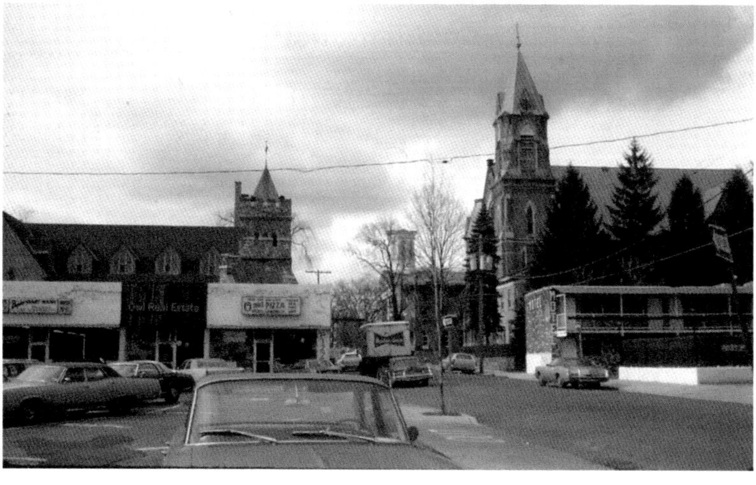

Before Congress Park Center filled the Broadway frontage once more, Bethesda Episcopal Church and the church adapted as Universal Preservation Hall were clearly visible on Washington Street. *Photo: Libby Smith-Holmes*

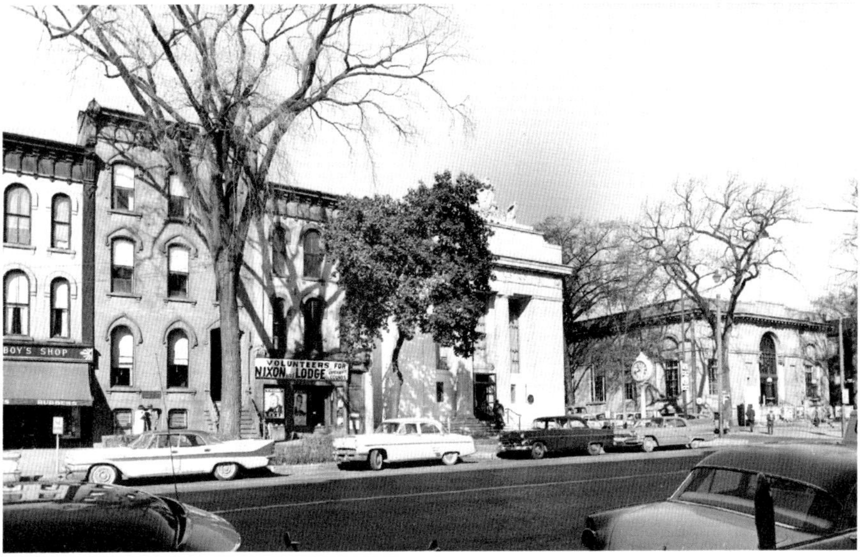

Broadway and Church Street, 1960. Only a few of the original elms remain and will soon fall victim to the elm beetle.

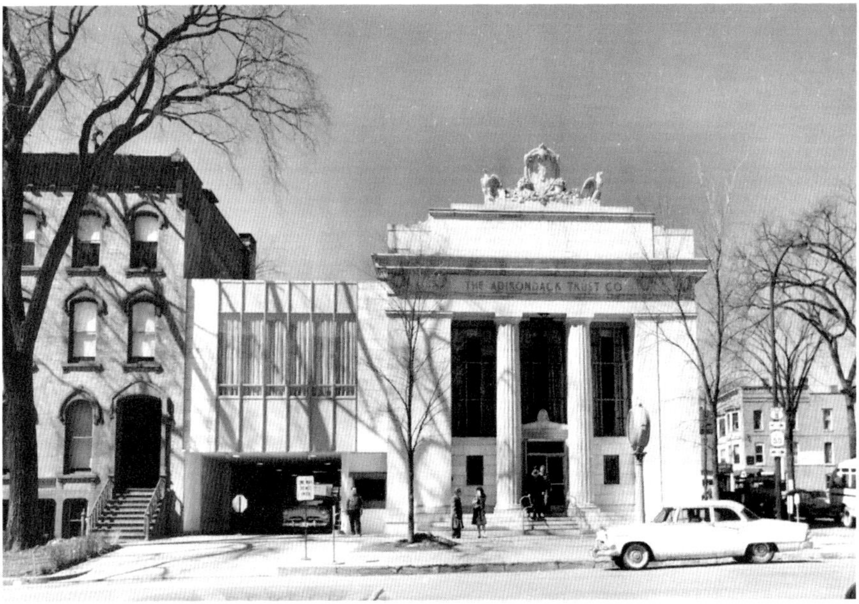

The Adirondack Trust Company, in business on Broadway since 1902, is still independent, locally owned and deeply invested in the community through its main office, nine branches and three insurance offices.

bonds issued by the fledgling corporation. At $50 per share, citizens and businesses were encouraged to invest in the enterprise. In two years, $1.5 million was raised. This was leveraged sufficiently to build a 150-unit motel on lower Broadway, the first travelers' resource built in decades. The stockholder-owned hotel opened in August of 1964 and operated successfully until 1981, when a national chain bought it. The hospitality industry was back.

Engine of Commerce

A Chamber of Commerce, established in 1918, had been operating for half a century. It had grown modestly, as had business organizations elsewhere. After mid-century, the Greater Saratoga Chamber of Commerce had benefited from the wisdom gained in hosting diverse populations of sophisticated visitors, and then had seen the world of recreational entertainment profoundly change. It dealt with local concerns but sought a national reach. In the late 1960s, it took on new life.

Business leaders, residents, students, preservationists, city planners and historians banded together to save the downtown business district. They began with a vision for revitalization called the Saratoga Plan of Action (SPA).[46] A volunteer committee met frequently and consistently. With the guidance of Saratoga Associates head Robert Bristol, a miniature streetscape was built and citizens were invited to play the "game" of removing or changing buildings in the downtown, with frank discussion about the effects. While the physical landscape itself was considered, concepts of façade preservation and public amenities such as plantings and sidewalk treatments were developed. These resulted in shared objectives being elevated to agreements for lasting visual improvements in the Special Assessment District and Capital Improvement Register.

When asked, the city planner for this most successful period in the city's history said, "Leading families stepped up." The heads of those families, when posed the same question, credited "an engaged citizenry." There was consensus that the private sector was determined to succeed and local government was willing to let them. Those who drove the successful initiatives expressed that voluntarism, laced with talent, lay at the heart of the good that began to result.

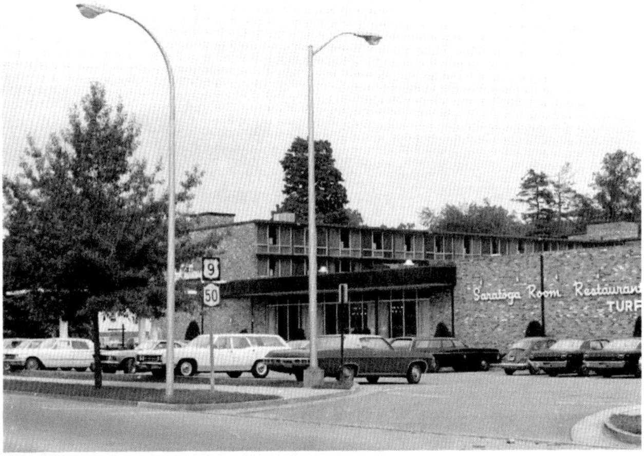

The Holiday Inn was built by local investors as the first new hotel in Saratoga Springs in many decades.

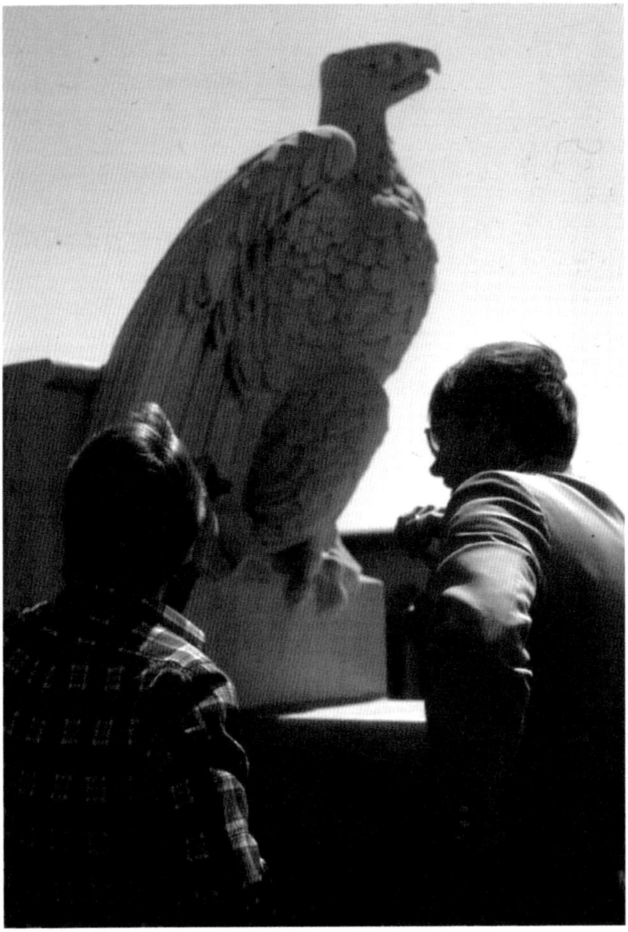

The marble eagle was placed atop the Adirondack Trust Company bank in 1916 as an emblem of vigilance in challenging times. The imposing edifice was designed by Alfred Hopkins. President Charles Wait is at right. *Photo: Saratoga Springs Preservation Foundation.*

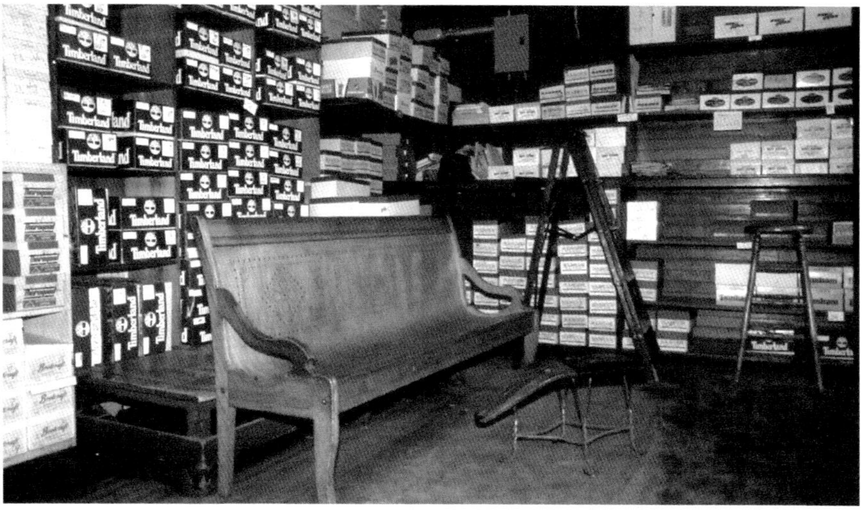

Mabitt's and its next-door neighbor Farmer's Hardware persisted on Broadway into the late twentieth century, providing basic needs to residents. The present mix of local and chain store specialty shops draws students, visitors and residents downtown. *Photo: Saratoga Springs Preservation Foundation.*

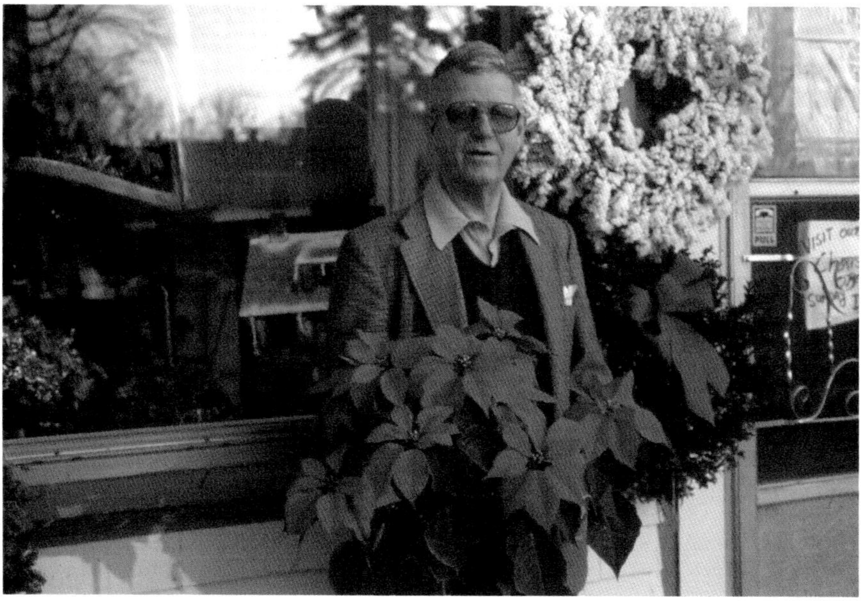

The late Charlie Dehn represented one of the city's older locally owned businesses, a garden store and florist shop with twenty-two greenhouses in operation on Beekman Street since 1892. *Photo: Libby Smith-Holmes.*

Fortuitous Circumstance

Before the idea of health retreats or heritage tourism, many people had found their way to the springs; when travel became a recreational adventure, by steamer and carriage or by railroad, they came by the thousands. In the 1950s, Americans were seeing their country by car, and the interstate highway system was built. Many small towns and cities were adversely affected by the placement of the highways. For Saratoga Springs, the interstate fell just right. The draft plan of Route 87, "the Northway" from Albany to Montreal, ran straight through the mansion at Yaddo. Reasonable heads prevailed. When completed, the Northway began to deliver an endless stream of visitors to exit 14 just east of Yaddo, where the visitor is welcomed by the still rural, tree-lined boulevard of Union Avenue running between the majestic racecourses.

Industrial Diversification

Grande's Industrial Park was established, attracting a national food distributor, a container company and the printing company for a number of national magazines. Saratoga Hospital raised its sights and objectives, growing to serve a broad area. With the help of benefactors from families that stayed close to the city despite the downturn, specialty treatment centers were founded.

The Chamber of Commerce commenced an energetic program to rebuild the local economy. Its objectives included restoration of tourism year-round and diversification of industry and business to provide a stable growing economy. Chamber Executive Joe Dalton led the organization into the twenty-first century.

The great Victorian past was recalled in designing the streets, from lighting fixtures to park benches. Leaders developed annual events from the theme, making Saratoga Springs a regular destination once again for people from local and regional areas and from far away. A friendly family environment gave more visitors the idea that Saratoga Springs might be the right place to live.

To replace the old Convention Center that had burned in 1965, a new City Center was opened with an adjoining first-rate hotel. The hotel has changed hands several times to stronger national-brand ownership. Now the Saratoga Hilton, it brought world-class accommodation back to town.

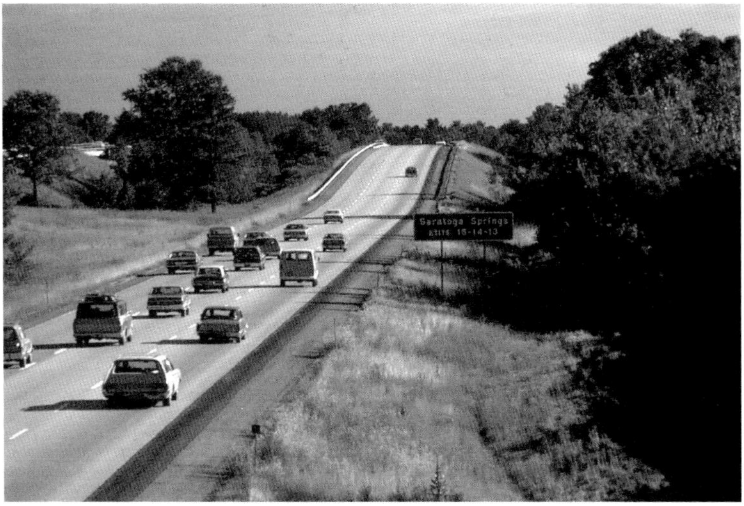

The Northway (Interstate 87) swung around Saratoga Springs close enough to allow easy commuting but far away enough to preserve the downtown core. *Photo: Libby Smith-Holmes*

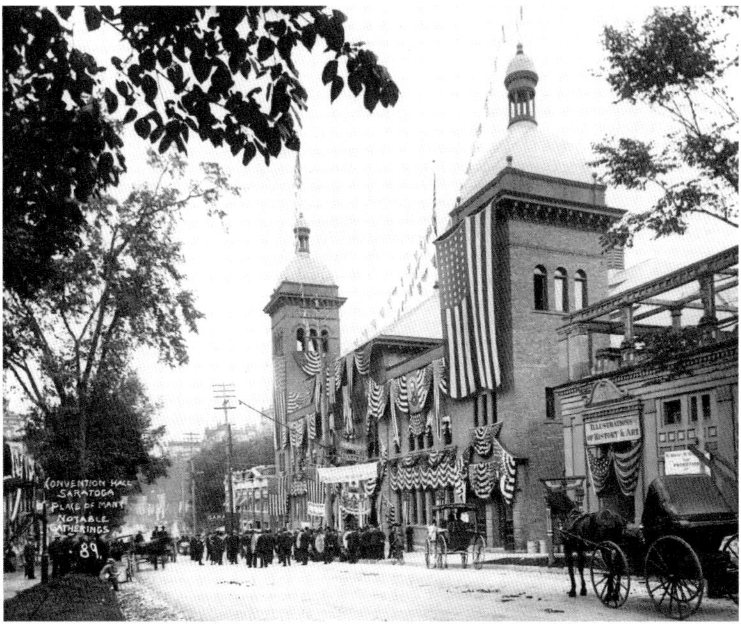

Convention Hall, built in 1893 at the edge of Congress Park, could hold five thousand people for meetings, concerts and sporting events. Its loss by fire in 1965 was a final insult to Saratoga's downtown and an incentive for improvements that continue today.

Colleges

Skidmore College had begun in 1903 as Lucy Skidmore Scribner's Young Women's Industrial Club. It grew up in some purpose-built buildings and many of the houses to the east of Congress Park.

By 1960 the difficulty of operating in more than eighty adapted structures was evident, and officials began looking at other possible sites. It was heard that other cities were making overtures to attract Skidmore away from Saratoga Springs. In an extraordinary stroke, board member J. Erik Jonsson and his wife, Margaret, donated sufficient funds to purchase a 650-acre tract of the old Woodlawn estate on the outskirts of the city. The college's board and president rose to the task. In October 1961, they voted to purchase the land and begin the construction of a brand-new campus. Masterful planning and design ensued. Dr. Val H. Wilson was followed in 1965 by Joseph C. Palamountain Jr., Skidmore's fourth president. In 1971, the former women's college began admitting men to the regular undergraduate program and established the University Without Walls, a distance learning option for liberal arts studies. A period of steady growth and academic enhancement has taken the college to national standing.

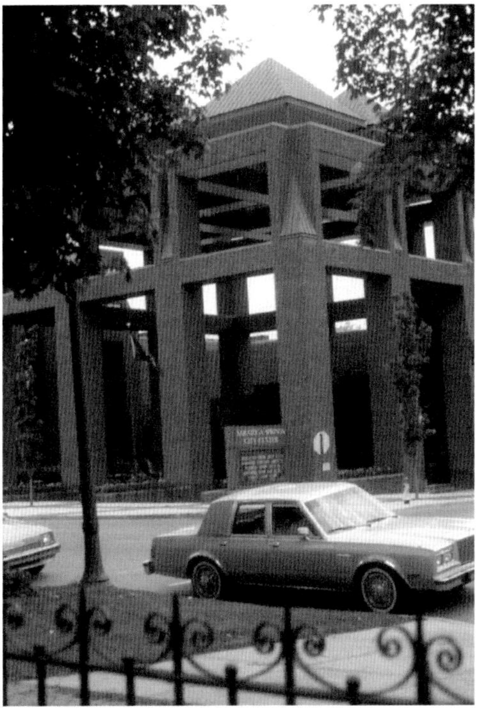

In 1984, work began on the Saratoga Springs City Center and the adjacent hotel, which work together and with the local Convention and Tourism Bureau to attract return business from conventions and events. *Photo: Saratoga Springs Preservation Foundation.*

Another leading educational institution came to Saratoga Springs in 1971 when Empire State College, a branch of the State University of New York, established its statewide headquarters here. Empire State took over some of the former Skidmore College

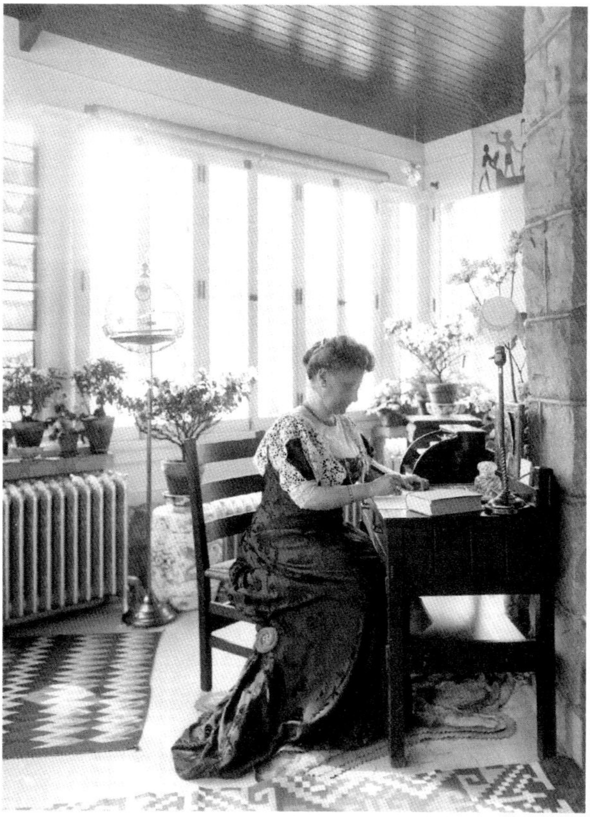

Lucy Skidmore Scribner at work on the porch, 1903.

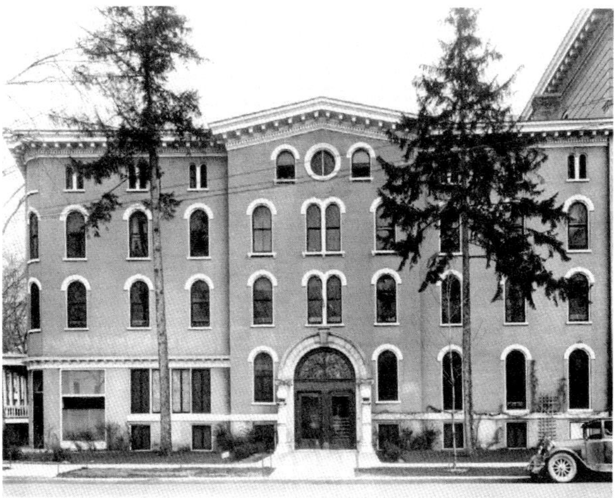

Skidmore Hall, formerly Temple Grove.

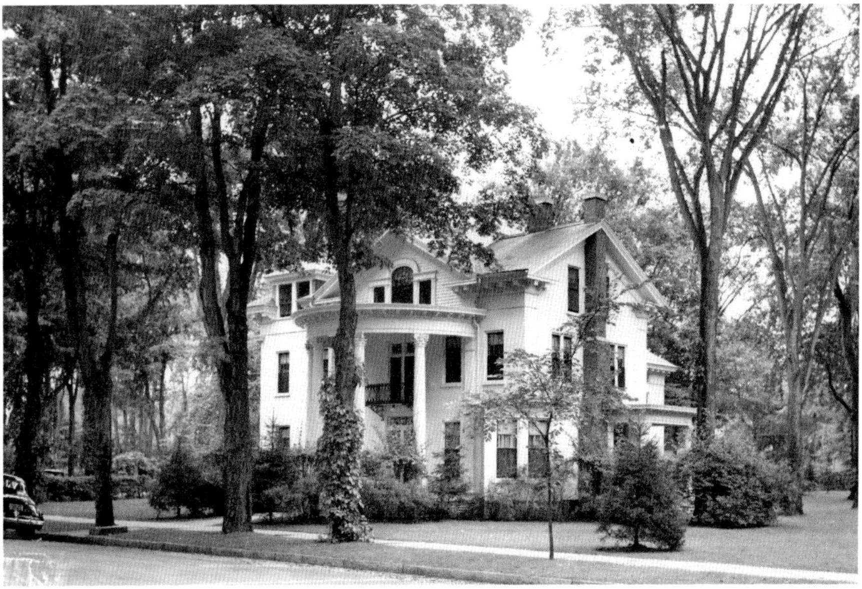

Scott House became the headquarters for the short-lived Verrazano College, then a real estate office before returning to private ownership as a single-family home.

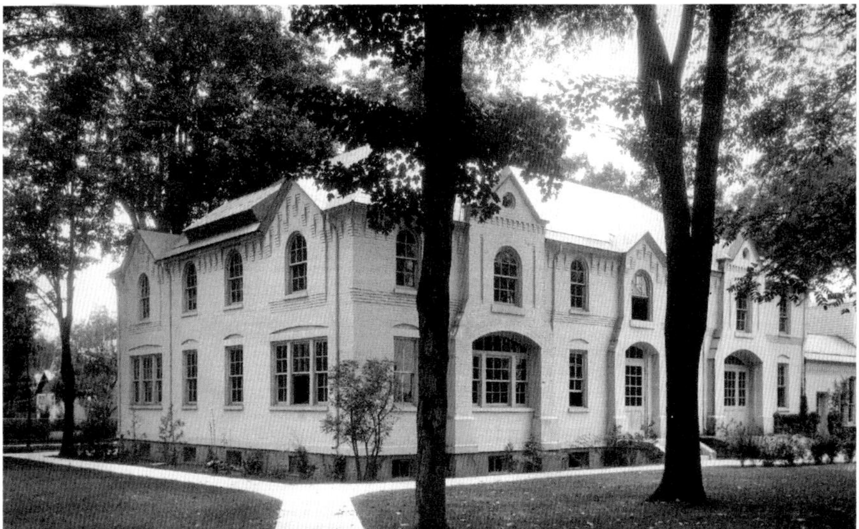

Hathorn art building, 1923.

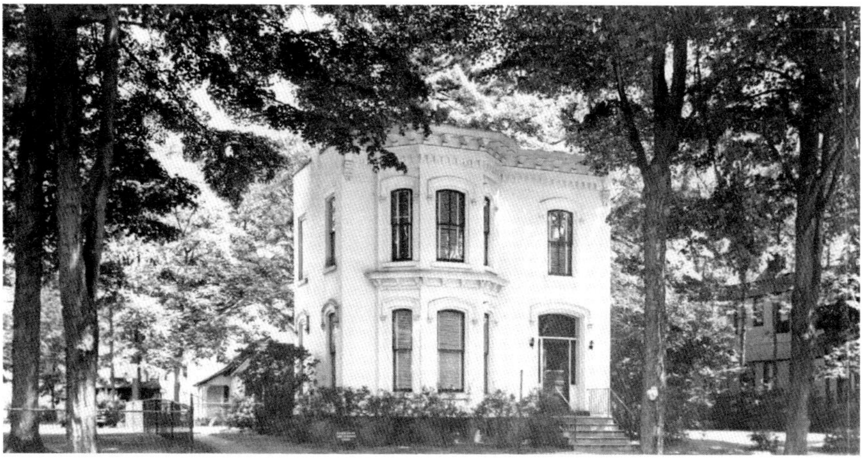

The home economics building.

buildings east of Congress Park and has built new structures to serve its needs. Empire State conducts an expansive program at thirty-five locations around the state and through distance learning, reaching adult students regardless of location with undergraduate and master's degree academic and professional programs.

Yaddo

Katrina Trask eventually married her longtime admirer, George Foster Peabody, who had been a close friend to both of the Trasks. Peabody helped Katrina seal her legacy by putting Yaddo into the corporate form that would endure. The results have been historic. Since 1926, more than two thousand artists have been nourished by the solitude and natural setting. The opportunity to work without interruption was accomplished by dedicating the four-hundred-acre retreat to residencies for future generations of writers, composers, painters and other creative artists. This strong foundation was to serve new expression in literature, musical composition, choreography, film, painting, performance art, photography, printmaking, sculpture and video.

John Cheever once wrote that the "forty or so acres on which the principal buildings of Yaddo stand have seen more distinguished activity in the arts than any other piece of ground in the English-speaking community, and perhaps the world." Collectively, artists who have worked at Yaddo

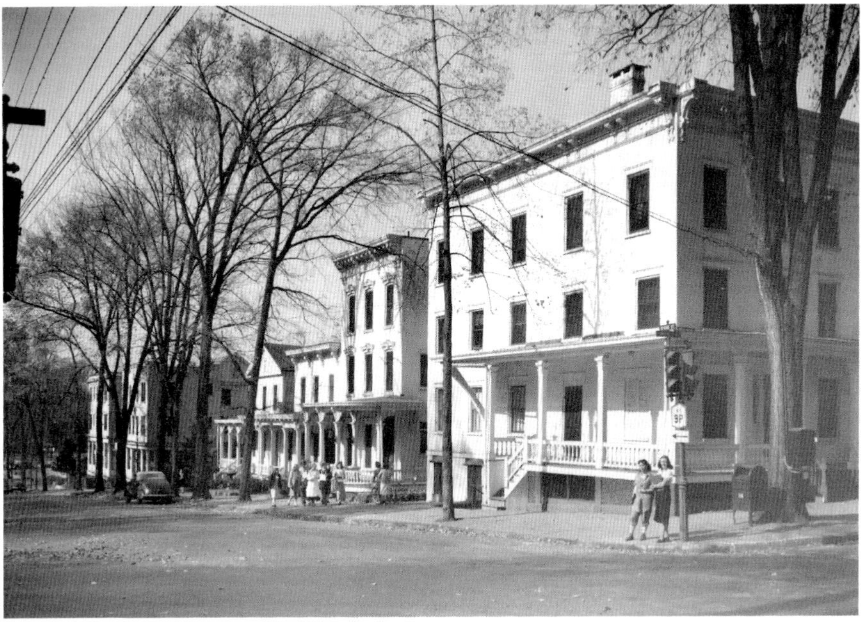

Skidmore students walking to class on Spring Street when the campus was downtown.

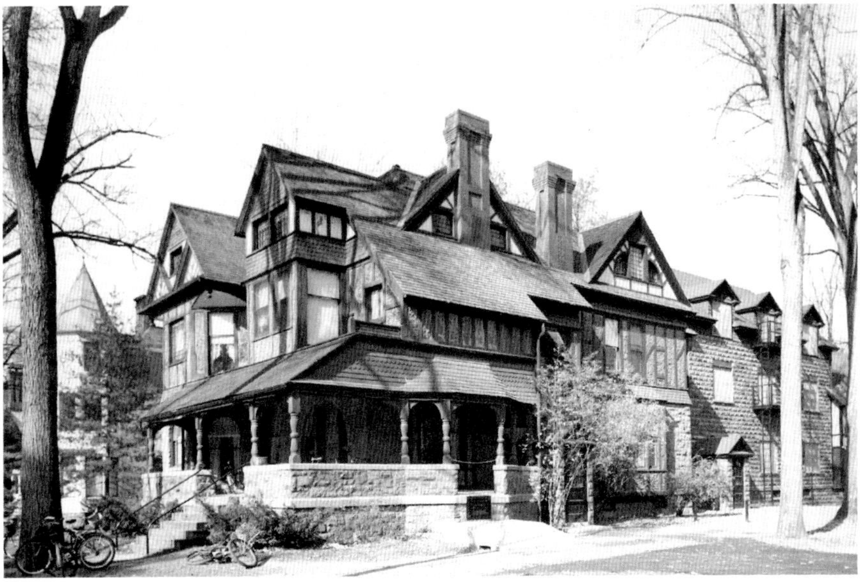

Ross house.

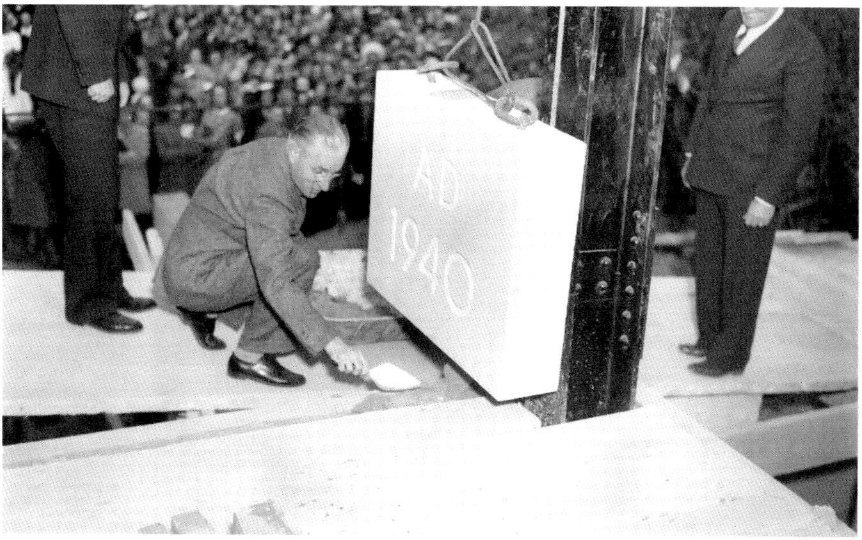

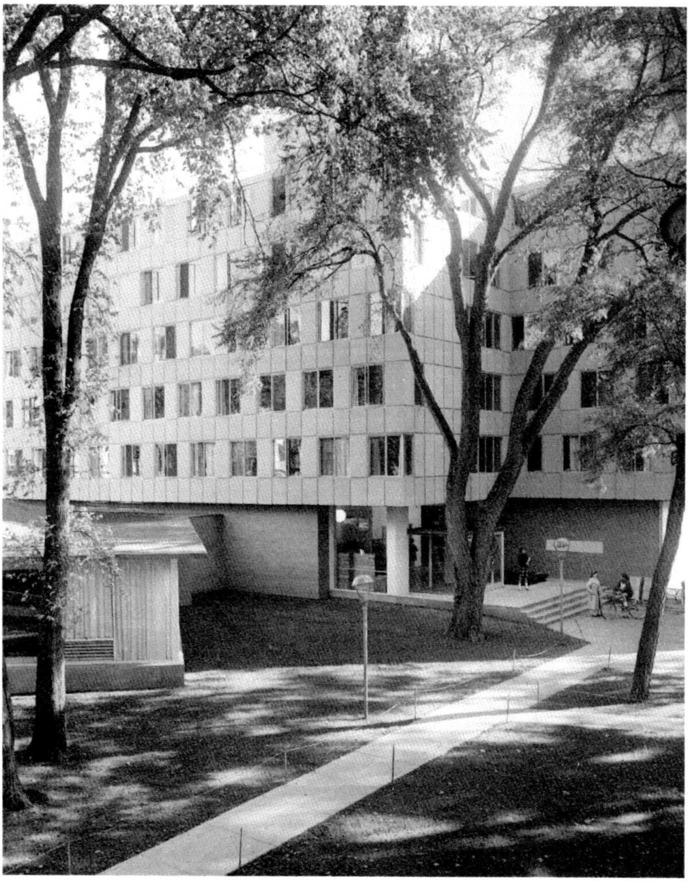

Above: The cornerstone for a new library was placed in 1940 at the corner of Union Avenue and Circular Street.

Right: Moore Hall, a dormitory on Union Avenue, was always out of scale with its neighborhood in size, style and color. The "Pink Palace" is scheduled to be replaced by a condominium building.

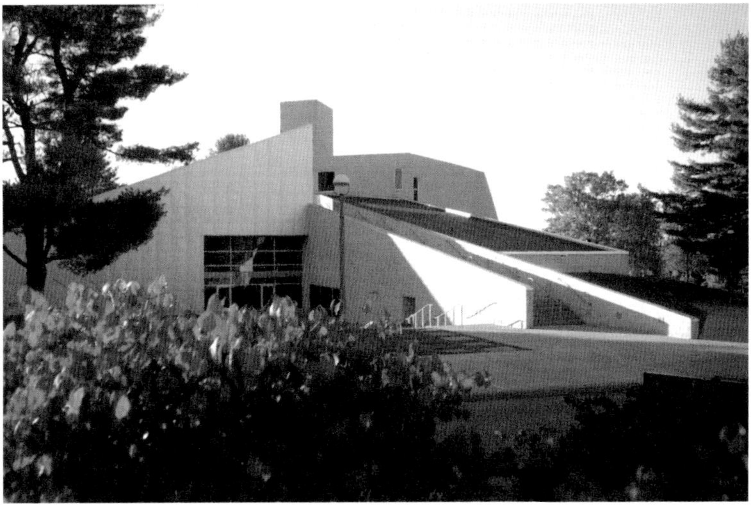

Adventurous architecture continues to appear on Skidmore College's Jonsson campus, where the Tang Teaching Museum brings innovative exhibits to challenge the minds of students, residents and visitors. *Photo: Skidmore College*

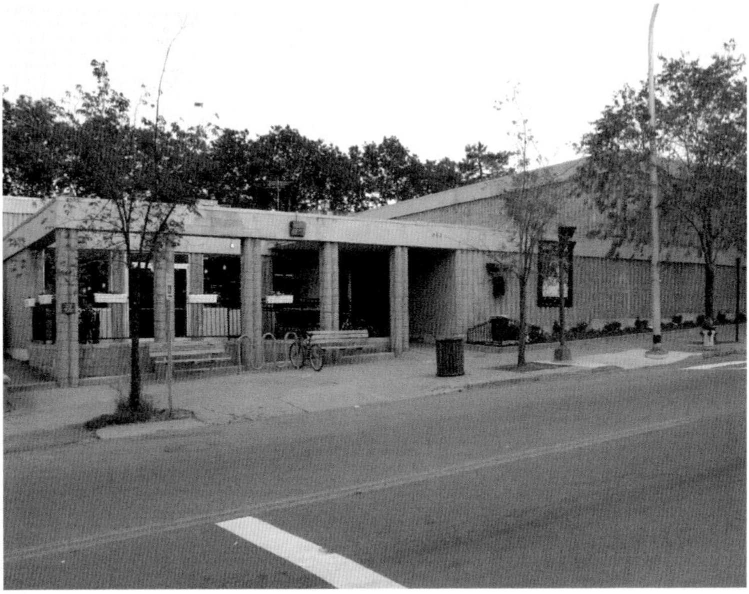

Meeting community needs from 1971 to 2006, the YMCA held the city's only year-round public pool. A new condominium building replaces it at the edge of Congress Park. *Photo: Saratoga YMCA.*

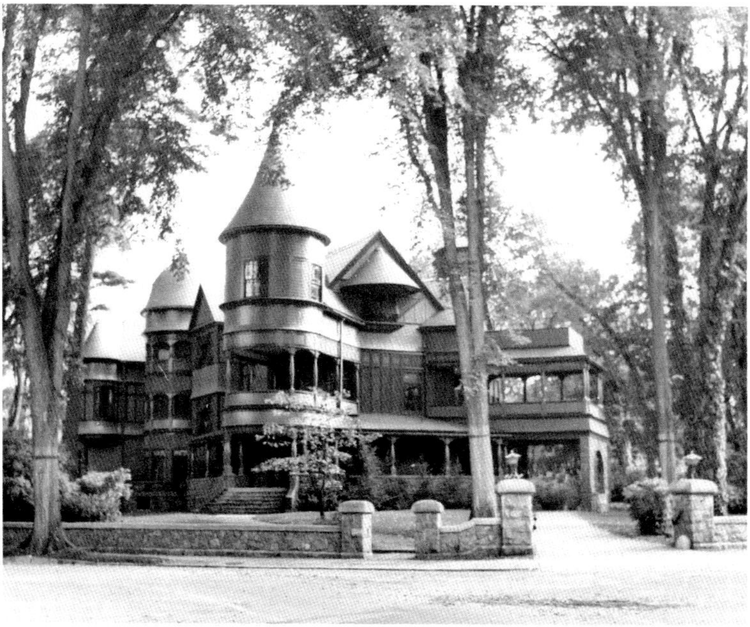

The Mabee house, at the corner of Union Avenue and Circular Street, built just prior to 1900. It burned down in 1937 and the location was taken up by Skidmore College's library.

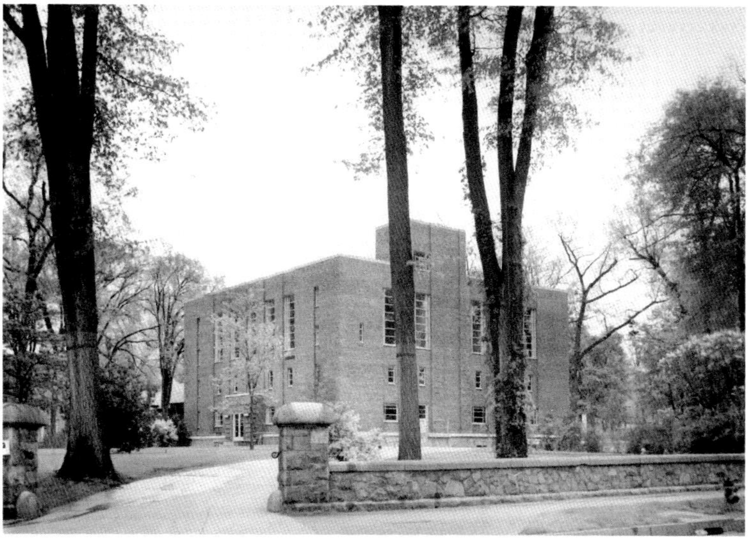

The Skidmore library for the downtown campus after 1940. It became the administration building for Empire State College.

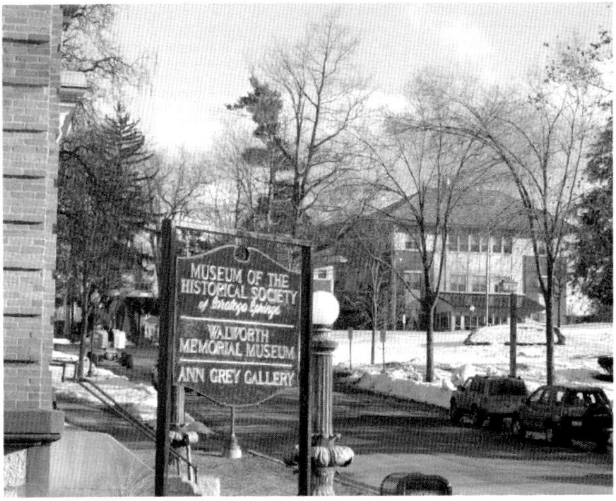

Empire State College's new headquarters building rises above Congress Park in the space that formerly held a mansion and Skidmore College's library. *Photo: Libby Smith-Holmes*

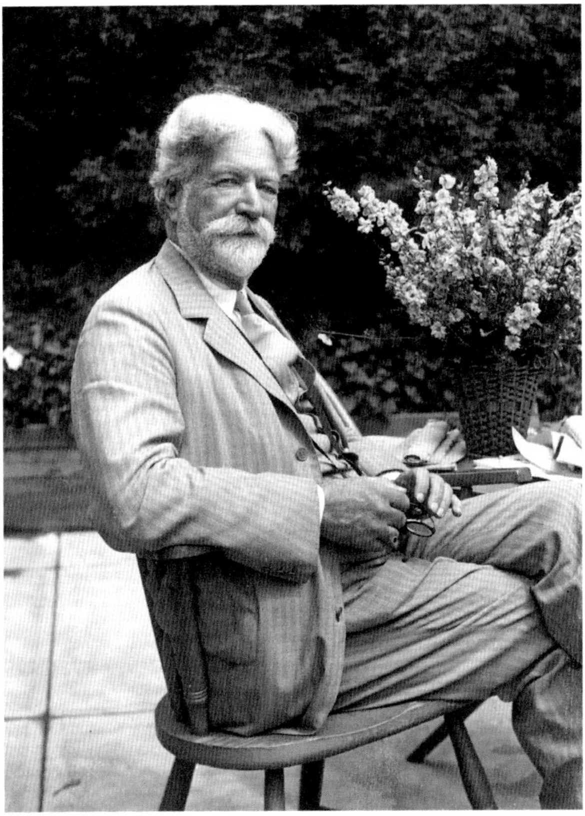

Financier and philanthropist George Foster Peabody (1852–1938) was a longtime family friend who married the widowed Katrina Trask in the last years of her life. He was instrumental in realizing her dream of Yaddo as an artists' retreat.

have won 62 Pulitzer Prizes, 24 MacArthur Fellowships, 58 National Book Awards, 22 National Book Critics Circle Awards, 106 Rome Prizes, 1 Nobel Prize (Saul Bellow, who won the Nobel Prize in Literature in 1976) and countless other honors. Many books by Yaddo authors have been made into films. Writers since Cheever's day include James Baldwin, Carson McCullers, William Carlos Williams, Truman Capote and Sylvia Plath; in music, composers such as Leonard Bernstein and Aaron Copland have frequented Yaddo; and visual artists including Milton Avery, Clyfford Still and Jules Olitski have benefited from their residencies at Yaddo. Others include Philip Guston, Patricia Highsmith, Langston Hughes, Ted Hughes, Alfred Kazin, Ulysses Kay, Jacob Lawrence, Katherine Anne Porter, Mario Puzo and Virgil Thomson.

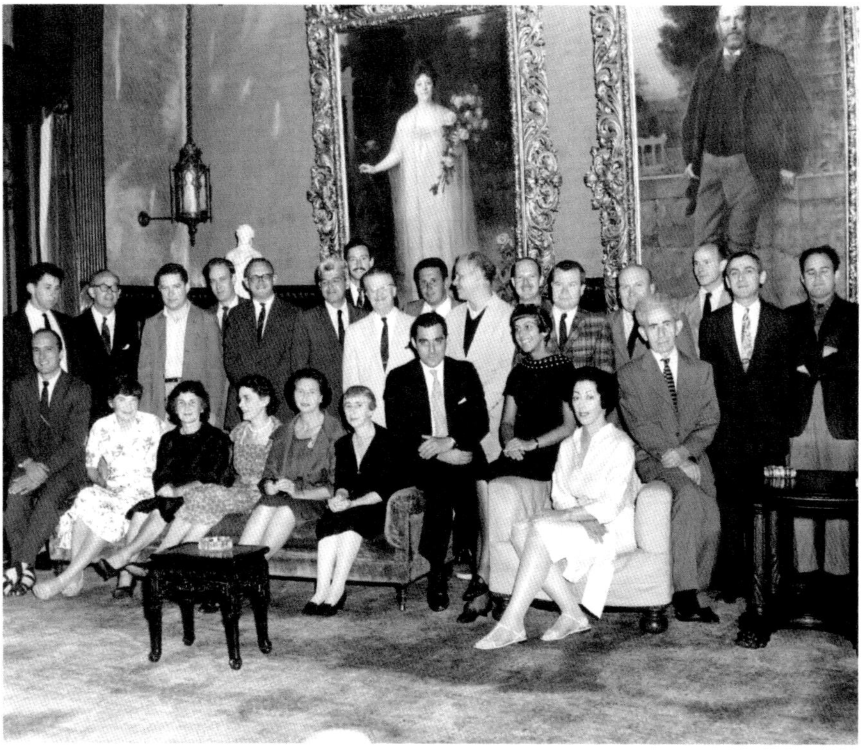

The "class portrait" of those enjoying productive residencies at Yaddo in August 1960 includes a typical mix of writers and visual artists, including Hortense Calisher (seated front right) and her husband, Yaddo Director Curtis Harnack (standing, with mustache). *Photo: Yaddo.*

Saratoga Spa State Park

At its height of usage, which occurred in the 1930s and 1940s, hydrotherapy was maintained as an effective medical therapeutic treatment. The spa provided service to the public at large, with a graded scale of pricing that gave access to all. Following the Second World War, the spa gave valuable restorative service to European concentration camp survivors. Attendance at the baths actually peaked in 1946, at which point doctors began using more pharmaceuticals to provide health solutions. By the early 1960s, the State Reservation was annually running a half-million dollar deficit.

The vision for the Spa State Park was about to transform with the addition of recreational amenities appealing to the postwar generations. The park occupied 2,500 acres and included two vast neoclassical bathhouses, the temple-fronted Hall of Springs and arcades designed to shelter water treatment patients laid out on a splendid grid among lawns and trees. The Spa Little Theatre had been built in 1934, serving first as a medical lecture hall and later as a stage for dramatic productions. Ethel Barrymore, Jimmy Cagney and other first-ranked stars had appeared, giving pre-performance talks out front.

The idea for a summer arts center recalled the bygone days when hotel and park facilities combined as venues for the best in performing arts. A Spa Master Plan of 1931 included some unfinished pieces. One of these was an amphitheater to be built into a natural sloping bowl in the northeast corner of the park. New York State Conservation commissioner Dr. Harold G. Wilm was authorized by the governor to explore the idea, and a study was made.

The pragmatic partnering of state and private resources again was effective. Artistic interest among state and local leaders gained agreement with the New York City Ballet (NYCB) and the Philadelphia Orchestra to create a new theater as their summer home. Good business judgment and capability responded to the government's call for private support.

It was necessary for the local leading families to organize substantial pledges from the community to build the amphitheater. They took action by founding a not-for-profit corporation, not only to build but also to operate the entertainment facility. Families who made Saratoga Springs their home year-round and some seasonal residents held fundraisers and personal appeals. When they were able to report to Governor Rockefeller $250,000 in pledges, the governor turned to members of his own family to support the project.[17]

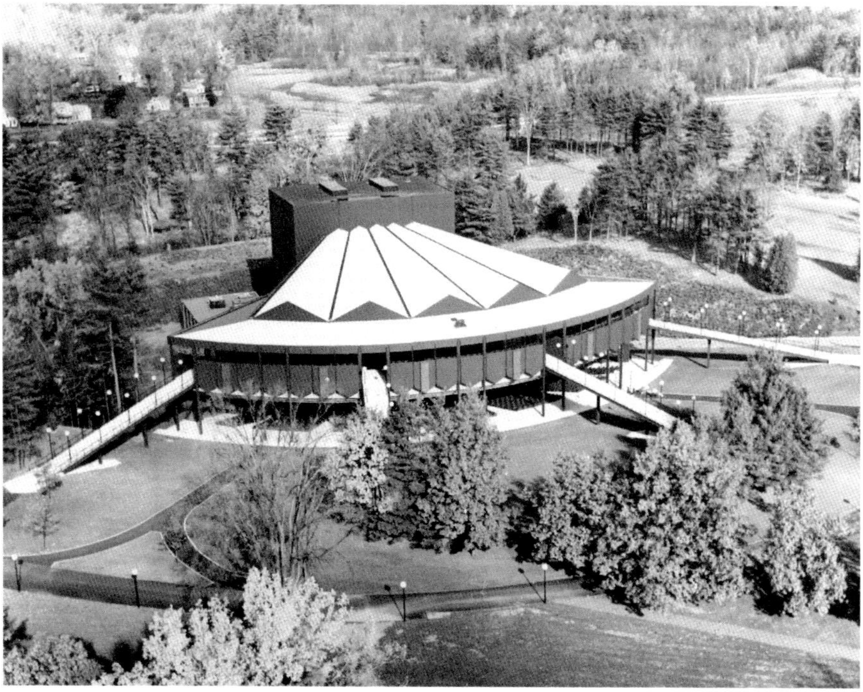

The Saratoga Performing Arts Center, known as SPAC (rhymes with "track"), has brought world-class culture and popular entertainment to the area for more than forty years. The building in the Spa State Park seats five thousand; thousands more enjoy performances from the lawn. *Photo: SPAC*

On July 8, 1966, the center opened as scheduled, with the New York City Ballet onstage with George Balanchine's *A Midsummer Night's Dream*. Both the performance and the venue got rave reviews in the newspapers of record in New York and Boston.

The Saratoga Performing Arts Center went on to entertain millions at more than one thousand NYCB performances, five hundred concerts by the Philadelphia Orchestra and full representation of popular artists and groups. Brilliant productions by Balanchine and Jerome Robbins alternated with shows by Johnny Cash, Elton John, the Boys Choir of Harlem and the greats of jazz. Yo-Yo Ma, Kathleen Battle and Pinchas Zukerman also drew their own crowds.[18] At the Spa Little Theater, a popular chamber music series introduces new music and performers along with old favorites in August, while the Lake George Opera presents fine regional productions in June.

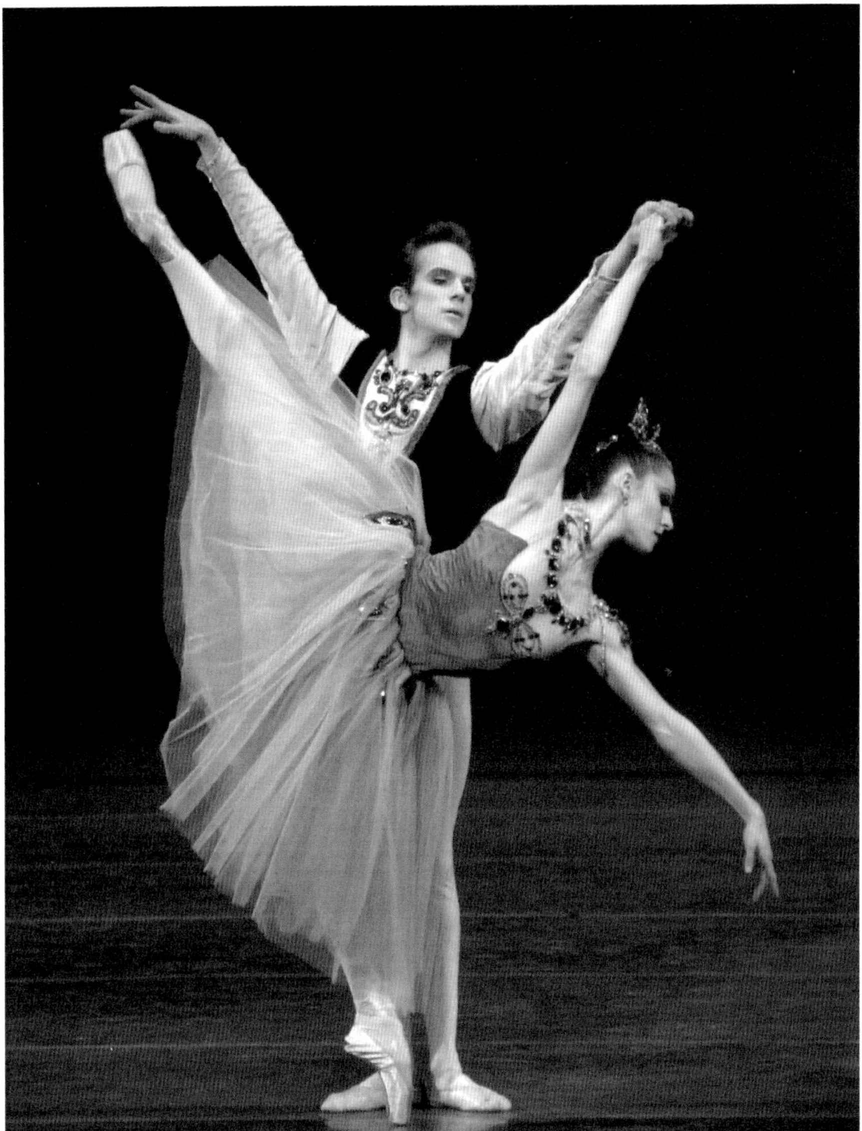

The New York City Ballet has delighted SPAC audiences since 1966. "Emeralds," from the ballet *Jewels*, choreographed by the late George Balanchine, remains an audience favorite. *Photo by Paul Kolnik, courtesy of the New York City Ballet.*

The Race Course Passes Another Century Mark

The Saratoga Race Course became legendary for upsets. Man o' War suffered his only defeat in twenty-one starts when he lost to Upset in the 1919 Sanford Memorial Stakes at Saratoga. (See "Stories Everyone Should Know About Saratoga Springs" at the end of this book.) The list of horses showing at the spa is a register of greats: Gallant Fox, Kelso, Secretariat, Affirmed, Alydar, Cigar and Fourstardave, who won at Saratoga for eight straight years and had a street in Saratoga Springs named after him when he retired. The weeklong Travers Festival features various special events, including the Travers Ball, which draws celebrities to the spa city. The venue is an elegant Old World horse track in the country that has ushered in a new era for racing's most fortunate and countless fans.

At the beginning of the twenty-first century, horses are still heroes in Saratoga Springs. Funny Cide, locally owned by several former high school pals, won the Kentucky Derby in 2003 and was thereafter celebrated on each appearance at the racecourse. When Birdstone defeated Smarty Jones at Belmont in 2004, preventing him from clinching the Triple Crown, owner Mary Lou Whitney, a perennial Saratoga Springs celebrity, graciously apologized for the slight.[49]

The Saratoga Race Course is widely considered to be the most beautiful racetrack in North America and is among the top sports experiences in the country. In the new millennium it looks forward to another quarter

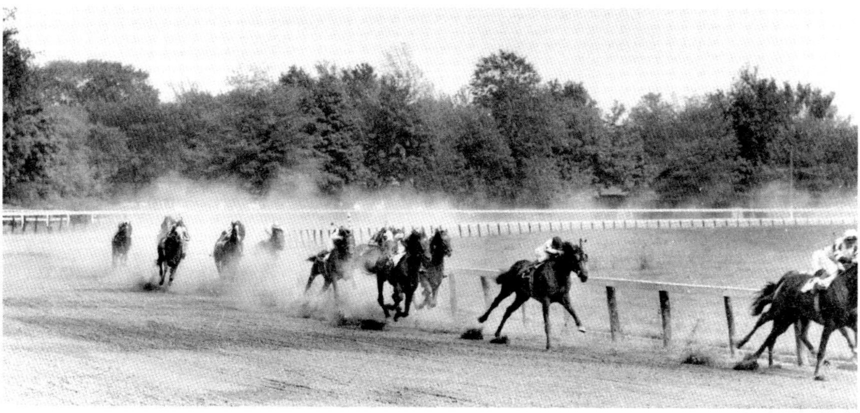

The excitement of horses pounding around the final turn at the historic Saratoga Race Course is a predictable thrill for six weeks every summer, even if the results may be unexpected.

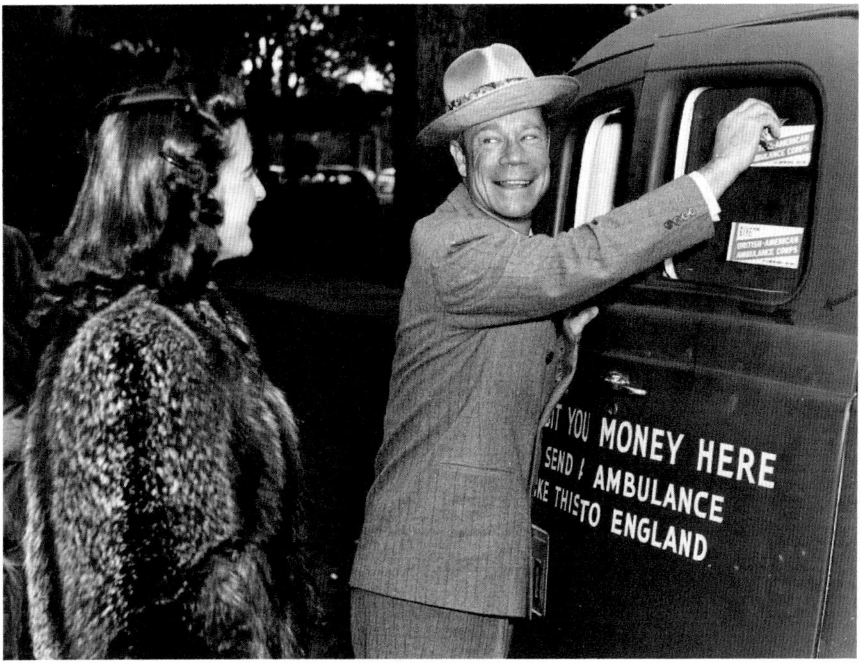

At the racetrack, comedian Joe E. Brown, appearing at the Spa Little Theater in 1940, shows his signature grin as he helps raise money to send an ambulance to Britain, where the war was already in progress.

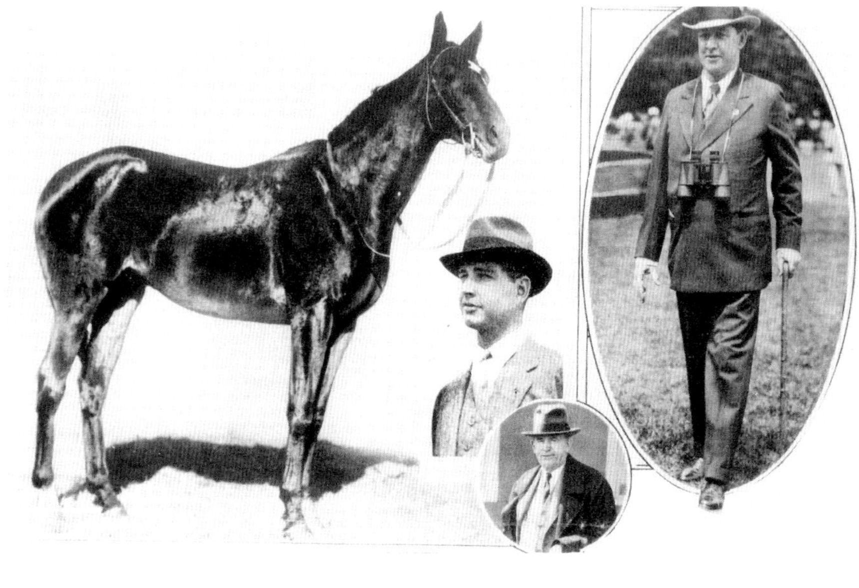

Saratoga cameo: a Whitney, a jockey and a winning horse.

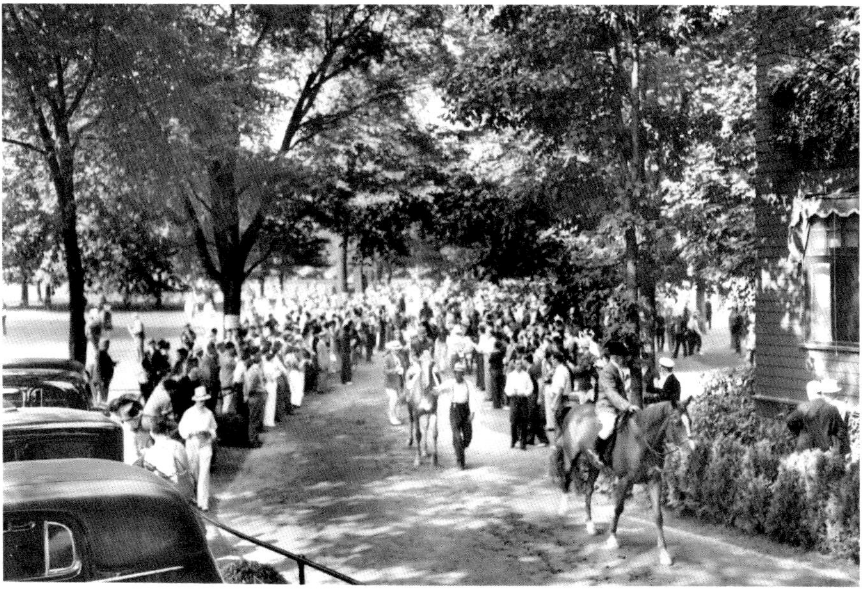

Visitors to the racecourse have always enjoyed watching the jockeys and horses coming to and from the paddock area and the track.

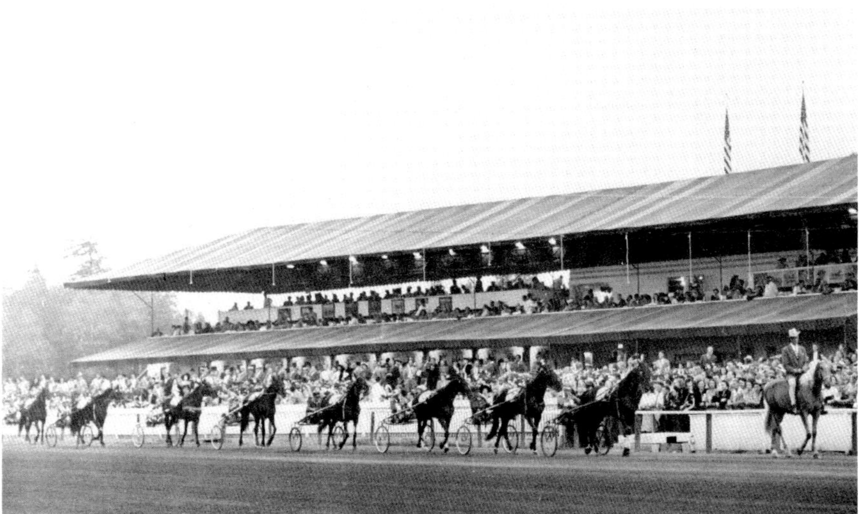

Harness racing began here with Standardbred horses at a separate half-mile track in 1941. Also called the Racino, it is operated as the Saratoga Gaming and Raceway, with video gaming machines and racing simulcasts.

century of operation under the New York Racing Association. The literary sportswriter Heywood Hale Broun once observed that a day at the Saratoga races is like being "transported by a time machine into a sporting print."[50]

The harness track continued, with a smaller but faithful following. Electronic gambling, now blessed by New York State, had been brought in to support revenues, adding a new generation of gamesters. A longtime local resident recalled in 1940, when moviegoers went to the Congress Theater and saw W.C. Fields, as Cuthbert J. Twillie, putting an accurate cast on gambling in *My Little Chickadee.* The rube cardplayer, looking over his hand, asked, "Is this a game of chance?" Twillie replied, "Not the way I play it, no."[51]

Historic Preservation and Open Spaces

An important factor in the revival and growth of Saratoga Springs has been the guiding vision of the community as "the city in the country." This perspective means preserving the open, green spaces at the edges and concentrating development in the core of the city, following the

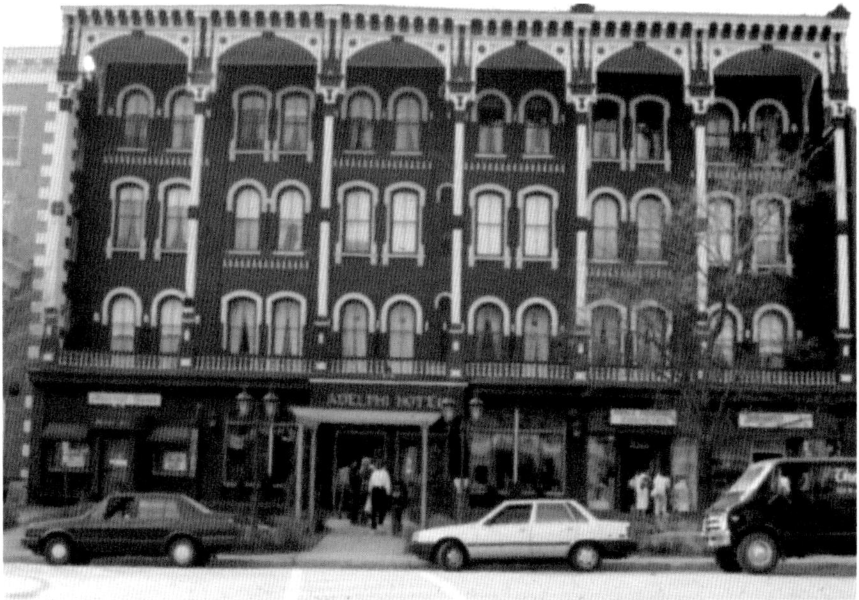

The Adelphi Hotel, built in 1877, was due for demolition a century later until Sheila Parkert and Greg Siefker bought, stabilized and reopened it in 1980. Over the next twenty years they restored the thirty-nine rooms in eclectically pleasing styles.

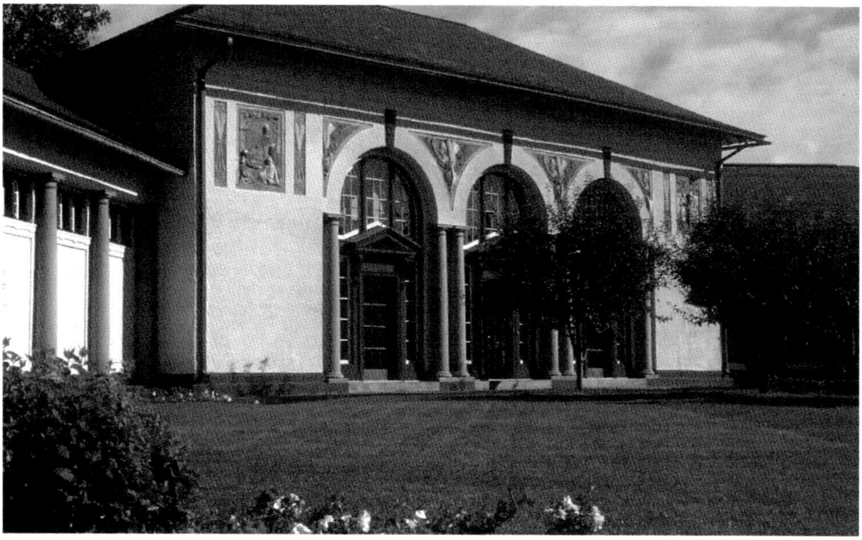

Built in 1915, this elegant trolley station was a depot for interurban lines that linked area communities. The station became a "Drink Hall" for tasting mineral water from 1940 to 1965; it now houses the Heritage Area Visitors' Center.

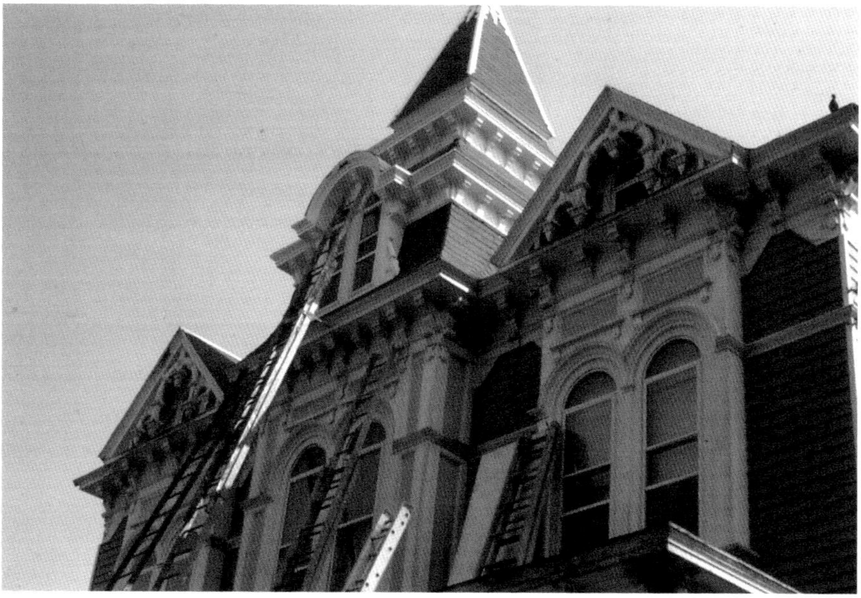

As Saratoga Springs regained a sense of its history, many of its salvageable buildings were renovated by new owners who recognized the value of architecture appropriate to its setting.

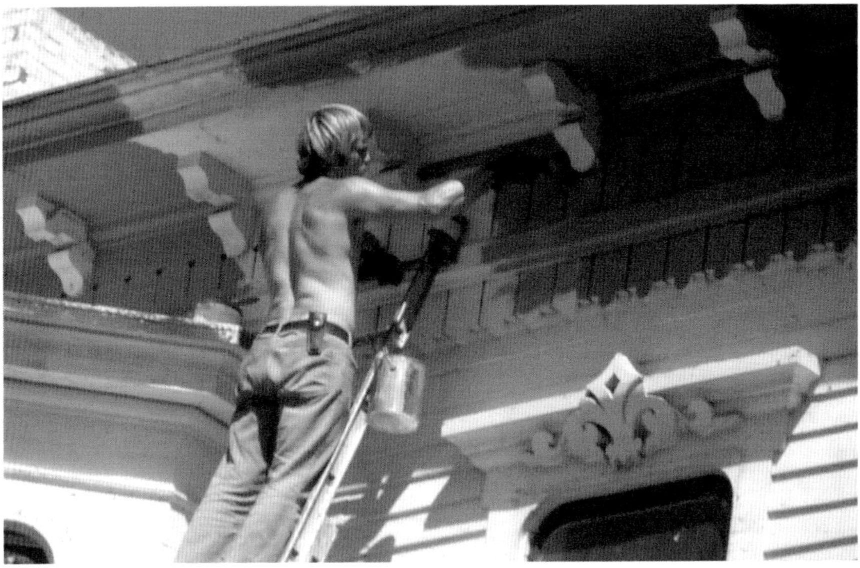

Older buildings take constant maintenance. Restoration efforts have been helped by grants and technical assistance from the Saratoga Springs Preservation Foundation, which filled a civic need starting in 1977. *Photo: Libby Smith-Holmes for SSPF*

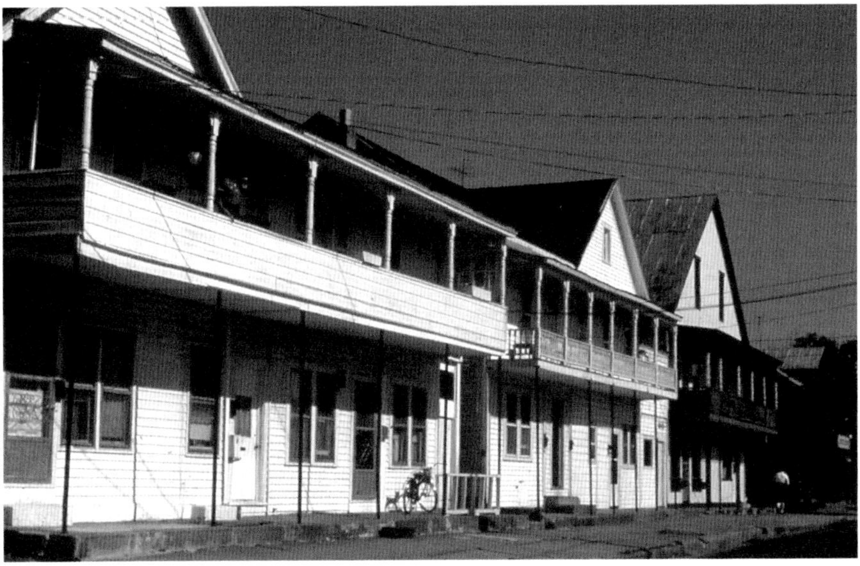

Beekman Street, in the heart of the West Side, now is recovering from neglect as studios and specialty shops have created a new arts district. *Photo: Libby Smith-Holmes for SSPF*

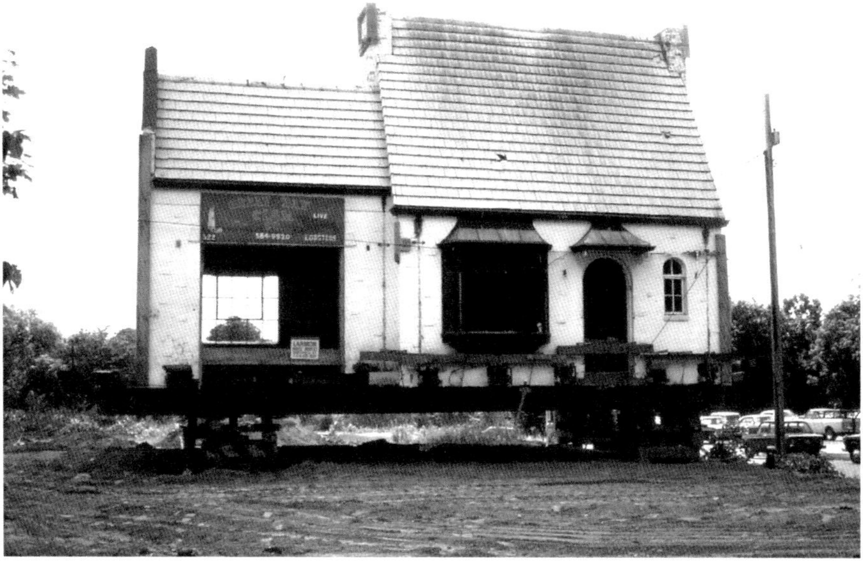

Who could have predicted that a 1933 Pure Oil gas station would not only be worthy of salvage, but would be valuable enough to be moved in 1978 to Spring Street, added to the National Register of Historic Places and be reborn as a popular bakery? *Photo: Libby Smith-Holmes for SSPF*

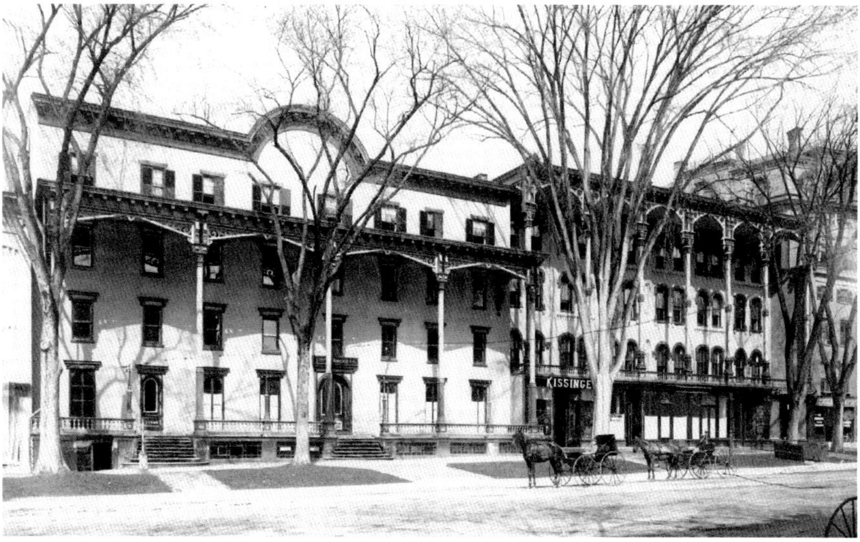

The Rip Van Dam and Adelphi Hotels, Broadway. The Van Dam, built as the American in 1840, underwent updates in Victorian times and in the twentieth century. The Adelphi, built in 1877, was part of the great façade including the United States Hotel that ran north on the west side of Broadway.

original growth pattern in contrast to the creep of suburban sprawl seen in nearby areas.

While individual efforts to preserve specific buildings, most notably the Canfield Casino, were successful, many residential areas and commercial structures were run-down or inappropriately altered by the mid-1970s. This state of affairs prompted concerned citizens to form the Saratoga Springs Preservation Foundation in 1977. This nonprofit group, supported by members and grants, has become the leading advocate for the preservation of Saratoga Springs' unique architectural, cultural and landscaped heritage. Beginning with a façade easement program for downtown commercial blocks, the program brought restored building exteriors into a pleasing uniformity of appearance.

Working with the city's Planning Board and its Historic Review commission, the Preservation Foundation was instrumental in establishing six local historic districts in Saratoga Springs, each with its own charm and character reflected in the historic architecture of that neighborhood. The organization today holds tours of historic properties, provides technical guidance to owners wishing to renovate their buildings and encourages good stewardship of our architectural heritage.

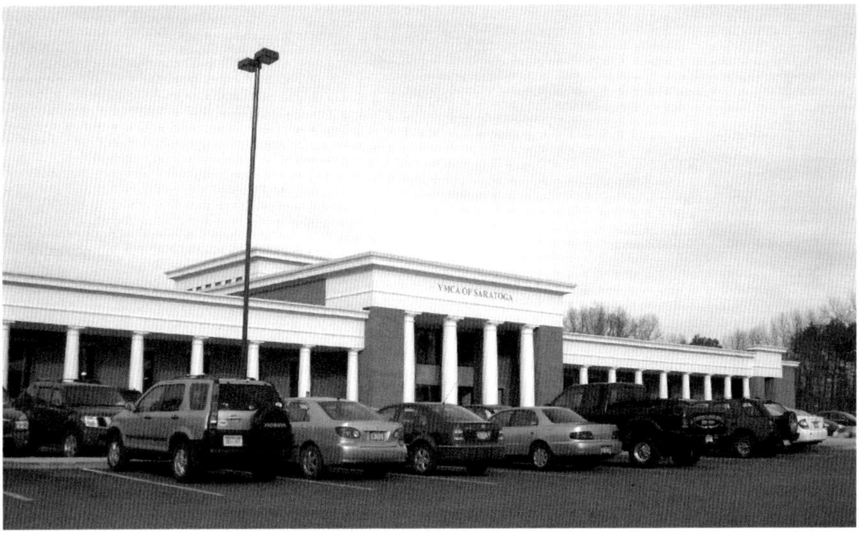

The YMCA moved to its West Avenue building and opened in 2006. In addition to well-utilized sports and fitness facilities, the Y also sponsors First Night Saratoga, a citywide New Year's Eve festival. *Photo: Saratoga YMCA*

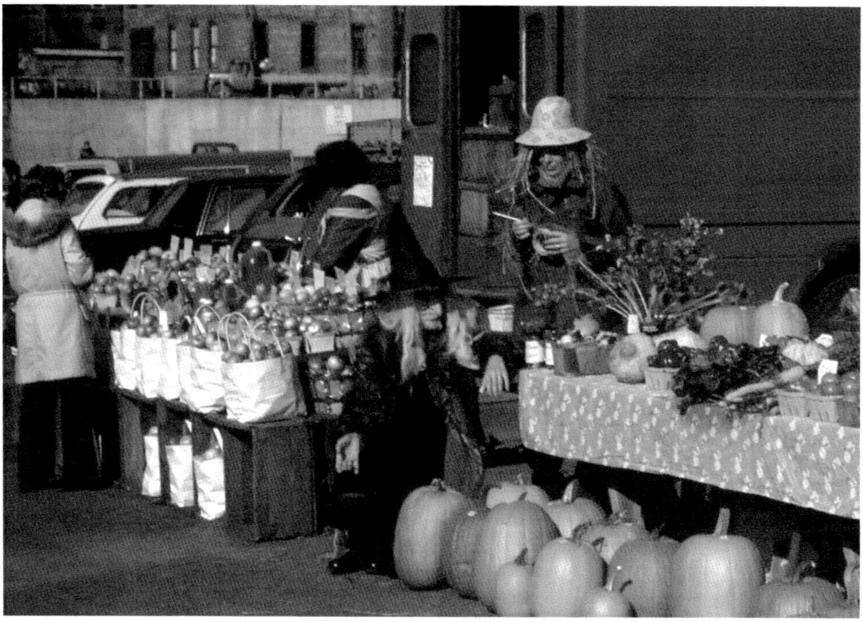

The twice-weekly Farmers' Market now has its own home under pavilions built near High Rock Spring, a place of lively commerce and social interaction. *Photo: Libby Smith-Holmes for SSPF*

Concerned that scenic and recreational open spaces were being lost or overlooked, a group of local residents and professionals in appropriate fields banded together as the Open Space Project of the Saratoga Institute in 1987. They produced an open space plan in response to the master plan introduced at that time. The resulting document, developed over seven years' time with plentiful community input, makes a management package that complements efforts to preserve historic structures and areas by guarding recreational, ecological and natural resources. City Council unanimously adopted *The City in the Country—The Open Space Plan for Saratoga Springs* in 1994.

Among the Open Space Plan's achievements are forty-seven miles of on- and off-road bicycle trails throughout the city, a two-mile nature trail in the Bog Meadow Wetland and Railroad Run, a strolling and bicycle path on the West Side converted from an abandoned railroad track. Still in development are an extension of Railroad Run through the property of the new YMCA and into the Saratoga Spa State Park and the new Spring Run Trail running along Excelsior Avenue connecting High Rock Park to the Bog Meadow Trail, with land purchased for a new, linear park.

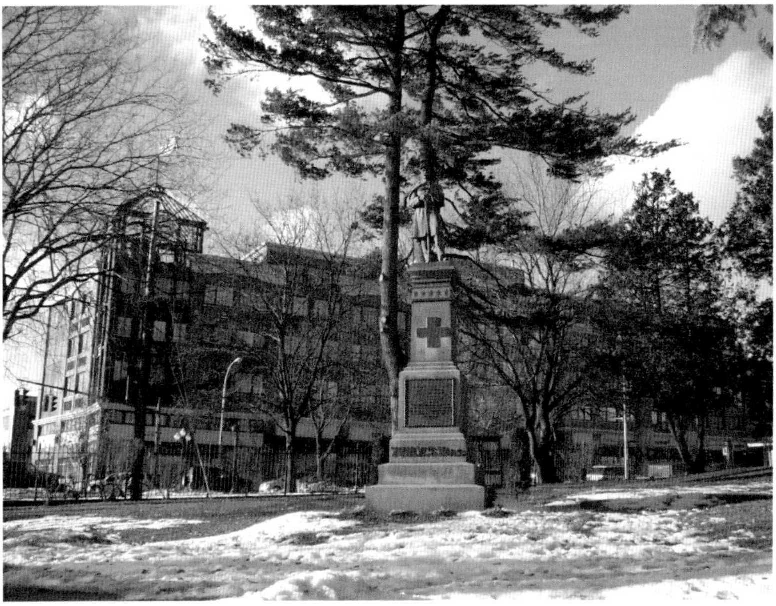

Congress Park Center, a mix of retail and residential spaces, fills the same street profile and mass as its distant predecessor, the Grand Union Hotel, as seen from the Civil War Memorial in Congress Park. *Photo:Libby Smith-Holmes.*

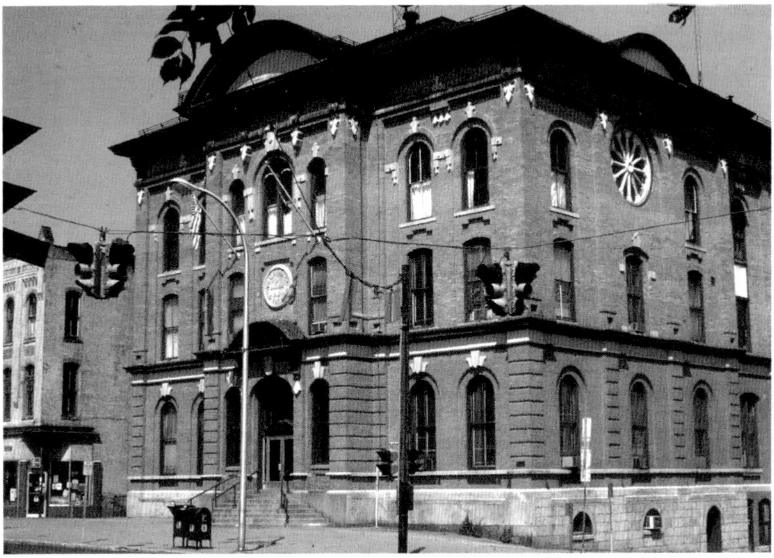

City hall. The building remains in service into the twenty-first century.

Some actions have been accomplished by citizen action opposing development incompatible with the open space vision, such as a proposal to change the rural character of the entrance to the city at Northway exit 14 and a truck bypass that would have altered a portion of the Spa State Park. But most of the actions have been proactive. For example, the South Broadway approach to the downtown area became a boulevard that eases traffic into the city. Proponents of the plan also worked on cleaning up the Kayaderosseras Creek and protecting the Petrified Sea Gardens and the Loughberry Lake Watershed. They worked with the city to provide a permanent home for the Farmers' Market under new pavilions at High Rock Park. Looking to the future, the citizen group held Next Steps & Beyond Forums to promote reasoned dialogue on the future of downtown, the concept of Smart Growth, the Route 50 corridor and public access to Saratoga Lake and Lake Lonely.

In light of the more complex and technical issues involved in its mission, the Open Space Project has evolved into Saratoga PLAN (Preserving Land and Nature), a countywide, independent organization with professional staff. Part of its success has been its ability to approach serious issues with a sense of optimism and fun, through art exhibits, entertainment and sociable gatherings, combined with success in finding grant funding, plus determined work behind the scenes, all with an adventurous sense of exploring possibilities for enhancing the high quality of life in Saratoga Springs.

Saratoga Springs' efforts to preserve its historic structures, neighborhoods and open spaces have received state and national recognition for downtown revitalization, for the development and maintenance of recreational trails, for commitment to the building of community partnerships and for its achievements, devotion and resourcefulness.

The Memory Keepers: The Historical Society in Saratoga Springs

Beginnings

In many ways, the story of the Saratoga Springs Historical Society echoes the ups and downs of the city, as both grew, reacted and adapted to changing times. In October 1883, a group of interested citizens filed a charter with the New York secretary of state for "The Historical Society of Saratoga, including the Upper Hudson, Lake George and Lake Champlain." The purposes of the organizers were historical, patriotic, artistic and literary. From their initial meeting they envisioned a permanent home with a library, picture gallery "and other accessories."[52] Many of the Historical Society's founders were also part of a commemorative movement that established the Saratoga Battle Monument, a 155-foot-tall obelisk in nearby Schuylerville that was started in 1877 and nearly complete by 1883.

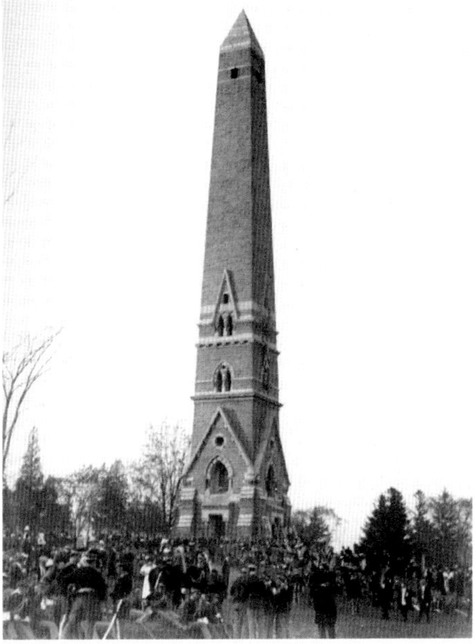

Many of the Historical Society's founders have worked together to raise private funding for the Saratoga Battle Monument in Schuylerville, completed in 1888 and dedicated in 1912, when it was deeded to New York State.

Among the members of the first board of trustees were men and women who were civic leaders, both year-round and summer residents from a wide area. For an Upstate village, or for any time or place, they were a well-educated and sophisticated group, with a prevalence of lawyers, bankers and writers. One of the guiding lights of the organization was Ellen Hardin Walworth, educator, civic leader, poet, essayist and author.

Although the Historical Society was started with enthusiasm and high goals, little information is available about what they did because no minutes survive from the early period. We do know that the society set up its first museum displays of loaned objects in 1899 in the Pompeiia or House of Pansa at 260 Broadway.

After several of the founders died, the Historical Society lost its early momentum, but Mrs. Walworth revived the group in 1911, an act of courage in a bleak period for Saratoga Springs. The next year, the Historical Society was allowed to use one of the rooms on the second floor of the Canfield Casino, which had been purchased by the municipality from Richard Canfield. The museum was reestablished in its new home, where it continues to flourish nearly a century later. Captain James M. Andrews served as its first curator.

The organization was reorganized and added "County" to its long name, making it the Historical Society of Saratoga County. In 1916, officials convened a special meeting to encourage the New York State Senate to purchase the Saratoga Battlefield and to maintain the battle monument. In a plea that echoes through the years, the society urged a campaign for membership. Despite a bank balance of ninety-eight cents in 1917, members continued to prepare research papers on historical topics and to meet in one another's homes for mutual edification and light refreshments.

At the annual meeting in 1923, the name was simplified to the Saratoga Historical Society. The next year, Miss Evelyn Barrett (later Mrs. Britten) was appointed temporary secretary, starting a key relationship that would benefit the organization for many decades. The trustees remembered the contributions of the late Edgar Truman Brackett, who "among the many demands of a busy life… found time to interest himself in the furthering of the aims and purposes of the Saratoga Historical Society and became one of its officers."[53]

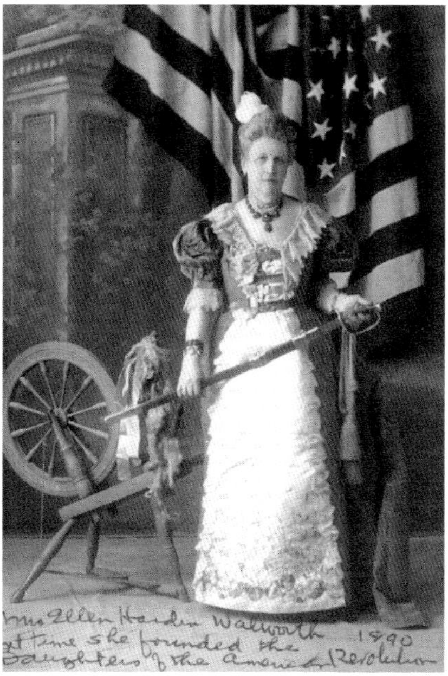

Ellen Hardin Walworth, an accomplished educator, was also one of the founders of the Daughters of the American Revolution (DAR). Her stand for preservation of vital documents led to the formation of the National Archives.

For many years, the museum could be open only in the warmer months because the Casino had no heat. In 1925, the museum acquired more wood and glass display cases so that it could exhibit all of the five thousand interesting artifacts that had been loaned or donated. Labels were typewritten on cardboard, supplemented by cautionary signs such as "Do Not Handle" and "Do Not Lean on the Cases."

Continuing the founders' interest in the Revolutionary War, the society played the major role in celebrating the 150th anniversary of the Battles of Saratoga in 1927 with a pageant and a Surrender Day

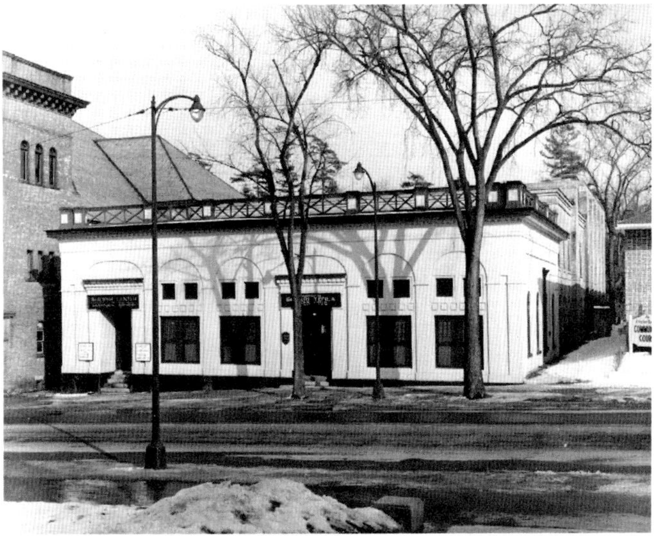

The House of Pansa, a recreation of a Pompeian villa, exhibited the Historical Society's first exhibits. It has in successive years housed a restaurant, a Masonic temple, a Jewish synagogue and, presently, a communications company.

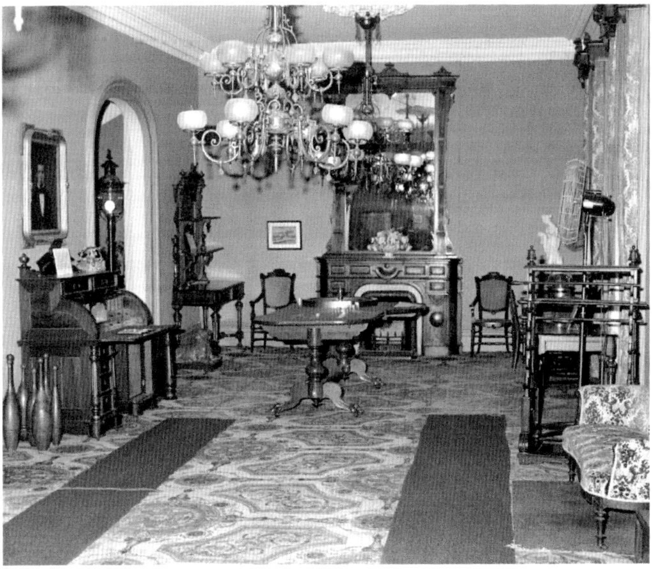

Canfield's high-stakes room. Here some of the highest-stakes games of the century were played after the Civil War. John Morrissey had modeled the business on descriptions of Monte Carlo.

banquet held in Victory Mills. Governor Alfred E. Smith acted as master of ceremonies that included speeches by dignitaries, which were carried to a large audience by radio station WGY. The society in subsequent years raised money for historic markers at the battlefield, Stark's Knob and for the World War I memorial in Congress Park. It encouraged student interest in history by sponsoring annual essay and oratorical contests at the high school, with cash prizes of five and ten dollars.

In 1935, Saratoga Springs attorney John A. Slade was elected president of the organization, providing calm, reasoned guidance and continuity through difficult times. Through the years of the national Depression, the museum continued to draw visitors every summer, especially during conventions held in the city. In 1936, the society advocated successfully for the federal government to take over ownership of the Saratoga Battlefield to make it a national shrine, now the Saratoga National Historical Park. The Historical Society continued to meet in members' homes around the area. The board of trustees in 1939 named Mrs. William Hay Bockes, officer of the organization for fifty-six years since its inception, honorary curator for life.

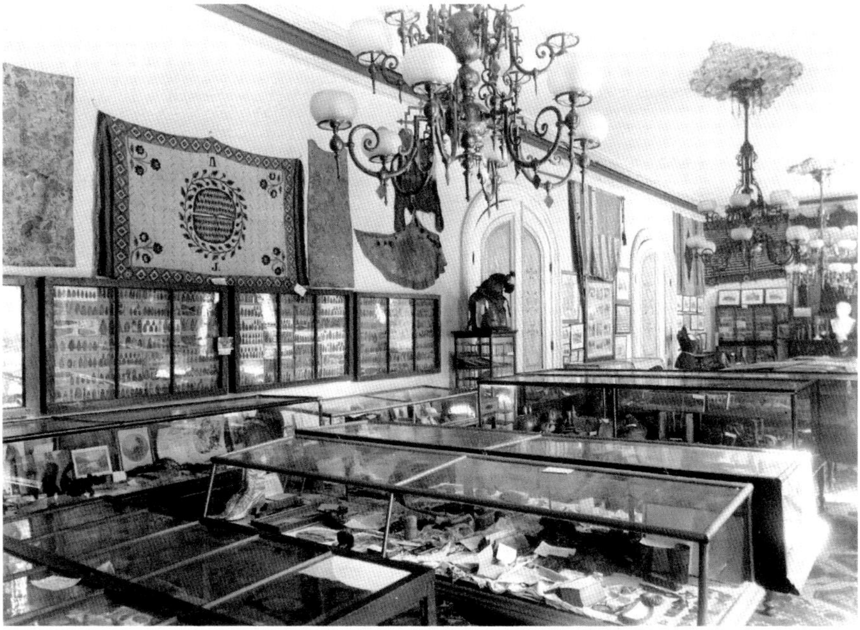

By 1925, the History Museum displayed a great variety of objects. Some were of genuine historical value and some were curiosities acquired by the well-traveled members. A loaned collection of china was later reclaimed by a family member.

During World War II, State Historian Albert E. Corry urged patriotic citizens to look carefully through any papers being given for salvage drives to avoid throwing away documents of historical interest. He also stressed the value of gathering the recollections of the area's oldest residents as well as records, photographs and letters. Members continued to give important pictures, artifacts, family documents and furnishings, including Mrs. Chauncey Olcott's donation of an eighteenth-century sedan chair used as a prop in her husband's play *Mavoureen* and later in their home Inniscarra as a telephone booth.

New Life

The years following World War II were discouraging times. Saratoga Springs was forced to redefine itself once again. Many saw little hope for a place where the razing of its magnificent hotels left gaping holes in the streetscape and where the old-time glamour was unlikely to return. Even the graceful elms and chestnuts that had been planted by Gideon Putnam along Broadway were falling victim to blight. President John Slade gave an impassioned speech at the end of 1952 extolling the city's glorious future, countering Melvin Heimer's statement that "Saratoga is dead and doesn't know enough to lie down," as published in his *Glorious Bawd, The Story of Saratoga*.

In 1952, Clara Walworth, granddaughter of Ellen Hardin Walworth, left her estate to establish a family museum at Pine Grove, in cooperation with the Historical Society. However, the condition of the house at 527 Broadway was so poor that the city attorney drew up an agreement to move the vast collection of Walworth family papers, books, letters and the furnishings from the mansion to the Casino. The Dutch door from the original 1815 house was installed to welcome visitors at the entrance to the new museum. With some difficulty, large beds, dressers, couches and other furnishings were carried up to the third floor and placed in the former servants' rooms to recreate some sense of Pine Grove's grandeur. Although technically a separate entity with its own board and modest endowment, the Walworth Museum and the History Museum are, for all practical purposes, operated together. Interest in the new displays boosted museum attendance to ten thousand in 1955.

During many of the years Evelyn Barrett Britten was involved with the society and its museum, she also served as city historian. Not only did she

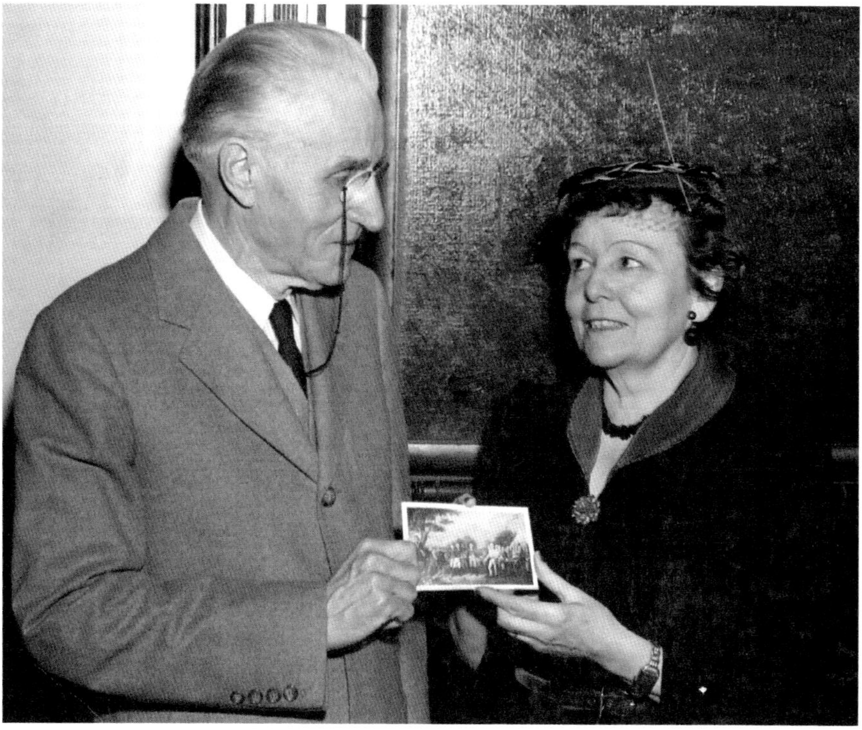

Attorney John Slade was elected society president for life after serving as head for twenty years; he served for fourteen more. Volunteer museum curator, city historian and society secretary Evelyn Barrett Britten served the organization for forty-six years. Both died in 1969.

keep the minutes, she also published monthly newspaper articles detailing the society's programs and attendees and wrote additional articles under the pseudonym "Jean McGregor." A collection of these articles, published as the *Chronicles of Saratoga*, provides views of the past that, while they may not pass every test of historical accuracy, remain good reading. As Minnie Clark Bolster states, "Without Mrs. Britten, there would be no museum."[54] Mrs. Bolster herself continued the tradition of long activity with the museum, starting in 1963.

In August 1943, Historical Society President John Slade wrote, with the endorsement of the trustees, a letter protesting a proposal to change the name of Congress Park to Memorial Park. Evidently, in a burst of mid-war patriotism, some city leaders felt that the present generation had no historical association with the name Congress and that it would be more fitting to acknowledge the park's various memorial sculptures, plaques and structures. Fortunately, the society's letter was persuasive enough to retain

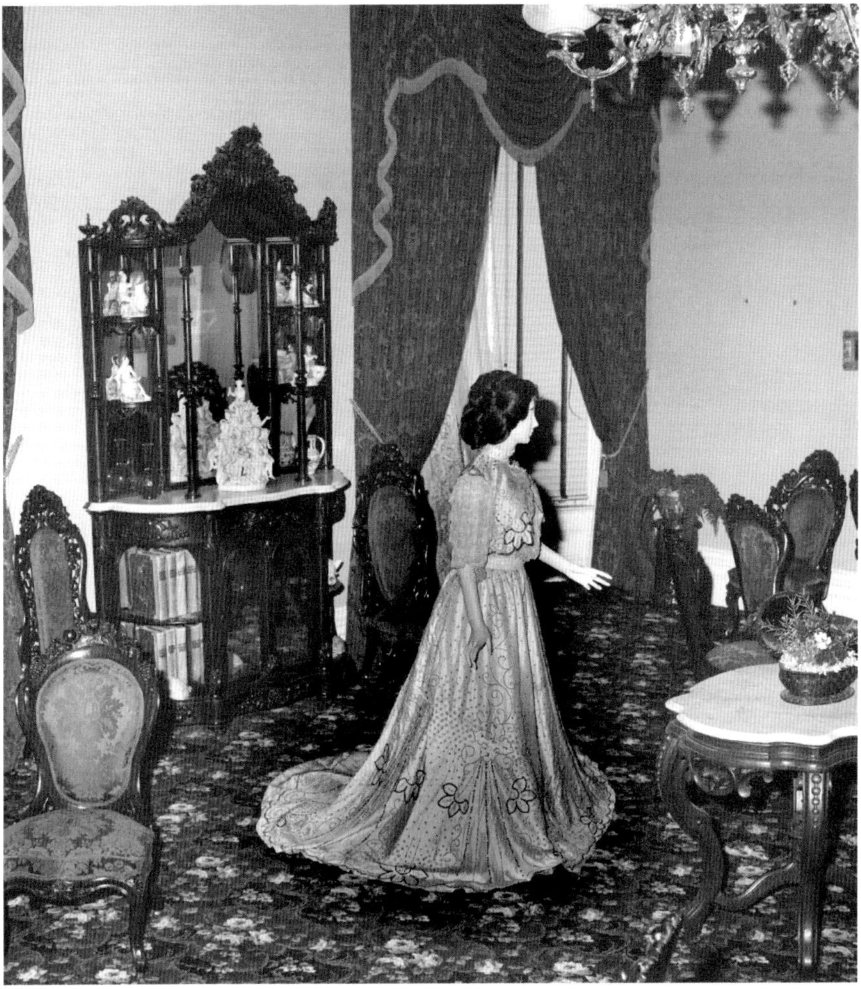

The second floor displays rococo revival Belter furniture in a setting that recalls Victorian parlors. Its décor and the mannequins' costumes are changed seasonally.

the original name. Mrs. Britten marshaled the forces to fend off an attempt to build a hotel in the park in 1956, an effort Beatrice Sweeney would have to repeat in the mid-1960s, when a hotel was proposed to be annexed to the Casino itself.

The Historical Society reinvented itself again in the late 1960s. It was clear that the organization's countywide focus was no longer needed, as nearby towns were forming their own history organizations. Permission was granted to the museum at Brookside in Ballston Spa to use the name Saratoga County

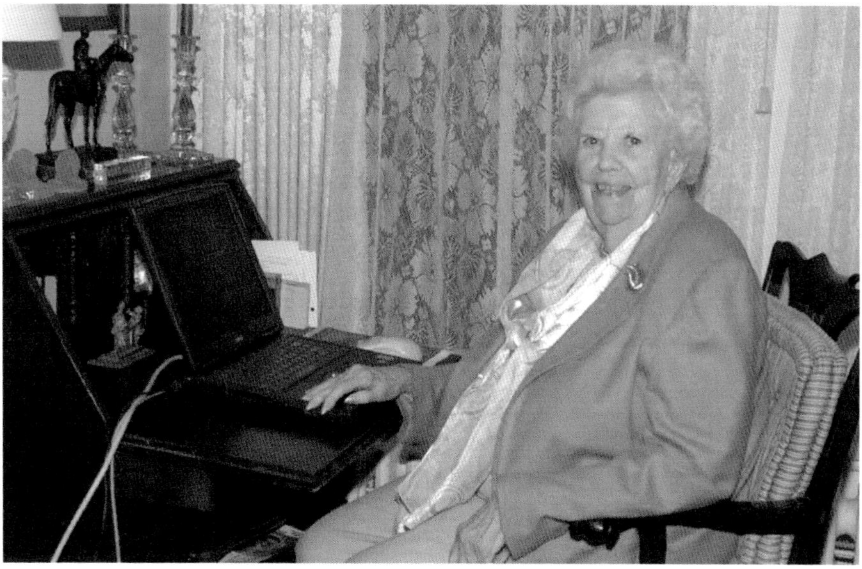

Minnie Clark Bolster continues the tradition of long involvement with the History Museum. She chaired the museum's successful annual antiques shows for more than thirty years and maintains her own extensive collections of Saratoga artifacts, scrapbooks and postcards. *Credit Ed Burke, the* Saratogian *newspaper.*

Historical Society. The officers changed the organization's name to the Historical Society of Saratoga Springs, amended the charter and restructured the board in 1971, the year of the first fundraising Antiques Show. A corps of trained volunteers helped with admissions, gave guided tours and maintained the costumes, which now numbered more than one thousand. Interest was emerging in preserving some of the city's historic buildings and neighborhoods, many of which were in a sad condition of disrepair.

In 1972 the society took on new challenges—raising money to help restore the Casino and the Congress and Columbian Springs, with replicas of John Clarke's pavilions. Both were ultimately successful campaigns to which the city, the society and its members contributed generously. Beatrice Sweeney was instrumental in getting a large grant for the Casino. The Congress Spring pavilion was replaced in 1976, but the two-thirds-sized replica of the domed Columbian pavilion was not erected until the 1980s, with help from the Urban Cultural Park program.

Mrs. Sweeney, in her fourth year as full-time, volunteer director as well as serving as the city historian, stated that it was time to modernize the museum and establish more professional management. One of the accomplishments of Mary Dougal, the museum's first professional director,

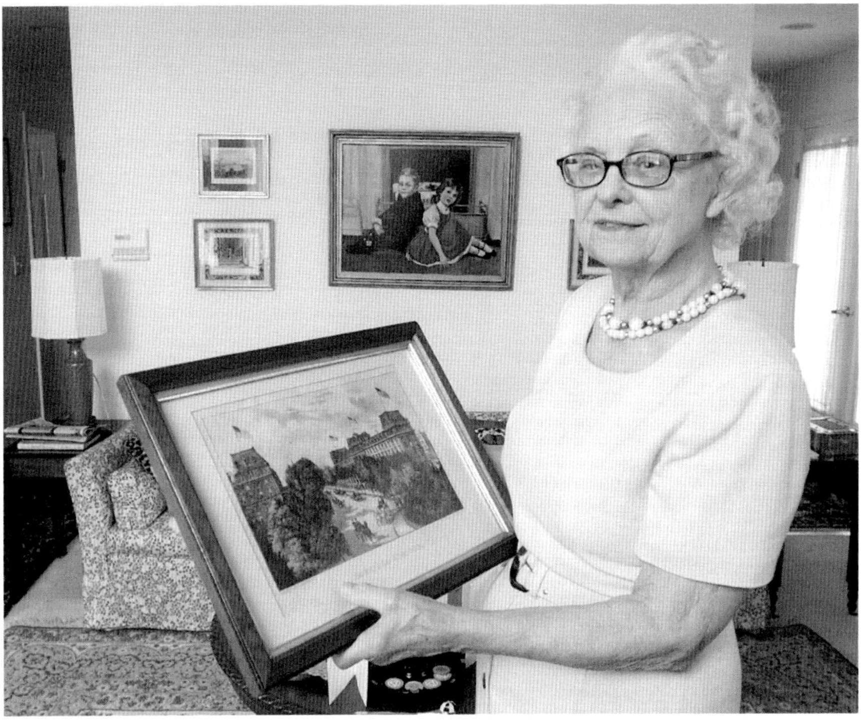

Beatrice Sweeney provided the vital link between the old, volunteer-run museum and the present professional operation. She established the archives and oversaw the modernization of exhibits and operations. *Photo by Ed Burke, courtesy of the* Saratogian.

was to establish an educational program in the schools. She remembers the winter of 1973–74 as being "very, very cold—the building was under restoration and there was no heat and no working bathrooms."[55] The collections were selectively edited to reflect the revised focus on Saratoga Springs, with some items going to other, more appropriate museums. When the city installed heat throughout the Casino in 1975, it became possible to open the museum and run the education programs year-round. The name "Chips" was chosen from public contest submissions for the new museum newsletter.

The exhibits redone in the 1970s remained for several decades under a succession of directors and a variety of one-term presidents. The first-floor room served as an art gallery until the Saratoga County Arts Center moved into the old library at the corner of the park and took over exhibit functions for local artists. A series of important museum exhibits was launched with "Honorable Work," detailing black history in the spa city, followed by major exhibits focusing on local businesses, neighborhoods, natural and built landscapes and Congress Park itself.

The archival collection of local photographer George S. Bolster was bequeathed in trust to the museum in 1989. Of the 375,000 negatives, 315,000 were pictures Bolster himself had taken to document weddings, graduations, fraternal groups and street scenes. The remaining items are in the series that George Bolster called "Old Saratoga," made between 1900 and 1960, primarily by Harry B. Settle. Other well-known photographers—such as Jesse S. Wooley, Gustave Lorey, Seneca Ray Stoddard, C.C. Cook and H.C. Ashby—are also represented in "Old Saratoga." Some date back to the 1850s. The entire archive provides an incomparable window to the past, for which Saratoga owes Bolster a great debt of gratitude. A successful book published in 1990 presented the community's history through a selection of Bolster Collection photographs; this book also draws upon the archive.

For several years the operation was run from Bolster's original studio on Phila Street, with paid staff and its own trustees. When this arrangement proved too costly, the collection and its curator moved into the museum's third floor. The collection now has been merged with the museum, under a part-time curator, sustained by sales of the popular photo prints.

When the Casino building closed for six months of necessary repairs in 1992, the resulting loss of revenue caused museum trustees to come up with creative fundraising projects. Extra effort to promote the two-day August Antiques Show, a raffle and a benefit piano recital by City Historian Martha Stonequist, combined with timely grants and a bequest, resulted in firmer financial footing for the Historical Society. Business savvy trustees directed the museum's management to specific goals and objectives that have succeeded both in achievements and fiscal security despite a lean budget. In 2004, a new orientation gallery and enlarged gift shop opened on the Casino's first floor, funded by generous individuals, local businesses, organizations and foundations. The large upstairs gallery, once crowded with curio cabinets, was home for several decades to the static Evelyn Barrett Britten Hall of History. Now it is used to present new exhibits each year, often drawing upon the expertise of guest curators. In 2003, the organization changed its public identification to the Saratoga Springs History Museum in recognition that the term "historical society" had negative connotations of a stuffy, exclusive club. That image is belied by the dynamic, dedicated board, committed professional staff headed by James Parillo and a cadre of loyal, skilled volunteers. All strive to make

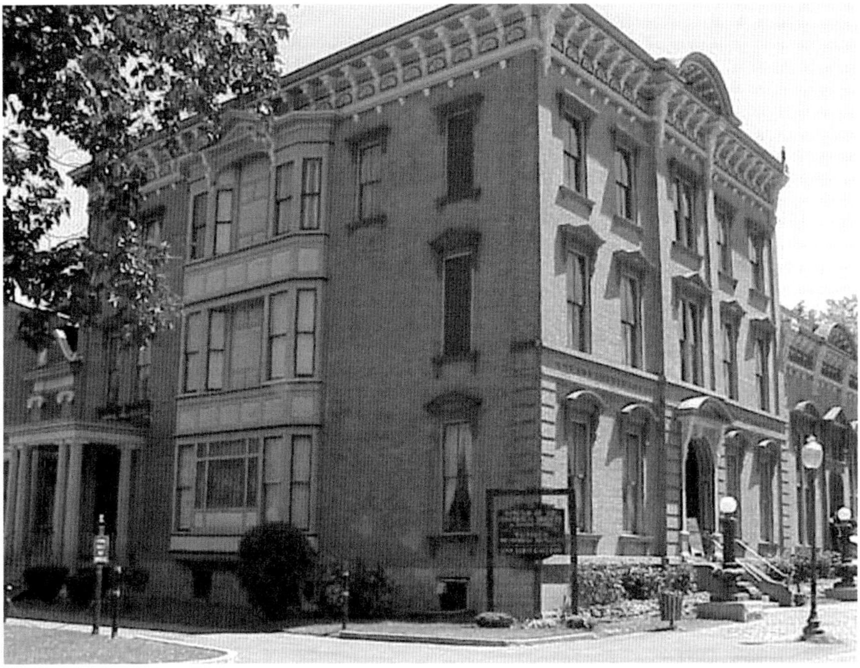

The Canfield Casino, home to the Saratoga Springs History Museum and the Walworth Museum, presides over Congress Park and welcomes residents and visitors to the heart of the community. *Photo: Libby Smith-Holmes*

exhibits, programs and events engaging and enjoyable as well as instructive. For example, the annual holiday open house has grown into a celebration of lively entertainment at the lake houses. When the big band starts up in the Casino's ballroom, well-dressed attendees kick up their heels, filling the room once again with life and laughter.

The museum in the new millennium is still the keeper of Saratoga Springs' community memories through its varied collections. Among the items are fifteen hundred costumes, the Bolster photographic collection, the Walworth Museum and the Beatrice Sweeney Archive, containing thousands of maps, prints, books, business records and other documents. These are available to researchers upon request. Exhibits and monthly programs explore the area's fascinating personalities and happenings. Educational programs reach hundreds of students in local schools, while college interns study and research topics of mutual interest. The museum is living its motto: "Telling the story of Saratoga Springs."

Appendix I
First Americans

The human experience in New York State before recorded history is usually divided into five periods or stages of development. They are classified, from the earliest, as Paleo-Indian, Archaic, Transitional, Woodland and Contact periods.

The Paleo-Indian is the period following the last glacial recession of the Ice Age. The environment was part tundra, the populations consisting of small bands of hunters following the game herds. There is evidence from this period along the shore of Saratoga Lake.

The Archaic period is evident in Saratoga dating from approximately nine thousand years ago in habitation sites along navigable waterways. Subsequent periods are evidenced by significant artifacts collected and studied recently.

In late Woodland times, the Mohicans were predominant in the Saratoga region. In the early Contact period, the more aggressive Mohawks are recorded as taking over the area. Archaeological investigation today includes the examination of trade goods introduced by the Dutch settlers.

The New York State Museum is an excellent resource on this subject.

Appendix II
The Battles of Saratoga

With the end of the wars known as the French and Indian, a new spirit was active in the North American colonies. The colonists had found strengths and capabilities, and had advanced their concepts of rights and freedom. The American Revolution was the result. The English king determined to hold onto North America. A sweeping plan had been developed, and it involved the Hudson-Champlain Valley. The terrain was now well known. The distances were vast in relation to the communications required for a campaign of long duration.

A three-pronged attack would split the New England colonies away from New York and those farther south. The central thrust would proceed down Lake Champlain and the Hudson Valley to Albany. This approach had been tested in 1776, and ended when a remarkable flotilla, manufactured by the colonials' army on the shores of Lake Champlain, had stymied progress of the British troops until winter closed in.

It was thought that 1777 was to be "the year of the hangman" for the American Rebels. The two-hundred-mile battle from Quebec to Albany would be undertaken by a strong force led by energetic Major General John Burgoyne. Like almost all of British generalship of the day, John Burgoyne was a well-rounded man. Educated, a member of Parliament, a playwright and wit, now seasoned from battles during the Peninsular Wars, he was popular with his troops. His code of conduct called for officers' technical capability. He treated the enlisted as thinking men.[56] As events had persuaded leaders on both sides to their positions on revolution, the ambitious general had come around to the conviction that the rebellion of the colonists must be put down. Burgoyne was high spirited, adventurous and a player in all respects.

The campaign went well at first. Then the considerable baggage of the expedition, obstacles encountered and the resistance put up by the revolutionaries slowed the advance of Burgoyne's juggernaut through the summer. Events elsewhere and the emergence of resourceful leadership on the colonials' side brought the critical confrontation to the fields and forests along the Hudson River, the eastern shore of the Saratoga region.

On September 19, 1777, the king's troops and the colonial forces fought to a standoff; on October 7, the colonials broke through and routed Burgoyne's army. Burgoyne pulled back eight miles north and settled into defensive fortifications on the hillside of Philip Schuyler's holdings in old Saratoga. After a well-executed, brief siege by the impassioned Americans, Burgoyne surrendered.

These battles were decisive. The news of the outcome breathed new life into the hopes of the Revolution's leaders. Philadelphia had just fallen, but an entire British army had been captured. In Paris, Benjamin Franklin's ministrations brought the support of the French king to the American cause. Within a few short years, some of the leaders of the American Revolution came to see for themselves the locale of the momentous events.

Appendix III

Museums of Saratoga

Brookside Museum
Saratoga County Historical Society
6 Charlton Street
Ballston Spa, NY 12020
www.brooksidemuseum.org

The Children's Museum
69 Caroline Street
Saratoga Springs, NY 12866
www.cmssny.org

The Frances Young Tang Teaching Museum and Art Gallery
815 North Broadway
Saratoga Springs, NY 12866
www.skidmore.edu/tang

National Museum of Dance and Hall of Fame
99 South Broadway
Saratoga Springs, NY 12866
www.dancemuseum.org

National Museum of Racing and Hall of Fame
191 Union Avenue
Saratoga Springs, NY 12866
www.racingmuseum.org

New York State Military Museum
See page 156 for address and information

Saratoga National Historical Park
648 Route 32
Stillwater, NY 12170
www.nps.gov/sara

Saratoga Springs Automobile Museum
Spa State Park
110 Avenue of the Pines
Saratoga Springs, NY 12866
www.saratogaautomuseum.org

Saratoga Springs History Museum
The Canfield Casino in Congress Park
1 East Congress Street
P.O. Box 216
Saratoga Springs, NY 12866
www.saratogahistory.org

Appendix IV
Saratoga Springs History Museum Hall of Fame

The Saratoga Springs History Museum maintains a Hall of Fame. Each year, candidates are considered for their significant and enduring contributions to the life of Saratoga Springs. Two recent examples here are Frank Sullivan and Lena Spencer.

Frank Sullivan

Journalist, humorist, author; the "sage of Saratoga"
Francis John Sullivan was born in Saratoga Springs on September 22, 1892, to Irish immigrant parents, through whom he was also related to the late Judge Michael Sweeney and television host Ed Sullivan. As a child he worked as a pump boy serving spring water at the racetrack, meeting turn-of-the-century luminaries like Diamond Jim Brady and Lillian Russell. He attended Saratoga Springs High School, working part time for the *Saratogian* newspaper before graduating in 1910. His talent blossomed early, earning him a scholarship to Cornell University, where he graduated in 1914. Sullivan returned to Saratoga Springs and worked for the newspaper again until he was drafted in 1917. After two years as a second lieutenant in the infantry, he moved to New York, ultimately ending up as a reporter and feature writer for the *New York World*, where he became a columnist in 1924.

As a humorist, Sullivan was known for his gentle touch and for the collection of fictitious characters he created to give voice to his observations on life: Aunt Sally Gallup, Martha Hepplethwaite, the Forgotten Bach (a member of the Bach family who was tone-deaf) and Mr. Arbuthnot, the cliché expert. Sullivan wrote his column until the *World* closed down in 1931, but he had also been writing humor articles for the *New Yorker* since 1926 and continued to do so until the 1950s. He also contributed to *Harper's*, *Atlantic Monthly*, the *Saturday Evening Post*, *Good Housekeeping*, *Vanity Fair* and other magazines. His twelve books include *Broccoli and Old Lace* and *A Pearl in Every Oyster*. He often wrote fondly of Saratoga Springs. A critic described Sullivan as "the master of undersimplification—he could take the clearest and most obvious commonplace and…reduce it to its ultimate complexity."

During the 1920s, Sullivan was a frequent member of the Algonquin Round Table, that legendary lunchtime gathering of wits from New York's literary and theatrical worlds. The crackling conversations often appeared in print, and the celebrities met later for parties featuring poker, charades and more wit and laughter.

A lifelong bachelor, Sullivan returned to his childhood home in Saratoga Springs in the 1960s, stating that it was "the most cosmopolitan small town this side of Europe; tolerant, urbane, often rowdy, but kind to the visitor." Sullivan was a good friend to all in the vicinity of the house he shared with his sister Kate at 135 Lincoln Avenue, often stocking up on small presents to delight neighborhood children. He often wrote in bed, in his pajamas. Two of his typewriters are in local collections. Until his death in 1976, he kept up an active correspondence with his many friends, who included Admiral Nimitz, Walter Lippmann and his showbiz cronies from the 1920s. He is buried in St. Peter's Cemetery. Perhaps the most fitting epitaph is: "Frank Sullivan was a Saratogian."

Collections of Frank Sullivan's publications and correspondence are at the Cornell University Library and the Beatrice Sweeney Archive of the Saratoga Springs History Museum.

LENA SPENCER

Patron of the arts, promoter of folk music, proprietor of Caffè Lena

Pasqualina Rosa Nargi was born in 1923 in Milford, Massachusetts, the youngest of eight children. After high school, she worked in her father's Italian restaurant while harboring ambitions of becoming an actor and singer. When she married sculptor Bill Spencer, they began to pursue the dream of opening a coffeehouse where audiences could enjoy accessible arts, especially performances by musicians in the emerging folk movement.

In 1960, they found the perfect place—a run-down building at 47 Phila Street in Saratoga Springs. Caffè Lena opened in March 1961.

The Caffè never made much money; over the years, friends and supporters would have to hold fundraising events to keep the building up to code and the doors open. Early on, Bill Spencer became disenchanted with the struggle and returned to Boston. Lena soldiered on in the cause of the arts until her death in 1989.

Few doubt that real magic was created at the Caffè. The unadorned room with its small tables, mismatched chairs and tiny stage became a legendary home for musicians getting their careers started. Arlo Guthrie, Bob Dylan, Joan Baez, Don McLean, David Amram and Rosalie Sorrels are just a few of the artists who played here and rose to greater fame and acclaim. Skidmore girls and their dates numbered high among the early audiences, but the Caffè soon drew people of all ages from the Capital District and throughout New England. Volunteers served aromatic teas, coffees and tasty pastries that Lena made in the small kitchen. Lena sat at a table at the head of the stairs, with Pasha, her Siamese cat, to welcome all comers and to collect the cover charge and food payments.

But the secret of the Caffè was the way that Lena nurtured talent and encouraged young performers. She invested many hours talking with "her" musicians, who became as close as family members. She took care of their needs, finding them meals and places to sleep when they could not afford hotels. When a group of friends gathered after the regular performances, the laughter, playing and singing often went on well into the night. In 1985, Lena wrote, "Every single person who graced our tiny stage, the great, the near-great, the not-so-great, they are all, in their own way, responsible for my still being here. I've lasted for some twenty-five years. I've done some things right, I've done some things wrong, but right or wrong, I've always tried to do the best I could. And I couldn't have done it without the help of God and a lot of love from a lot of wonderful people."

Adjacent to the Caffè room is a theater known as the Black Box, where Spencer fostered productions of plays ranging from *The Mouse Trap* to avant-garde works finding their first airings. Spalding Gray, John Wynne-Evans and David Hyde Pierce were among the actors who were part of the scene in the 1970s and '80s. Lena herself enjoyed appearing in some of the works. The company that started here became Home Made Theater.

Lena Spencer's contributions to the Saratoga arts scene were recognized in 1987 with a Doctor of Humane Letters degree from Skidmore College and by the first Life Achievement Award presented by the Saratoga County Arts Council in 1889.

Caffè Lena continues to operate as a not-for-profit organization to perpetuate Lena Spencer's dream of providing a home for folk musicians to get their start and to perform for the public. The success of the undertaking can best be measured in the rapt expressions on the faces of dedicated "folkie" pilgrims who mount the stairs at 47 Phila Street as if they are entering a shrine.

Appendix V

Stories Everyone Should Know About Saratoga Springs

Edited from a presentation by Chris Millis as "Ten Stories every Saratogian Should Know,"[57] presented as a program for the Saratoga Springs History Museum. Several personalities not already covered previously in the book are included here, an example of the many stories and many people who contributed to Saratoga Springs' legend.

As Saratoga Springs' popularity, profile and population soar in the new millennium, new neighbors are being drawn in to enjoy its unique charms and prime location. It is again a desirable destination in which to live and play. The secret of Saratoga Springs, if it ever was a secret, is out. And as they say, you can't put the toothpaste back into the tube.

Every Saratogian should know at least ten good stories about Saratoga as a rudimentary foundation of local knowledge. Because if there is one thing our town ain't—it's boring.

Today our communities continue to surrender, in ways large and small, their oddness and singularity to a modern culture of sameness: sameness in architecture, in commerce and, strangely, even in its citizens. As we toss what makes us special into the wood chipper of progress we should think hard about what will be spit out the other end. Will we like it? And can we live with it? Now more than ever our stories, like this brief list, have assumed a sudden urgency. They are not mere quaint anecdotes; they are who we are and how we got here. Let's treasure them by retelling them.

To help illustrate the point, consider this passage written by native son Frank Sullivan from the introduction he penned in March 1947 to his high school classmate Evelyn Barrett Britten's *Chronicles of Saratoga*. "The Sage of Saratoga," as he was known, Sullivan was an American author and humorist best known for his work with the *New Yorker* and his association with the Algonquin Round Table. He writes:

> *It is probably human nature to take your hometown for granted and, if you are young and venturesome, or even old and venturesome, to be more interested in places where you are not than in the place where you are. But sometimes I think Saratoga Springs has more than her share of sons and daughters in whom familiarity has bred an indifference to the rich and picturesque history of their town…* [Saratoga Springs] *is a merry place, full of color and vivacity, and humor and gaiety. It is the most cosmopolitan small town this side of Europe; tolerant, urbane, often rowdy, but basically kind to the visitor, and do not let any visitor say different, just because he's had one bad afternoon at the track.*

MAN O' WAR

If there is a single story every Saratogian probably already knows, it's that the greatest thoroughbred racehorse of all time, Man o' War, lost just one race, to a horse named Upset, and it happened over on Union Avenue.

Man o' War (Fair Play-Mahubah, by Rock Sand) was foaled March 29, 1917, at August Belmont II's Nursery Stud in Lexington, Kentucky (the Belmont Stakes is named for August's father). During World War I, Belmont II joined the U.S. Army at age sixty-five. While serving in France, Belmont's wife named the new foal My Man o' War to honor her husband. The "My" was later dropped.

Because of his military service, Belmont II decided to liquidate his entire 1917 yearling crop. In 1918, at the yearling sales in Saratoga Springs, the Belmonts sold Man o' War at auction for $5,000 to Samuel D. Riddle, who brought him to his farm near Berlin, Maryland, and owned him through his entire racing career and retirement. "As soon as I saw him," said Riddle, "he simply bowled me over."

As a two-year-old, Man o' War, affectionately known as Big Red, was trained by Louis Feustel and ridden by Johnny Loftus (a Hall of Fame jockey who died March 23, 1976). On August 13, 1919, at Saratoga Race Course, Man o' War entered the Sanford Memorial Stakes with a six-race winning streak. We all know what happened next.

In 1919, mechanical starting gates were not widely used. Horses circled behind the starting line and then lined up behind a tape strung across the track. When the race starter dropped a flag, the tape was jerked out of the way. Apparently, on this day, a substitute starter was having trouble getting the horses lined up properly. The horses were still circling and fussing and Man o' War was either backing up or completely turned around when the starter suddenly jerked the tape. He "was almost left at the post," reported the *Louisville Courier-Journal.*

Even with the lousy start, Man o' War, an 11–20 favorite, was third in the six-furlong race as the field headed for the wire in the last eighth. Blocked by other horses, including Upset, Man o' War was forced to go wide. He was game, but he could not overcome the lost ground. He was still gaining speed as he came up short by just half a length. Upset, who at 115 pounds carried 15 fewer pounds than Man o' War, was the 7–2 long shot. Big Red went on to beat Upset in all six subsequent meetings. Interestingly, Upset's jockey's middle name was Sanford.

After an inquiry, Man o' War's jockey, Loftus, was cleared but in 1920 the Jockey Club refused to renew his jockey's license. Though Loftus ended the

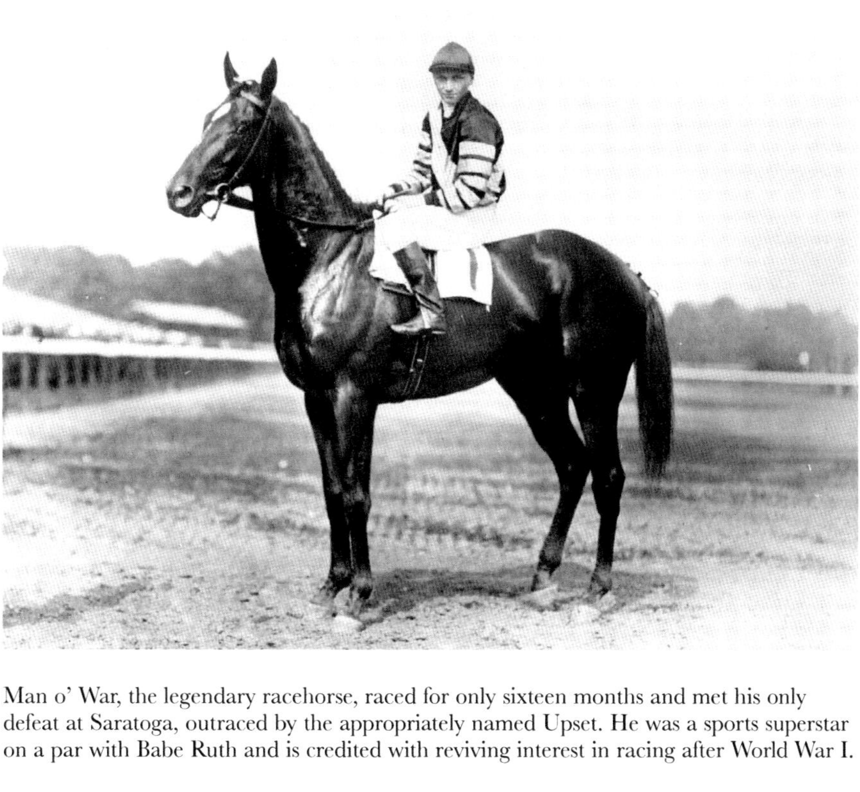

Man o' War, the legendary racehorse, raced for only sixteen months and met his only defeat at Saratoga, outraced by the appropriately named Upset. He was a sports superstar on a par with Babe Ruth and is credited with reviving interest in racing after World War I.

1919 season as the nation's top money winning jockey, he decided to retire to become a horse trainer.

As a three-year-old, Man o' War won all eleven of his races, with Clarence Kummer aboard nine times, including the Belmont, Preakness and Travers. In the Lawrence Realization at Belmont, Man o' War, the 1–100 favorite, beat Hoodwink by one hundred lengths (not a misprint).

In his final race at Kenilworth Park in Windsor, Ontario, Man o' War faced the great Sir Barton, who in 1919 had become the first horse to win the Triple Crown, though it would not be known as such for another decade. Officially, it was a three-horse race (since match races were not allowed in Canada) but the third horse was "scratched" before the start. Man o' War won the $75,000 purse and $5,000 Gold Cup, besting Sir Barton by seven lengths.

When Riddle was told that Man o' War, as a four-year-old, would have to carry over 138 pounds, he retired his horse to stud. Man o' War held American records for the fastest mile, $1\frac{1}{8}$ miles, $1\frac{3}{8}$ miles, $1\frac{1}{2}$ miles and $1\frac{5}{8}$ miles. Man o' War won twenty of twenty-one starts in his career for a lifetime earnings of $249,465 (the most of his day). He was inducted into the National Museum of Racing and Hall of Fame in 1957. *Blood-Horse* magazine ranked him number one of the top one hundred U.S. thoroughbred champions of the twentieth century.

As a sire, Man o' War produced more than sixty-four stakes winners and two hundred champions. He sired Belmont winners American Flag and Crusader. Both colts earned U.S. Champion 3-Year-Old Colt honors and Crusader was voted U.S. Horse of the Year. Among Man o' War's other famous offspring were Battleship, who won the 1938 English Grand National steeplechase; and War Admiral, the 1937 Triple Crown winner. Another of his offspring, Hard Tack, sired Seabiscuit. His son War Relic was his most successful sire. Tiznow, Honour and Glory and Bertrando are all sire-line descendants of Man o' War.

Man o' War died of a heart attack November 1, 1947, at the age of thirty. He is buried at the Kentucky Horse Park beneath his life-size statue created by noted American sculptor Herbert Haseltine.

Timothy Murphy

The Battle of Saratoga was not fought within the city limits of Saratoga Springs, but its stories are nevertheless an important foundational piece of our local and national heritage. The Battle of Saratoga has been hailed by many as one of the most important battles in military history. Indeed, the *New York Times Magazine* proclaimed the victory at Saratoga "the Most Important Battle of the Last 1,000 Years." Every Saratogian should know at least one good story about this critical turning point in our young nation's history.

On the morning of October 7, 1777, twenty-six-year-old Timothy Murphy, son of Irish immigrants from County Donegal, was engaged in the second battle at Saratoga as one of the five hundred riflemen of General Daniel Morgan's famed corps of Kentucky Riflemen. As the British army, under the command of General "Gentleman" John Burgoyne, attempted to outflank the American positions on Bemis Heights, Timothy Murphy climbed a tree and took aim with his Swiss, double-barreled Golcher rifle.

Murphy's first fatal shot, said to have been from roughly three hundred yards, mortally wounded General Simon Fraser. Fraser was leading a charge against the colonists. As a result of his death, the maneuver failed and ultimately led to the British defeat. The next day, General Fraser succumbed to his wounds. Murphy next set his sights on General Burgoyne's aide-de-camp, Sir Frances Clarke. Clarke had galloped onto the field with Burgoyne's order to retreat. Murphy fired at Sir Clarke twice, the second shot killing him before he fell from his stirrups. The death of these eminent officers threw the British ranks into utter chaos. The British lines withdrew in bitter defeat. Murphy's shots directly resulted in Burgoyne's demoralizing surrender of his entire army, an event unheard of in the annals of British military history.

The victory at Saratoga gave the inspired, but tattered, Continental army something it had sorely lacked through the campaigns of 1775 and 1776—hope. But more importantly, the victory at Saratoga brought France into the war as a powerful ally to the American revolutionaries, supplying much-needed money, equipment and manpower. The victory, and the news of French alliance, also encouraged many Americans to finally join the far-from-certain military campaign to win independence from our British masters. After Saratoga, thousands of beleaguered colonists began to think, "Hey, we could actually win this thing." Timothy Murphy, a young Irish immigrant in a field in Saratoga, fired the shots that won the battle that turned the tide of the war that gave birth to our great nation.

At the Saratoga Battlefield, not far from where Murphy fired those shots, on a two-hundred-foot square, stands a stone monument in tribute to his patriotism. The marker was donated September 20, 1913, by the Saratoga County Ancient Order of Hibernians, an organization that has existed in our city since the late 1880s and continues its good works today with over one hundred members. Each October at the monument, the Hibernians perform a solemn wreath-laying ceremony with a color guard, bagpipes and a few words to honor Murphy's contribution to our independence.

CHARLES FERDINAND DOWD

Time and again, history has been written in our great city. Every Saratogian should know the name Charles Ferdinand Dowd (1825–1904). Dowd was principal of Temple Grove Seminary, now occupied by Skidmore Hall on the corner of Spring and Circular Streets, across the street from the east entrance to Congress Park. Temple Grove Seminary was originally established in 1855 by Reverend Luther F. Beecher and a Mr. Carter, then principal of the Saratoga Female Seminary, a school for young women. The two men formed a partnership and constructed a new building to serve as a boarding school in the winter and a hotel in the summer. It was renamed the Saratoga Female Seminary at Temple Grove. By 1860, Mr. Carter was gone and the school, renamed Temple Grove Institute, soon closed.

Principal Dowd purchased and reopened the school in 1868 and served as its head, co-principal with his wife Harriett, for the next thirty years. He made many improvements to the campus, including steam heat, an innovation for its time. Temple Grove rose to become one of the highly successful select schools for young ladies in the Eastern United States. After Dr. Dowd's retirement, the school continued under the stewardship of his son, Franklin, until 1900. In April 1903, the grounds and building were purchased by Mrs. Lucy Scribner and were christened the Young Women's Industrial Club. In 1911, the club was renamed the Skidmore School of Arts and in 1922 it was chartered as Skidmore College. Mrs. Skidmore Scribner was a 2006 inductee of the Saratoga Springs History Museum Hall of Fame.

But it is important that Saratogians remember the eminent Dr. Dowd because, right here in Saratoga Springs, he perfected and lobbied the railroad to institute standard time. As far back as 1869, Dr. Dowd had advocated the system of four time belts based on every fifteen degrees of longitude. It was during this year that he presented his plan at a railroad convention. It was enthusiastically approved and he was asked to work it out in detail over the course of the next year. More than eight thousand computations were necessary. It was a tremendous task that Dr. Dowd performed alone. It was therefore a tremendous disappointment to him when, after all his work, the plan received little attention at the following convention because of an ongoing rate war.

It was not until twelve years later that the railroad barons again got around to considering Dr. Dowd's plan. The confusion and anger of rail passengers over the discrepancies in local time variants had come to a boil. The country went on standard time November 18, 1883. Since that date, standard time has been adopted across the globe in increments of fifteen degrees longitude.

Dr. Dowd was famously modest about his achievements. He once listened politely on a trip out west as a fellow passenger explained to him how to set his watch back. Dr. Dowd never received any compensation from his work on standard time, just a small amount from his copyright on his pamphlets and an occasional pass from the railroad.

One afternoon during his daily walk, Dr. Dowd's grandson, prodded by his schoolteacher, asked him shyly, "Who invented standard time?" "Who do you think?" asked the doctor. "I think you did," his grandson replied. "Ask your mother," Dr. Dowd replied as he smiled and resumed his walk. "She probably can tell you."

Inside the First Presbyterian Church there was a bronze tablet honoring Dr. Dowd. The church, once located at 496 Broadway between the Collamer and Algonquin buildings, burned in 1976. The plaque read:

> *In memory of Charles Ferdinand Dowd, Ph.D. April 25, 1825–Nov. 12, 1904. A ruling elder of this church. Wise in council. Prudent in action, broad in activity. An educator, Far-reaching and ever-living in influence. In solving the problem of Standard Time he proved himself a world benefactor. As a grateful tribute this tablet is erected by his loving pupils.*

Today, a plaque honoring Dr. Dowd is located beneath an armillary, a sculpture showing the relation of earth to the sun, which stands behind the Adirondack Trust Company on the corner of Broadway and Church Streets.

City Street Names

A favorite aspect of any hometown history is the derivation of its street names. Who named them, and why? Every Saratogian should know the origins of the most recognizable street names in our city. Many of the early village streets were named by Gideon Putnam, Judge Henry Walton, Abel A. Kellogg (village president), Dr. John H. Clarke and village engineer Horace Kelly.

Broadway was originally named Broad Street (two words) by Gideon Putnam when he laid out the village. As time went on, it was renamed Broad Way (still two words) to distinguish it from regular old streets. Over the decades it was squeezed into a single noun for convenience.

Phila, Caroline, Washington and Putnam Streets are all derived from Putnam family names. Phila and Washington were children of Gideon and Doanda, and Caroline was a granddaughter. Phila, you can now tell visitors with confidence, is not an abbreviation for Philadelphia. Putnam Street had begun as an intersection with East Congress Street, running right in front of the Canfield Casino, but of course that portion is now contained within Congress Park. It extended in the other direction into the forest toward the upper village. The extension was known as Front Street. Front Street became Maple Avenue. The street was developed by Thomas Haywood Tompkins, who planted 360 maple trees along the road. The beauty of the shaded avenue brought about the name change through popular demand.

Circular Street was so named because of its curvaceous line, as laid out by John Clarke. North and West Circular Streets did not get their names until many decades later. Circular Street is the only street so named and so shaped in the whole United States. Local legend has it that a man from out west once mailed a letter to Frederic Menges, owner of Menges and Curtis, giving as the only address "Circular Street"—no city, no state. The letter arrived without delay.

Warren Street is named for Judge William Lafayette Warren, son of Revolutionary Patriot Captain John Warren. Lake Avenue was so named because it was the favorite route to Saratoga Lake before the current Union Avenue was established. Lake Avenue was a beautiful, wide, tree-bordered street.

Jumel Place is of course named for Madame Jumel, but Benedict Street is not named for Benedict Arnold. It is named for Elias Benedict who, in 1824, erected the first United States Hotel.

Van Dam Street is named for Rip Van Dam, Dutch landowner who owned the allotment on which High Rock Spring was located. He died in 1745. There is also a hotel downtown that bears his name, now converted to office space. Van Dam becomes Church Street, so named because it was the address for two of the first churches, the Universalist Church and the First Presbyterian, which in 1841 was converted into the Commercial Hotel. Lafayette Street is named for the Marquis de Lafayette, who was honored at a gala reception in Saratoga Springs in 1825.

Many residents have used the steep, but handy, Gardner's Lane as a shortcut, but few may recognize the name. It connects Broadway to Putnam Street and runs between Lillian's and N. Fox Jewelers on Broadway and spills out in front of the library on Putnam Street. This is actually a very interesting lane, one of the earliest lanes in the city. Before 1868 there was no street that ended at Broadway between Caroline and Spring Street (which used to be called Bath Street). In 1830, Robert Gardner, a village official, bought the strip of land that ran from Broadway to Putnam Street. It being inconvenient for him to hike over to either street, he wore a footpath up the hill to Broadway. Saratogians were more than happy to help him wear down that path and in a few years it came to be known as Gardner's Lane. For those who do a lot of walking downtown, it is still as big a convenience to pedestrians today as it was more than 175 years ago.

Walton Street was named for Judge Henry Walton, who once owned all the land north of Congress Street. Walton was surrogate court judge of Saratoga County from 1794 to 1808 and built the great country seat at Wood Lawn (two words). This, of course, is the origin from which Woodlawn (one word) Avenue is derived. The street was originally named Mathilda Street (after the judge's daughter), home to more than one gaming house, but was changed by the judge at the behest of many residents. William and Henry Streets were named for the judge's sons. Wood Lawn estate was later inhabited by Judge Henry Hilton and his family.

Walworth Street is named for Reuben Hyde Walworth, last chancellor of the state of New York. He is remembered as a great champion of equality laws in the United States and is credited with many of their early advances.

Bryan Street, located a few streets below North Broadway, is named for famed Revolutionary scout Alexander Bryan. He was the village's first permanent settler and the local restaurant, the Olde Bryan Inn, is Bryan's former home and tavern. Before the Battle of Saratoga, Bryan was able to report the position and troop strength of Burgoyne's army, aiding in their defeat. Hamilton Street is named for Alexander Hamilton, New Yorker and first secretary of the treasury, who was shot dead in a duel with Madame Jumel's husband, Aaron Burr.

South Street was the village's southern boundary for years until new and imposing homes were raised east of Broadway. Development in that area continued into 1861, when enthusiasm for President Lincoln caused that portion of the street east of Broadway to be renamed Lincoln Avenue. As more homes were built in the city, more streets were named for presidents, including Madison, Jefferson, Adams, Monroe and Harrison. Of these presidents, five-foot, six-inch Benjamin Harrison and his wife were frequent visitors to Saratoga Springs as guests of Judge and Mrs. John R. Putnam and of Mrs. Ellen Hardin Walworth.

Clark Street (with no "e") is named for Dr. (an honorary title) John Clarke (spelled with an "e," but the "e" was dropped in subsequent street signs). He was famous for bottling and promoting the water from Congress Spring. He once owned all the one thousand acres surrounding the spring. He also laid out the early lawns of Congress Park.

Franklin Square was renamed for Ben Franklin. For many years it was called Marvin Square in honor of pioneer residents Thomas J. and James M. Marvin. The brothers were actually behind the movement to change the Square's name in honor of the elder statesman, apparently satisfied with Marvin Street, also named for them and located on the west side.

Clinton Street was named for the New York governor, George, not the past president, Bill, or the New York senator, Hillary. Seward Street is named for William Henry Seward, secretary of state, engineer of the purchase of Alaska and frequent guest of the Walworths.

Division, one of the city's oldest streets, was so named because it divided Broadway between the north and south parts of the city. Catherine Street may be named for Frederica Catherine Napoleon, wife of Jerome Napoleon, younger brother of the French Emperor, or it may be named for Catherine Sedgwick, American author. Another claim on the street is that it is named for a granddaughter of Judge Walton.

There are many other excellent stories that merit a place in learning our city's colorful past. A few not included in this text are the Whitneys, the Vanderbilts, Diamond Jim Brady, Lillian Russell, crusading reform reporter Nellie Bly, Yale professor-turned-actor Monty Woolley, the Waits, the Dakes, the great fires that shaped our city, gangster Meyer Lansky or more recent notables such as celebrated authors Steven Millhauser and Russell Banks, actor David Hyde Pierce, hometown hero Fourstardave… Take your pick, the list goes on and on. And that is the beauty of Saratoga Springs—we may be a horse town, but we are no one-trick pony. Hopefully these stories have piqued your curiosity enough to initiate some of your own investigations into our local lore.

Notes

Chapter One

1. Study of Sir William Johnson's papers has recently established 1771 as the most accurate date of his first visit to these springs. He had visited Lebanon Springs and others previously. In his eminent work, *Reminiscences of Saratoga and Ballston*, William L. Stone gave 1767 for Johnson's visit to Saratoga, a citation erroneously perpetuated since 1875. Saratoga Springs City Historian's office.
2. The name Saratoga was used by Native Americans referring to a favorite hunting and fishing ground that included the eastern section of the present county of Saratoga. Saratoga was early and variously spelled Cheratoge, Sarachtitoge, Sarachtoga, Saractoga, Saraghtoga, Saragtoga, Saratoge, Saraktoga, Sarastogue, Schorachtoge, Sarasteau, Saraston, Saratogo, Sarantau, Serach-Tague, Serachtoga and Soraghtoga. It has appeared on an old map as So-roe-to-gos-land, according to the *Documentary History of the State of New York*. The name is generally taken to mean "hillside country by the great, or swift water."

   The shortened usage "Saratoga" for "Saratoga Springs" sometimes vexes the nativist instincts of residents of Saratoga County, the town of Saratoga and "Old Saratoga" (Schuylerville since 1831). It derives naturally from abbreviation by countless thousands of visitors and people from away. Any such usage in the book is undoubtedly in this context.
3. The first surnames here are written about in some detail in Stone, *Reminiscences of Saratoga*. Good access to surnames is published on census lists on the Internet by HeritageQuest and others.
4. Sylvester, *History of Saratoga County*, Village of Saratoga Springs (Part 2), iv—Mineral Springs. This good reference work is available online at www.rootsweb.com/~nysarato/Sylvester/chap28a.html.
5. Kettlewell, *Saratoga Springs*, 10.
6. Cleveland Amory's conclusion was that groups came to resorts as follows:

   Artists and sensory types in search of scenery and solitude
   Gentle people (professors and clergy people), solid people in search of the simple life
   The "nice millionaires" in search of a good place for their children to lead the simple life (as lived by 'the solid people')
   The "naughty millionaires" who wish to associate with the "nice millionaires" but who built million-dollar cottages and clubs, dressed up for dinner, gave balls and destroyed the simple life
   Trouble.

This extract is from Amory, *Last Resorts*, 23. Though writing a humorous sendup of resort life, Amory was a knowledgeable student and partaker through the sunny first half of the twentieth century.

7. New York State Library, Henry Walton Papers, 1822–1871, SC19956.
8. Ithaca College Museum of Art has hosted an exhibition of works by Henry Walton (1806–1865) and is a good resource on this and other significant American artists of the period.
9. http://inventors.about.com/od/sstartinventions/a/soda_fountain.htm.
10. Swanner, *Saratoga Queen of the Spas*.
11. Chambers, *Drinking the Waters*.
12. Waller, *Saratoga*.
13. Chambers, *Drinking the Waters*, 4.
14. Swanner, *Saratoga Queen of the Spas*, 34.
15. Ibid., 114.
16. Ibid., 28.
17. Ibid., 115.
18. "Fifty Years Ago," *Daily Saratogian*, September 12, 1877.
19. Davison, *Fashionable Tour*.
20. Kettlewell, *Saratoga Springs*, 8.
21. *Saratoga County Communities*, 2.
22. Amory, *Last Resorts*.
23. Ibid., 23.
24. Swanner, *Saratoga Queen of the Spas*, 116.

Chapter Two

25. The definitive work on architecture in Saratoga Springs is *Saratoga Springs: An Architectural History*, by James K. Kettlewell, published by Lyrical Ballad Book Store. Lyrical Ballad has been for some years the best antiquarian source on Saratoga Springs and related subjects.
26. Kettlewell, *Saratoga Springs*.
27. Kettlewell provides a good description of this church. Remarkably, the architect's fee of $250 was not paid.
28. Kettlewell, *Saratoga Springs*. This revolution in the hospitality trade was sparked by Isaiah Rogers's innovations at his Tremont House in Boston, publicized by William Havard Eliot in his *A Description of Tremont House, with Architectural Illustrations*, 1830.
29. Styles that can be found significantly in surviving buildings in Saratoga Springs include Federal, Italian, Second Empire and Beaux Arts/American Renaissance. Some singular examples of these styles in public buildings are Adirondack Trust Company; Trask Memorial (Spirit of Life), Congress Park; Trolley Station, now the Visitor Center/Urban Cultural Park; and Spa State Park buildings.

    The Craftsman or Bungalow style was popular from 1900 to 1935. Designs survive significantly, especially in residential areas, with some interesting examples in important public buildings.

Chapter Three

30. Kettlewell, *Saratoga Springs*; Waller, *Saratoga*.

31. *New York Times* obituary, March 28, 1887.
32. www.brooksidemuseum.org/vewebsite/exhibit1/e13441a.htm.
33. Bradley, *Such Was Saratoga.*
34. Heimer, *Fabulous Bawd.*
35. The following is taken from Frederick Phisterer's *New York in the War of the Rebellion*, 3rd ed. Albany: J.B. Lyon Company, 1912. Courtesy the New York Military Museum.

> *Saratoga Springs, Civil War: 77th Regiment, Mustered in: November 23, 1861; Mustered out: June 27, 1865*
>
> *Saratoga Regiment; Bemis Heights Regiment. This regiment, Col. James B. McKean, was organized at Saratoga Springs, and there, November 23, 1861, mustered in the service of the United States for three years. October 30, 1862, a new company was forwarded to the regiment, becoming Company K, the original company having been consolidated with Company F. At the expiration of the term of service of the regiment its members entitled to be discharged were forwarded to Saratoga, and there, under Col. Winsor B. French, mustered out December 13, 1864; the regiment was continued in the service, but, November 19, 1864, consolidated into five companies, A, B, C, D and E.*
>
> *The companies were recruited principally: A at Westport; B at Ballston; C, E, F and G at Saratoga; D at Wilton; H at Charlton; I at Keeseville; K at Gloversville; and second Company K at Saratoga.*
>
> *The regiment left the State November 28, 1861; served in the 3d Brigade, Casey's Division, Army of Potomac, from December, 1861; in 3d, Davidson's, Brigade, W. F. Smith's Division, 4th Corps, Army of Potomac, from March, 1862; in the 3d Brigade, 2d Division, 6th Corps, Army of Potomac, from May, 1862; and the battalion left ill the field was honorably discharged and mustered out, under Col. David J. Caw, June 27, 1865, at Washington, D.C.*

The New York Military Museum
The mission of the museum and research center is to preserve, interpret and disseminate the story, history and records of New York State's military forces and veterans. The collection is divided into the museum and the library/archives' holdings. Begun in 1863, the collection has not had a secure, permanent home until the governor announced in 2001 that the historic armory in Saratoga Springs, New York, would be renovated to house the collection. The building, designed by Isaac Perry and constructed in 1889, is a fine example of armory architecture that was popular in Upstate New York in the late 1800s.

The museum houses over ten thousand artifacts dating from the Revolutionary War to Desert Storm that relate to New York State's military forces, the state's military history and the contributions of New York's veterans. The artifacts include uniforms, weapons, artillery pieces and art. A significant portion of the museum's collection is from the Civil War. Notable artifacts from this conflict include the uniform of Colonel Elmer Ellsworth (the Union's first casualty) of nearby Mechanicville.

Included in the museum are significant holdings relating to New York's 27th Division in World War I and World War II and notable state military regiments such as the 7th (Silk Stocking Regiment), 69th (Fighting Irish), 71st and 369th (Harlem Hell fighters) New York Infantry.

The museum also owns the largest collection of state battle flags in the country and the largest collection of Civil War flags in the world. Of the over 1,700 flags in the collection, more than 60 percent are from the Civil War. The flags date from the War of 1812 through the 1991 Gulf War. The museum maintains an exhibit of its flag collection in the state capitol building in Albany, where the museum collection was originally housed.

The library and archive holdings in the Veterans Research Center include a 2,000-volume library of military and New York State history, over 6,000 photographs, unit history files, broadsides, scrapbooks, letters and maps. Highlights of the library and archives material include over 2,300 Civil War photographs, a collection of Civil War–era newspaper clippings arranged by New York units and New York National Guard service cards and service records dating from the 1880s to 1965.

The Veteran Research Center operates and archives the New York State Veteran Oral History Program and the Veteran Questionnaire Program. The Oral History Program actively collects interviews of New York State veterans from all eras. The largest part of this collection is of World War II veteran interviews. The Veteran Questionnaire Program, similar to the Oral History Program, solicits and preserves the written and photographic record of the state's veterans.

Its programs and services include a reference library and archives, research assistance, education programs and lectures. The museum's publications consist of *Genealogy Resources in the New York State Military Museum and Veterans Research Center*, *Veteran Oral History Program Self-Interview Packet* and the *Library and Archives Guide*. The New York Military Museum and Veterans Research Center is another good reason to visit Saratoga Springs.

The NY Military Museum and Veterans Research Center
61 Lake Avenue
Saratoga Springs, NY 12866
518.581.5100
http://www.dmna.state.ny.us/

36. saratogasynagogue.org/
37. *New York Times*, June 13, 1903.
38. Bradley, *Such Was Saratoga*, 117.
39. chipster.net.
40. www.roundlakevillage.org.
41. Swanner, *Saratoga Queen of the Spas*, 157. Dr. Swanner was a lifelong advocate of water therapeutics.

Chapter Four

42. Charles V. Wait, CEO of Adirondack Trust Company and trustee of Skidmore College (like his father before him), quoted in *Skidmore Scope* (Summer 2001).
43. Mary-Anne Fitzgerald (city historian), Information sheet, *History of the City of Saratoga Springs: The 20th Century*.
44. It is a coincidence of name. The original Grand Union supermarket, in New Jersey, was themed with each aisle representing a different state of the union.
45. Horne, *With the Strength of the Adirondacks*.
46. *Skidmore Scope* (Summer 2001).
47. Prominent families that stepped up for the building project and then went on to contribute administrative talent included the Waits, Dakes, Vanderbilts, Whitneys, Mathers, Paysons and others. Persistent advocates in the press were Duane LaFleche,

city editor of Albany's *Knickerbocker News*; and Fred Eaton, editor and publisher of the *Saratogian*. The Founding Board represented diversity in the community:
Elizabeth Ames—executive director, Yaddo
James E. Benton—mayor, Saratoga Springs
Reverend Benjamin W. Holmes—pastor, Bethesda Episcopal Church
Hoyt L. Irwin—chairman, Music Department, Skidmore College
Charles A. LaBelle—State Conservation Department
Dr. David E. Liston—State Reservation director
Mrs. Harry L. Loop—Saratoga Practice Club and private piano teacher
Robert N. McKelvey—State Commerce Department staff member and ballet aficionado
Bernard Serotta—Saratoga Art Show Committee
Mrs. Kathryn H. Starbuck—Skidmore, Yaddo, daughter of the founder of the former Starbuck Dept. Store
Angelo J. Tarantino—president, Saratoga Springs Chamber of Commerce
Newman E. Wait Jr.—president, Adirondack Trust Company
Val H. Wilson—president, Skidmore College
SPAC Commemorative Edition, 2005

48. The show goes on every summer at SPAC. www.spac.org/
49. Opportunities for interesting insight into thoroughbred horses and horse ownership can be found at www.racingmuseum.org/
50. Heywood Hale Broun, *New York Times*, July 2, 1995.
51. *My Little Chickadee*, Universal Studios, 1940.
52. *Saratogian*, October 1883.
53. Minutes of the Saratoga Historical Society, March 19, 1924.
54. Interview with Minnie Clark Bolster, January 2008.
55. Telephone interview with Mary Dougal, February 2008.

APPENDIX II

56. Ketchum, 75.

APPENDIX V

57. Millis's original ten stories profiled Spencer and Katrina Trask; Man o' War; Timothy Murphy; Charles F. Dowd; Frank Sullivan; George Crum and Aunt Katie Weeks; Gideon Putnam; Madame Jumel; and E. Berry Wall. The tenth section is on the origin of some street names in the city.

Bibliography and Resources

Amory, Cleveland. *The Last Resorts*. New York: Harper and Brothers, 1952.

Bradley, Hugh. *Such Was Saratoga.* New York: Doubleday, Doran and Company, Inc., 1940.

Butler, B.C. *From New York to Montreal*. New York: American News Company, 1873.

Carola, Chris, Beverley Mastrianni and Michael L. Noonan. *George S. Bolster's Saratoga Springs*. Virginia Beach: The Donning Company, 1990.

Chambers, Thomas A. *Drinking the Waters: Creating an American Leisure Class at Nineteenth Century Mineral Springs*. Washington, D.C.: Smithsonian Institution Press, 2002.

Corbett, Theodore. *The Making of American Resorts: Saratoga Springs, Ballston Spa, Lake George*. New Brunswick, NJ: Rutgers University Press, 2001.

Davison, Gideon M. *The Fashionable Tour in 1825: An Excursion to the Springs, Niagara, Quebec and Boston*. Saratoga Springs: G.M. Davison, 1825.

Durkee, Cornelius. *Reminiscences of Saratoga: A Compilation of Articles in the* Saratogian. 1927–28.

Heimer, Melvin. *Fabulous Bawd: The Story of Saratoga*. New York: Henry Holt and Company, 1952.

Horne, Field. *The Saratoga Reader: Writings About an American Village 1749–1900*. Saratoga Springs: Kiskatom Publishing, 2004.

———. *With the Strength of the Adirondacks: A History of the Adirondack Trust Company 1901–2001*. Hensonville, NY: Black Dome Press, 2002.

Joki, Robert. *Saratoga Lost: Images of Victorian America*. Hensonville, NY: Black Dome Press, 1998.

Ketchum, Richard M. *Saratoga: Turning Point of America's Revolutionary War.* New York: Henry Holt and Company, 1997.

Kettlewell, James K. *Saratoga Springs: An Architectural History 1790–1990.* Saratoga Springs: Lyrical Ballad Book Store, 1991.

McGregor, Jean [pseud. of Evelyn Barrett Britten]. *Chronicles of Saratoga, The Saratogian.* Saratoga Springs, 1947.

Moore, Heather, and Robert Jones. *The Architecture of Necessity: Skidmore's First Home in Downtown Saratoga.* Saratoga Springs: Skidmore College, 2007.

Saratoga County Communities An Historic Perspective. Ballston Spa, NY: Saratoga County Planning Board, 1980.

Smithgall, Kim, and Kathryn Gallien. "Tales of the City: Boom or Bust, Saratogians Work to Keep Downtown Thriving." *Skidmore Scope*, Summer 2001.

Sterngass, Jon. *First Resorts: Pursuing Pleasure at Saratoga Springs, Newport and Coney Island.* Baltimore, MD: Johns Hopkins University Press, 2001.

Stone, William L. *Reminiscences of Saratoga and Ballston.* New York: Virtue and Yorston, 1875.

Swanner, Grace Maguire, MD. *Saratoga Queen of the Spas, A History of the Saratoga Spa and the Mineral Springs of the Saratoga and Ballston Areas.* Utica, NY: North Country Books, 1988.

Sylvester, Nathaniel Bartlett. *A History of Saratoga County New York 1609–1878.* Interlaken, NY: Heart of the Lakes Publishing, 1878.

Waller, George. *Saratoga: Saga of an Impious Era.* New York: Bonanza Books, 1966.

The best repositories of material on Saratoga Springs are:

Saratoga Springs History Museum
The Canfield Casino in Congress Park
1 East Congress Street, P.O. Box 216
Saratoga Springs, NY 12866
saratogahistory.org

The Saratoga Room at the Saratoga Springs Public Library
49 Henry Street
Saratoga Springs, NY 12866-3271
www.sspl.org

Saratoga Springs City Historian
297 Broadway
Saratoga Springs, NY 12866
www.saratoga-springs.org